MICHAEL HAMPTON

# GESTURE DRAWING

## DYNAMIC MOVEMENT AND FORM

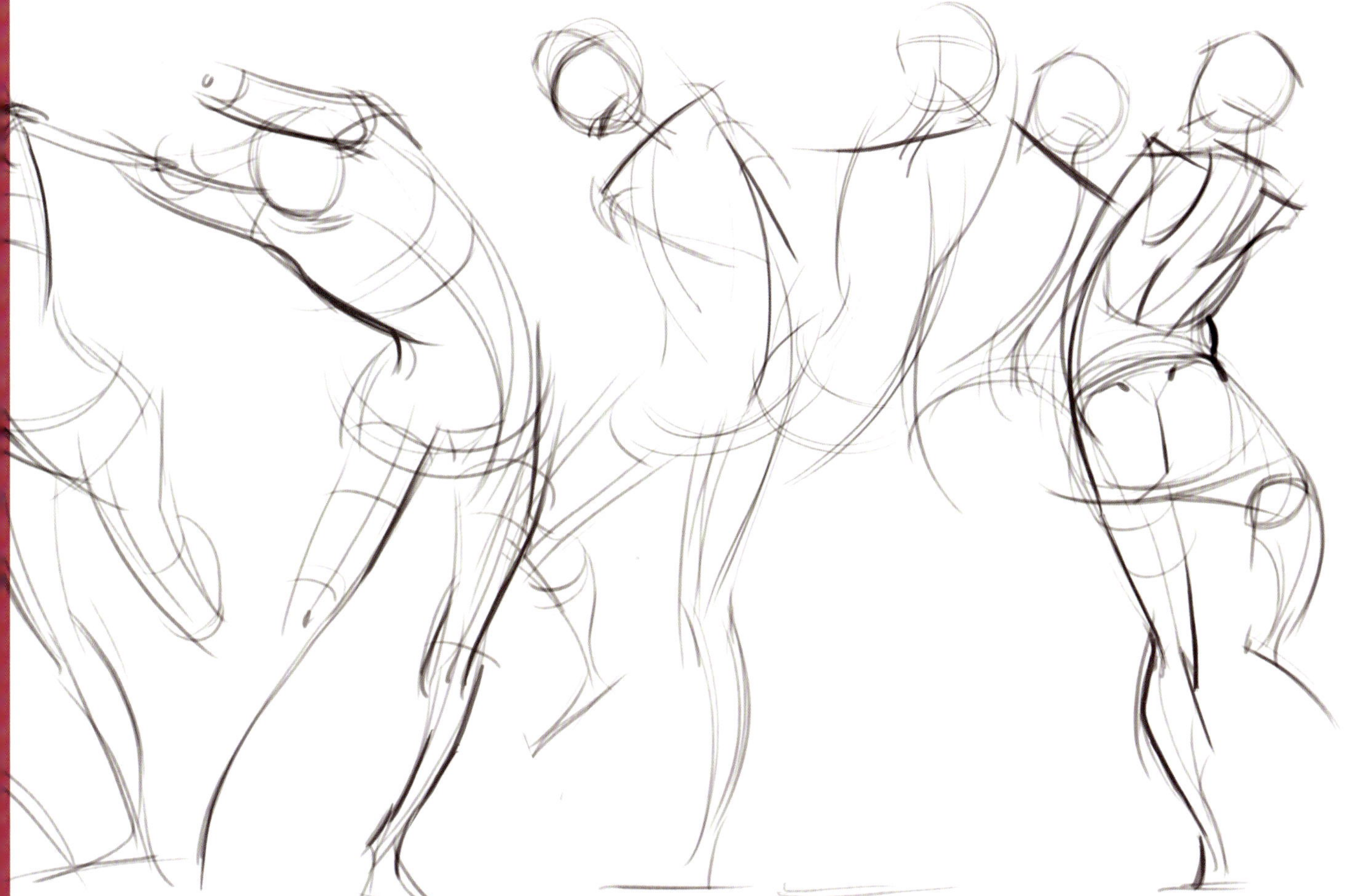

Gesture Drawing
*Dynamic Movement and Form*
Michael Hampton
www.figuredwrawing.info

*Special thanks to Proko and team for making these amazing references possible. As well as the InDesign Goblins! Without you, this book wouldn't exist. Thank you all for putting this together.*

Editor: Kelly Reed
Project manager: Lisa Brazieal
Marketing coordinator: Koryn Olage
Proofreader: Mike Beady
Cover design: Giselle Rey
Interior design and layout: Gisselle Rey and Gaby Granado
Cover Illustrations: Michael Hampton
Additional text by: Lia Alvarez Lopez.
Project Coordinator: J. Corvo Rubio

ISBN: 979-8-88814-241-7
1st Edition (1st printing, January 2025)
© 2025 Michael Hampton
All images © Michael Hampton unless otherwise noted.

Rocky Nook Inc.
1010 B Street, Suite 350
San Rafael, CA 94901
USA

www.rockynook.com

Distributed in the UK and Europe by Publishers Group UK
Distributed in the U.S. and all other territories by Ingram Publisher Services

Library of Congress Control Number: 2024937192

This book is printed on acid-free paper.
Printed in China.

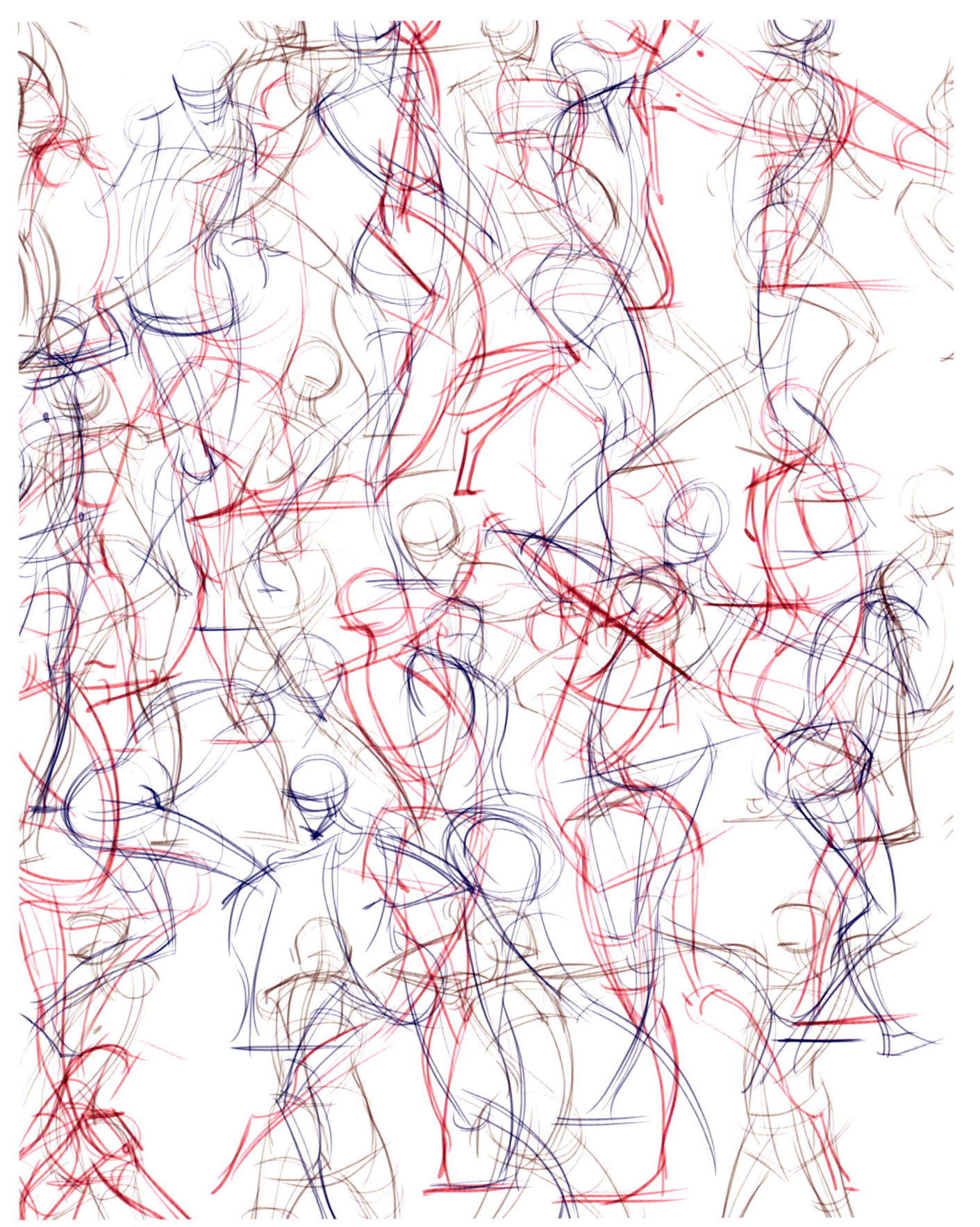

# FOREWORD

Despite its whimsical and often expressively nonchalant appearance, the practice of gesture drawing is anything but straightforward. At once fascinating and discouraging, elusive and accessible, gesture marks a paradox. Gesture drawing initiates a beginning and end while being reductively abstract in the service of representation.

One potential reason the practice and teaching of gesture drawing confuses is the split it initiates between the mind and the hand, or said differently, one's conceptual plan and kinetic execution. This scenario is described by Bernice Alice Rose, in her account of drawings history, as the artist at their most cerebral while simultaneously being autographic,

confessional, or intimate through the necessity of the personalized touch or mark.

What I take from this inherent split between concept and action intrinsic to the practice of drawing (especially at its earliest stages) is the necessity of embracing abstraction. If the idea of engaging with abstraction feels unduly complex, consider Leonardo Da Vinci's definition of line as being "neither matter nor substance and may rather be called an imaginary idea than a real object; and this being its nature it occupies no space." What we can learn from Da Vinci is that line is already a symbolic abstraction, as it exists nowhere in nature, it is exclusively an idea.

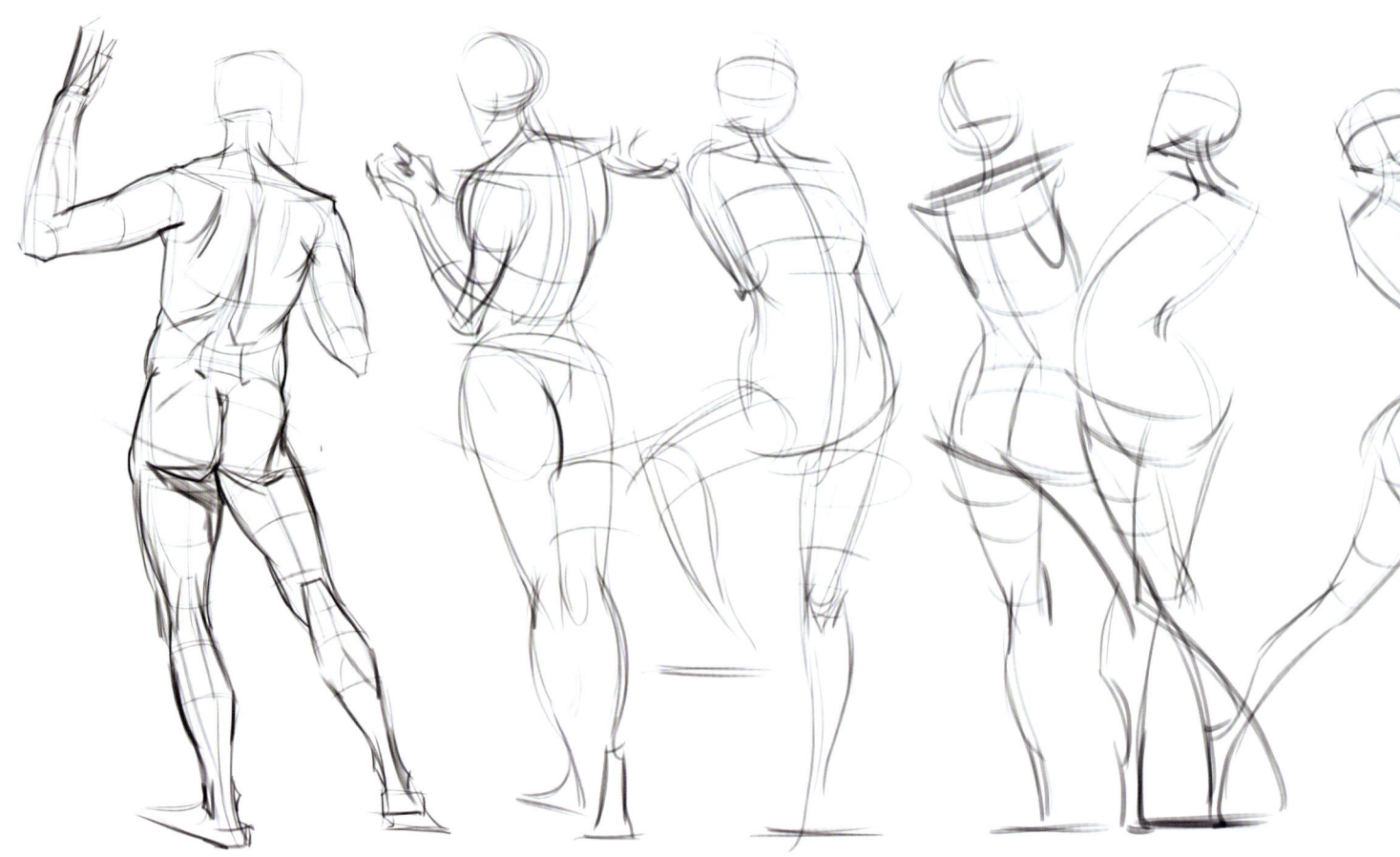

From this understanding, the challenge becomes choosing how we wish to orchestrate our use of line to represent our idea (of the figure). For me, this is the central challenge of making gesture drawings, namely, how does one match concept or intention to the most abstract/economical of means?

Gesture requires that we pair down our approach. Instead of identifying with the exterior or silhouette ask instead what animates the figure or is most essential to its design.

At this point, a study of other artists/authors on the subject of gesture may be illuminating, as every usage articulates the mind/hand split in different ways, communicating unique insights about the figure in the process. Conducting a survey of other instructional guides, it may be instructive to question, what is the "correct" way to make a gesture drawing?

Is the "correct" approach Andrew Loomis's long, sweeping Hogarth-inspired rhythms; George Bridgeman's densely managed forms; Glen Vilppu's Baroque-inspired rhythms; the relational rhythms of the Reilly method and its offshoots; a general mannequin figure such as that shown in *How to Draw Comics the Marvel Way*; Burne Hogarth's *Dynamic Figure Drawing*; James McMullin's direct *High Focus* contours; Michael Mattessi's pregnant "Force" asymmetries; and so on.

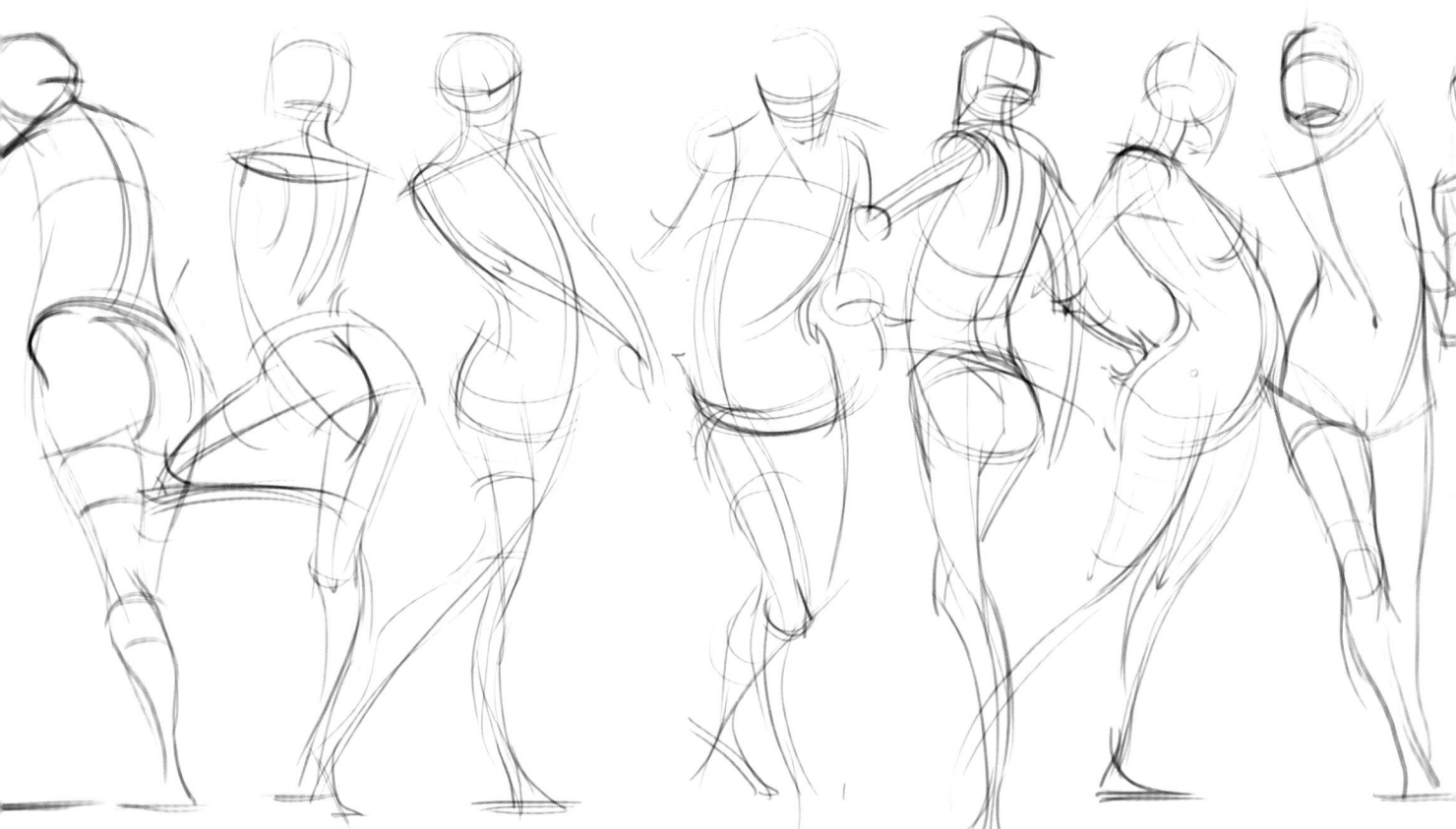

This list could go on indefinitely and the answer might be any one of them, all, or none. What I recommend is that you take your favorite elements from all and piece together a solution that works for you. To conclude this thought, what I'm advocating is an understanding of gesture as a stage and process, not a technique. The techniques of others may or may not be a great fit, what matters is that you decide for yourself what the gesture is setting up.

Yet another constant difficulty or frustration is that gestures are often made rapidly and condense a significant amount of information into a brief period of execution. For this reason, gestures, which I argue are highly conscious and representative of our concept in total, may seem deceptively simple, frivolous, or absent any planning. As such, the goal in this book is to slow down the act of gesture drawing and explain in detail the thinking process involved. With this laid

out, the difficulty of gesture may be more easily accessible and open to an actionable set of steps.

What matters most is that you, the artist, reconcile these concepts for your own interests and practice. This avoids the ridiculous trap of being caught in a "right" vs "wrong," linear vs tonal, or similar, approach and puts an emphasis on what you want the gesture to be setting up. It is my belief that strict adherence to a style, school, or workflow serves no productive role in artistic progress.

I suggest you survey as many different methods of gesture as possible and personalize your approach based on what you decide is most important to communicate. Not committing to one style may even mean you adopt multiple gesture drawing practices specialized for unique outcomes.

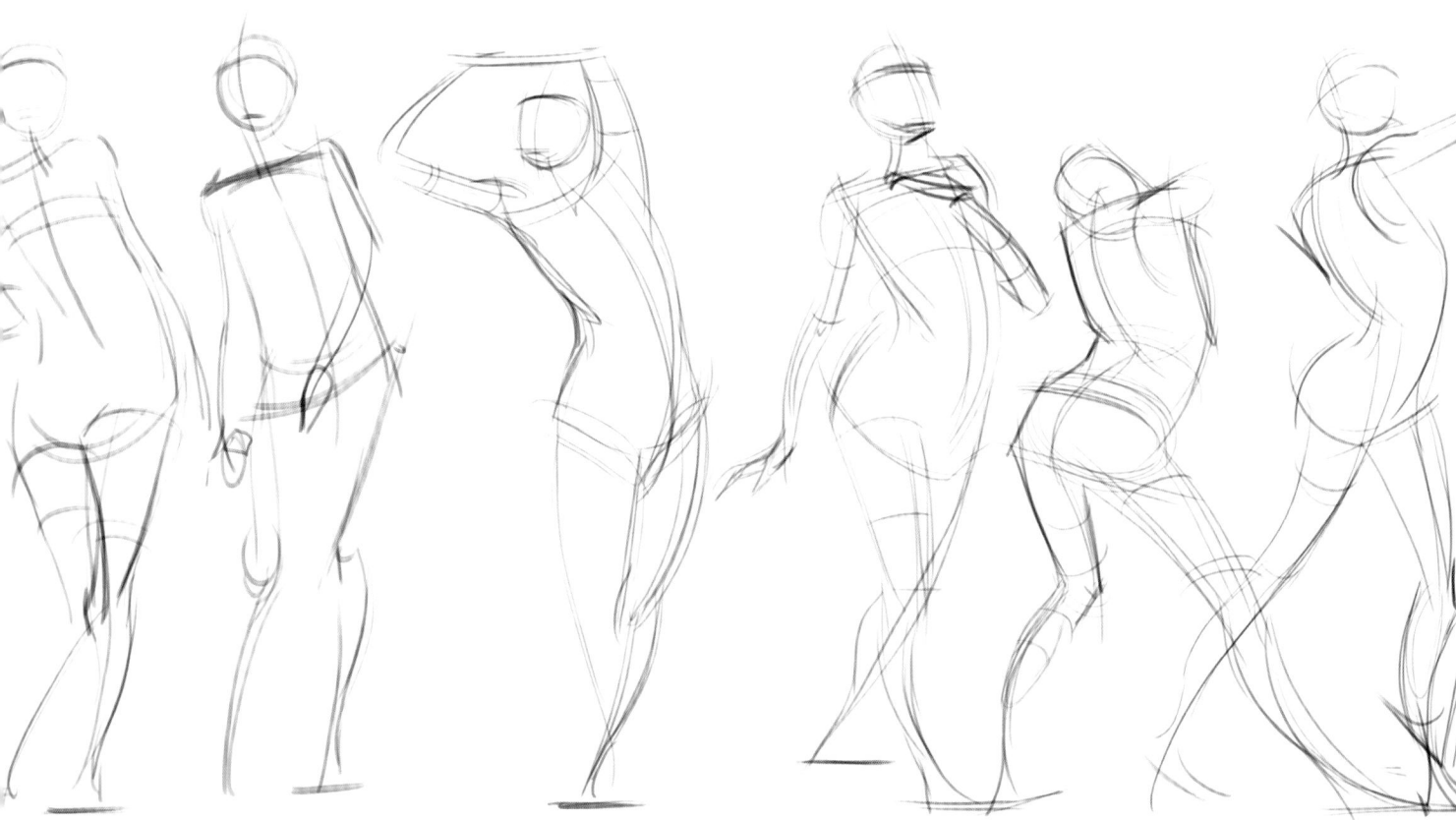

For example, I use one approach emphasizing line and rhythm for the analytical study of anatomy vs one emphasizing shape and design to facilitate the study of tone.

Regardless of the approach you choose, what ultimately matters most is that you intentionally plant a seed laying the foundation for your drawing. Thought this way, your drawing practice constitutes a language in which line, shape, perspective, and value allow for infinite expressive possibilities.

In what follows, I will be breaking down my thoughts on gesture drawing and contrasting two approaches that I move between in my own practice. These approaches represent extremes in their utility. The first, which favors line and the development of form, is an excellent tool of analytical investigation.

The second favors shape and is more effective at transitioning into light and shadow, composition, or design. My goal is to be as explicit with my thinking as possible and pull back the curtain on this exciting but ambiguous practice. As such, I hope this book will serve as an expansion to the chapter on gesture in my previous book, *Figure Drawing: Design and Invention.* While many of those concepts will be reviewed and repeated here, I hope that by addressing the subject of gesture independently that I am able to bring greater clarity to the subject and its practice.

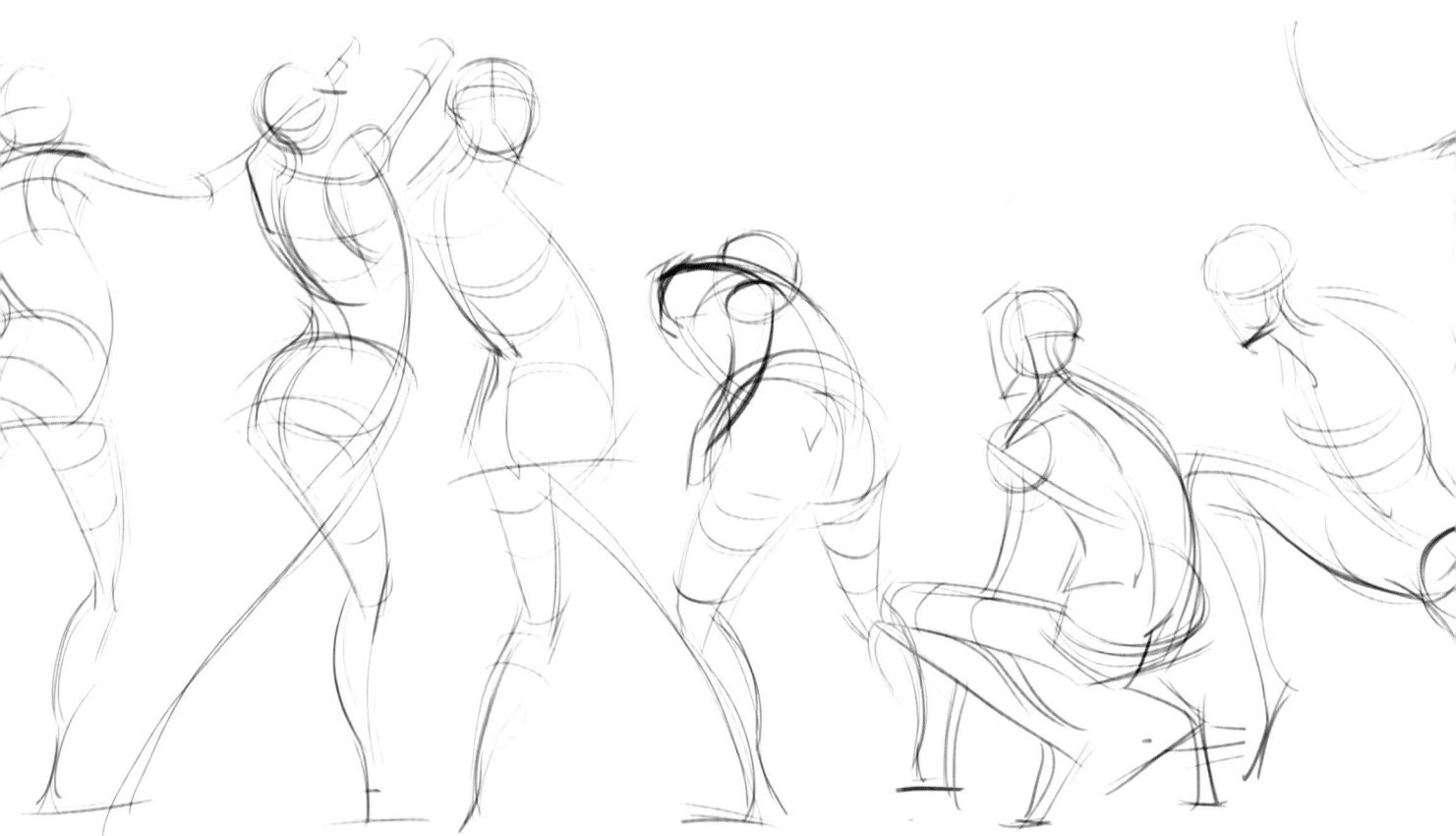

# CONTENTS

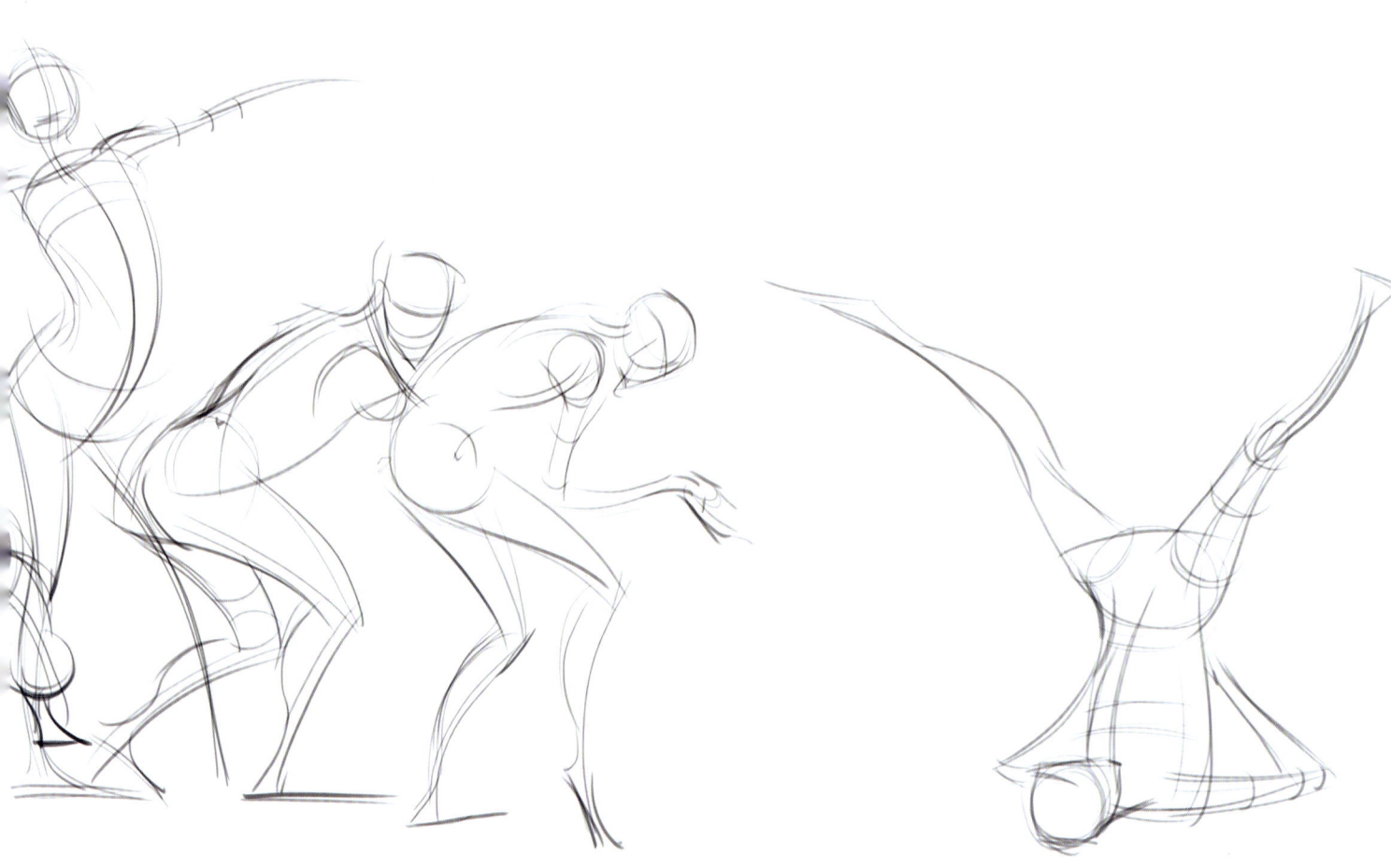

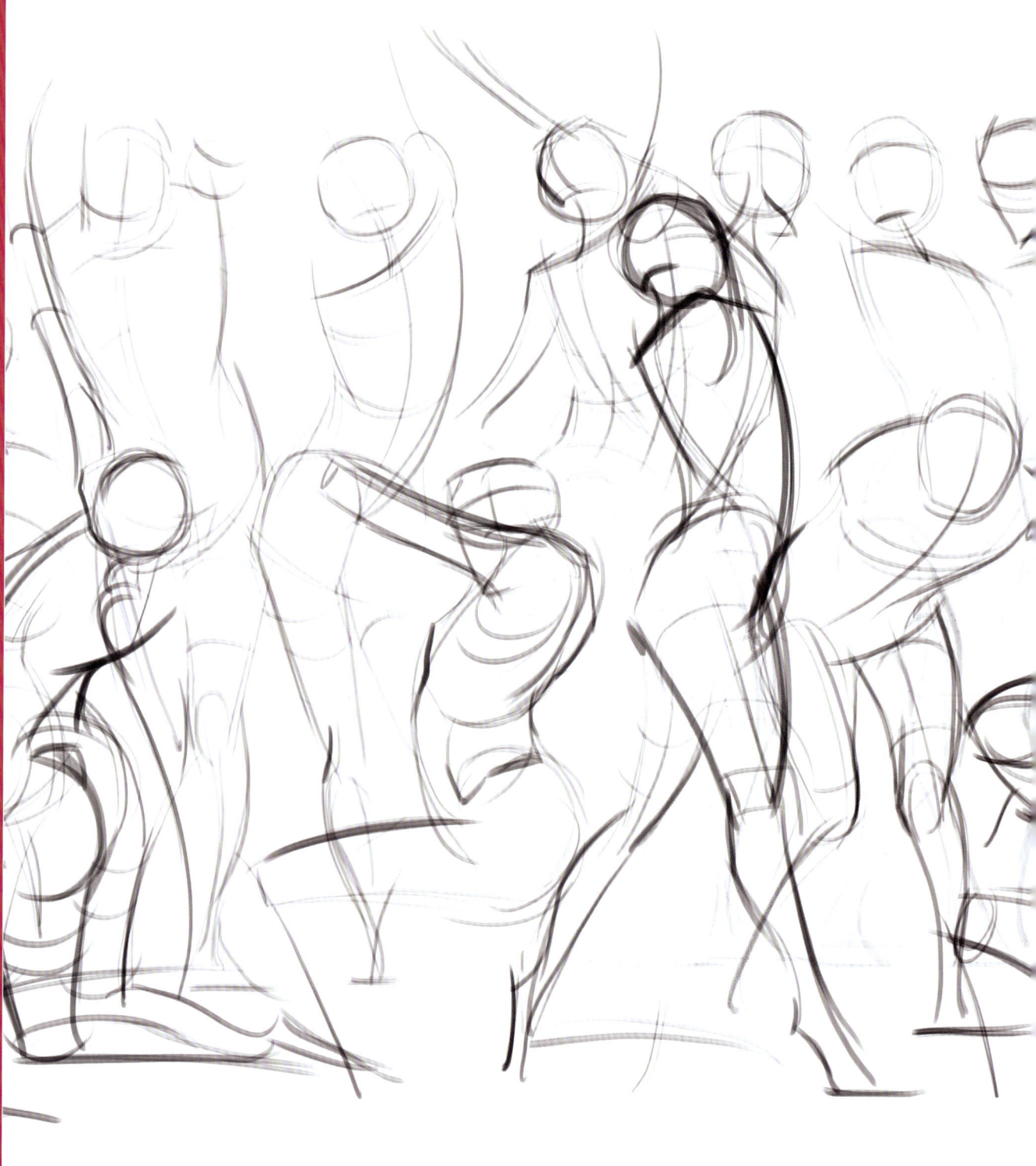

# WHY, WHAT, AND HOW?

I approach the subject of gesture by breaking down the problem into three categories: why, what, and how.

Before putting pencil to paper, pause and consider for a moment …

**Why** am I making the drawing? **What** is the subject? And **how** will I choose to represent it?

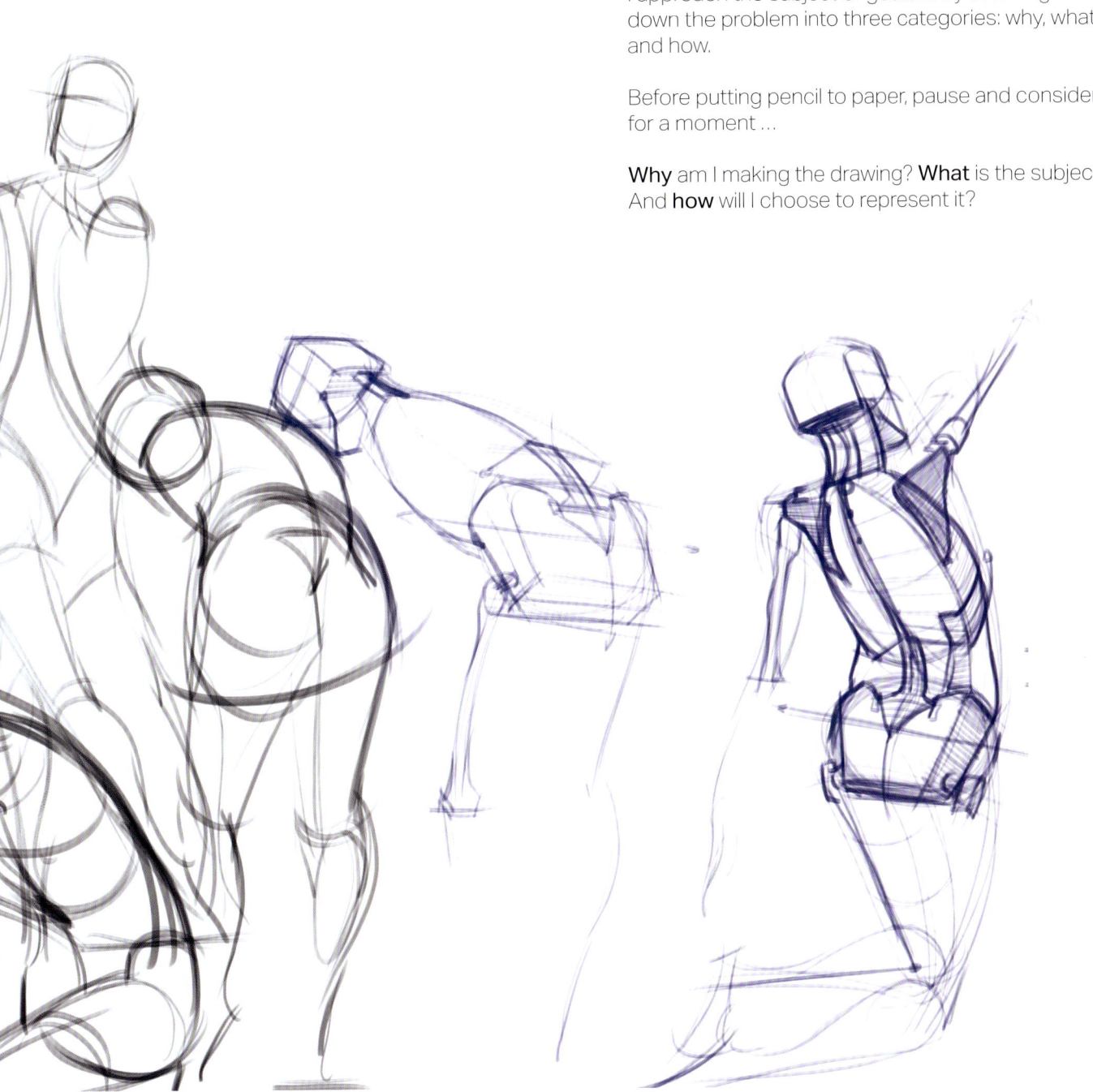

# WHY?

Let's look at these separately to expand the relevance of each and explore how they all overlap. The first question "why" is one addressed prior to the pencil or mark hitting the page. In other words, this is an issue of concept or your intended vision. When breaking down this important first category, I separate the "why" of my gesture into four concerns.

**IDEA / STORY**
**WEIGHT / BALANCE**
**MOVEMENT**
**PROPORTION**

To focus on this, think of your gesture only as a planning stage. The aim of this stage is exclusively to address the categories numbered above with an emphasis on communication … that's it.

We're not adding details, contour, or shadow. We're currently forming the reason(s) behind which we would devote the time to finish a drawing with those all-important details and realistic effects.

I'm encouraging you to think of the practice of drawing as an active language, not a static image, inert doodle, or passive attempt at copying the reference. Try and let go of the notion that the value of a drawing is in its ability to create a facsimile or only having worth if it achieves proximity to your reference.

Consider it this way, no matter how much effort or graphite you commit, your drawing will never be the reference. It will always be a drawing. And as a drawing your audience will respond to the mechanics of line and its implementation first and foremost. I'm suggesting we begin to think about the practice of drawing free from reference, or said differently, the only reference you should concern yourself with is your concept.

This leads us to the first item on our list.

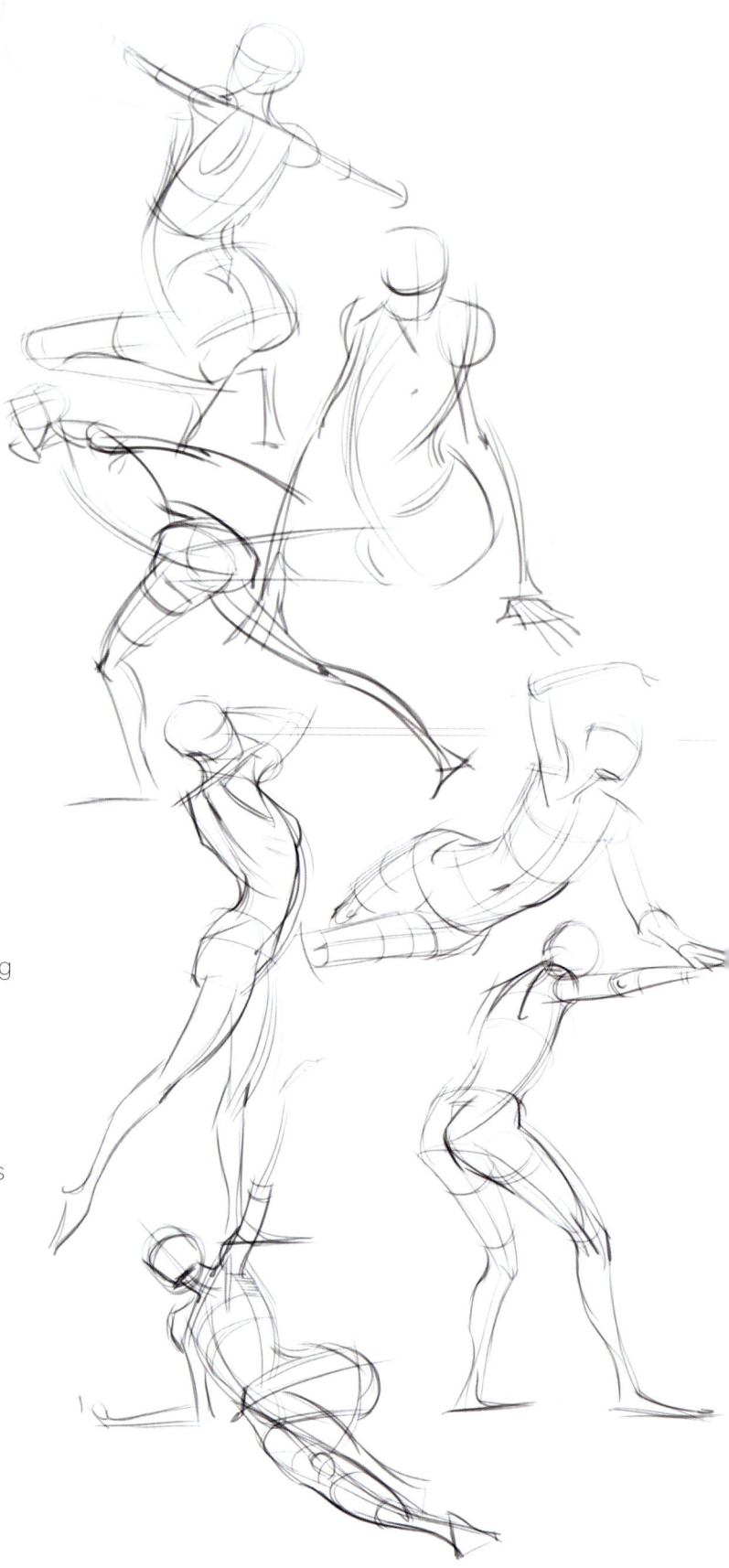

# IDEA AND STORY

Idea/story is simply (or not so simply) what you want to communicate, the larger concept or message you want your audience to take away. This could be something very direct, abstract, or anything in between.

Keep in mind that I'm advocating for a thinking of drawing which is the combination of abstract components (line, shape, perspective, value, etc.) and as such is inherently abstract. My emphasis throughout is that one productive way to think about your gesture is by embracing the abstract mechanics of the medium.

For example, in our drawing toolbox we have a straight line, a "C" curve, an "S" curve, which can all be used in varying configurations to create an array of effects or designs (symmetry, asymmetry, movement, economy, repetition, etc.). From this view it's easier to understand the ways your drawing works or comes to produce an experience on the part of the audience.

Again, I'm encouraging you to shift your thinking away from drawing as a medium tied to the "capture" of a reference to the formation of an experience.

But one step at a time …

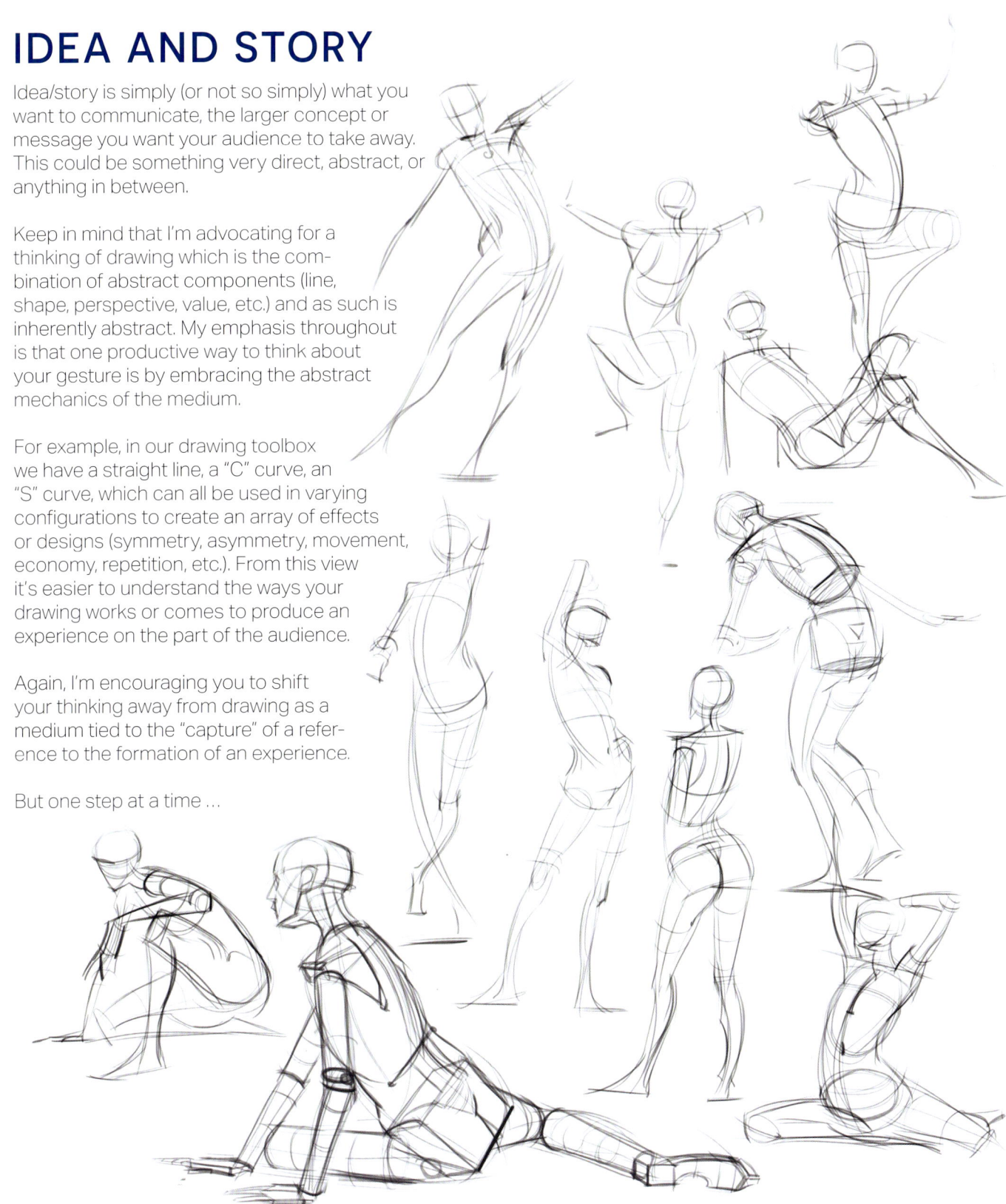

# IDEA

My first concern is always the "idea." By "idea," I'm referring to whatever the concept is. As our drawings are intended to be seen by an audience, this step is an opportunity to pause and reflect on what you want to say with your figure. Remember that the figure is just a vehicle for whatever message, mood, emotion, or experience you want to deliver.

Thinking this way might require, only for the moment, that you suspend an interest in copying or using a strict observational approach. Instead, I'm suggesting that we conduct an analytical investigation into what we see and want to say about the figure.

Let's pause for a moment and look at a historical example. Consider Leonardo da Vinci's famous image of the Vitruvian Man (Fig. 1). What interests me here is how an idea manifests at the level of abstract forms/shapes.

We do not see a carefully observed and copied subject in da Vinci's famous Vitruvian man. Instead, the Vitruvian man, is an idea about how the human form should be digested into idealized proportions. In da Vinci's drawing, we see the emphasis on the human body's connection with geometry to demonstrate a divine harmony between

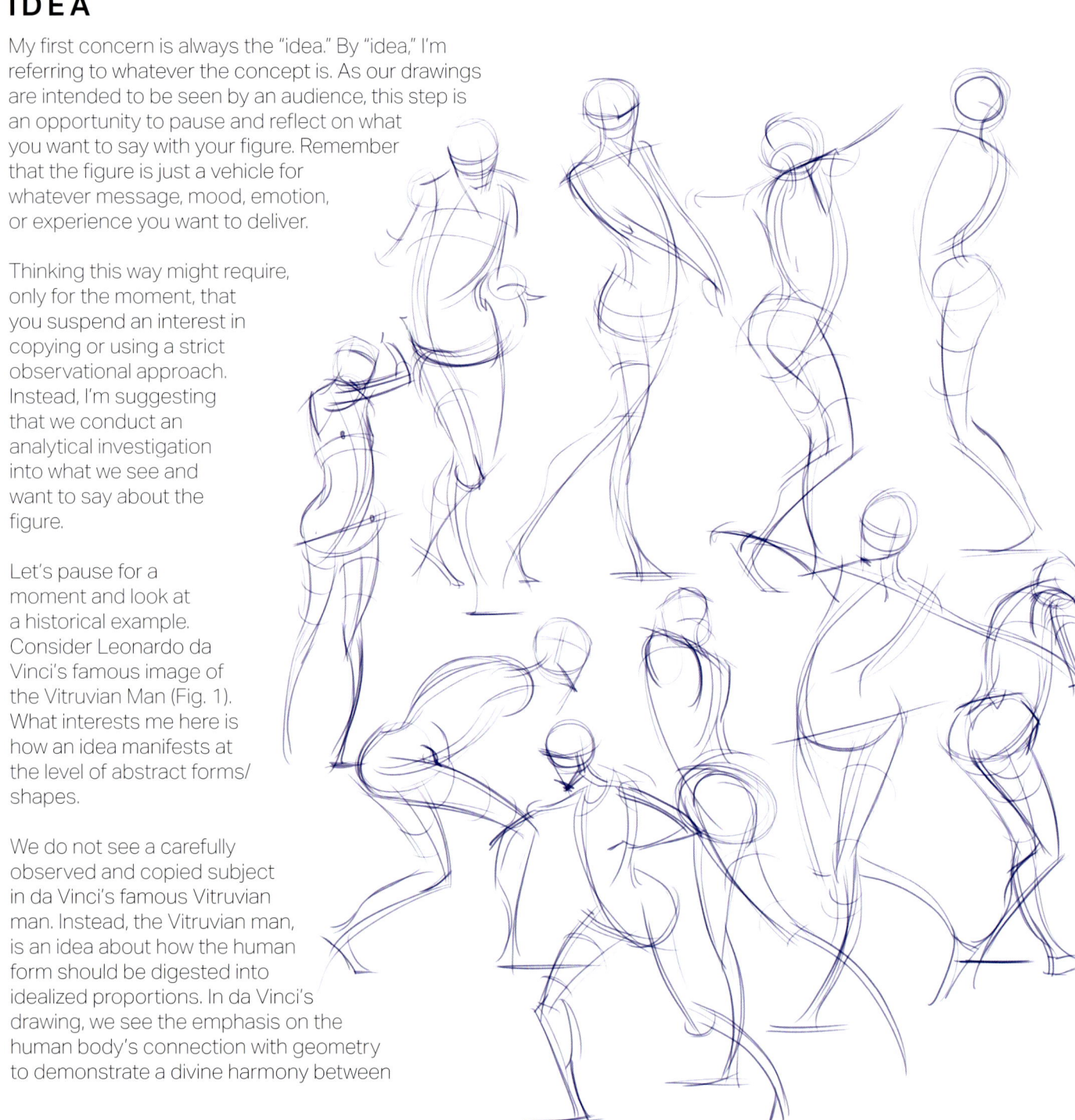

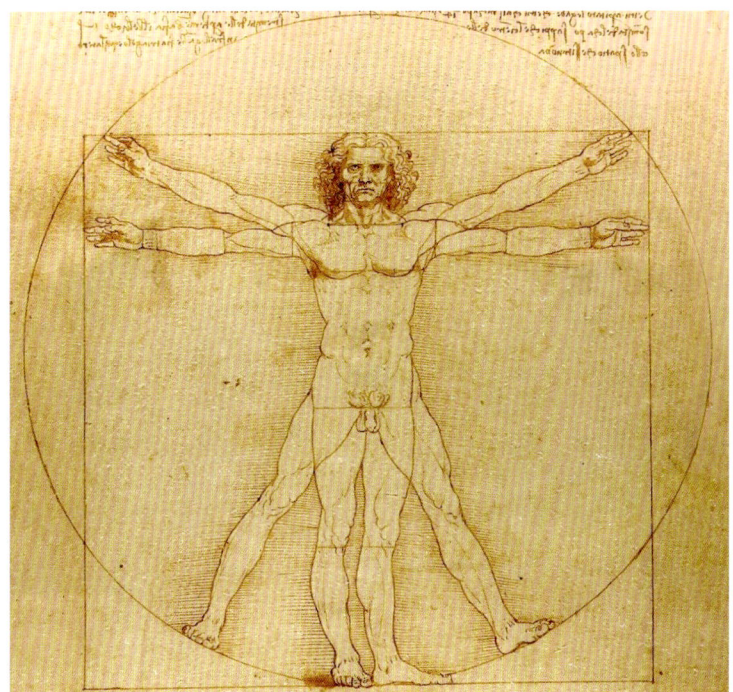

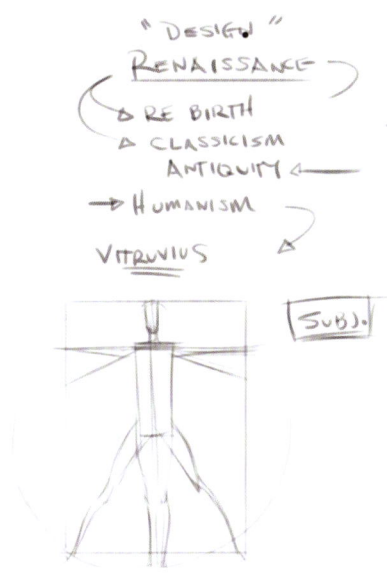

Fig. 1

the macro- and microcosms. Speaking to the symbolic value of these shapes for the Renaissance, John Hendrix has stated:

*"If the square is taken as the traditional symbol of the earth and the circle is taken as the traditional symbol of the divine, then the drawing represents man's ability to connect the celestial and the material by ascending to the one and descending to the other in his soul."*

In his Vitruvian Man, da Vinci illustrates a form of language describing essential geometries to be incorporated in abstracting from nature, specifically the figure. As such, the "idea" here is that the figure becomes the synthesis, or bridge, between these two geometries and the visual blueprint of the aesthetics of antiquity.

Further, the square and the circle (and geometry as a whole) directly relate to da Vinci's ongoing interest in a "transformation,"—or "the plastic molding of one shape into another without change of area or volume." For da Vinci, the Vitruvian Man stands at the center of an aesthetic preoccupation or an obsession with squaring the circle.

Your idea doesn't need to be this complex by any stretch. This is an example of how drawing practices might represent a blueprint for ideas through their necessary link to abstraction.

A more contemporary example of abstraction used in the service of connecting an audience with an artistic intention is found in character design.

While I am in no way a character designer, many of the students I work with do have character design as a creative goal. What fascinates me about character development is the ways in which abstraction, specifically abstract shape development, is core to the practice.

*Fig. 1 – Leonardo da Vinci, Vitruvian Man, c. 1490*

**15**

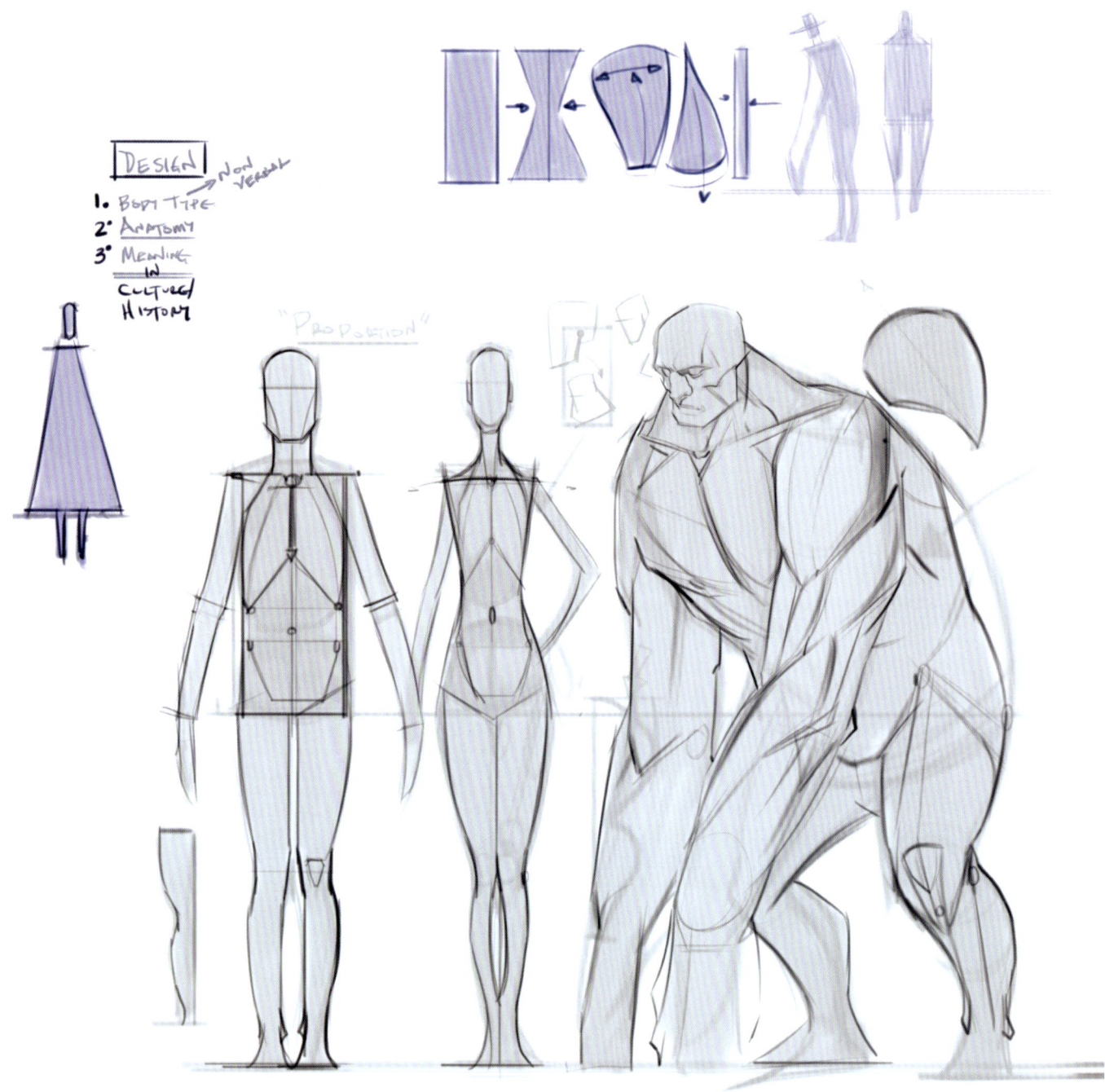

In this thinking, a hero would be defined with squares for its connections to stability is motivated by a heroine defined by a visual seductiveness using curves, challenged by a brute's top-heavy aggression, supported by the vulnerability of a depressed or anemic shape design of sidekicks, and, lastly, threatened by the primal angularity of a villain. What always struck me here is the way that abstraction, or the way we psychologically relate to a shape, is key to the emotive connection we develop for a character. I consider this stage gesture for its wonderful simplification and mobilization of artistic means to primary artist intent. So, with a couple of general examples under our belt, let's pause for a moment to consider: Why are we are making the drawing (painting, image, and so on)?

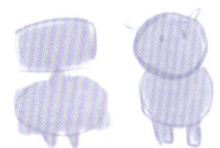 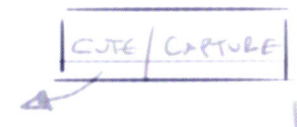 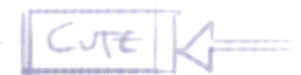

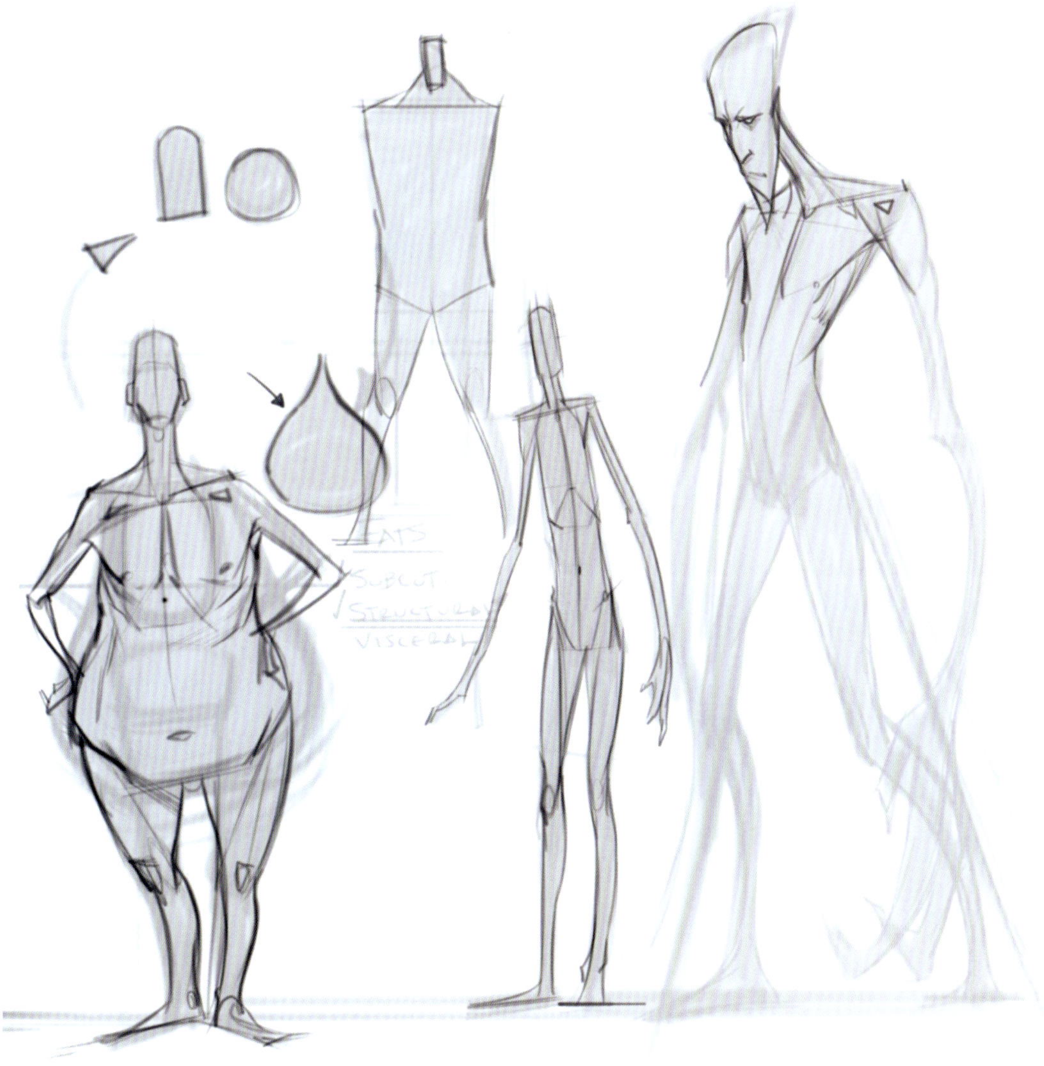

**WHAT'S IMPORTANT TO YOU TO SHOW?**
**WHAT IS IT YOU WANT TO SAY?**
**DO YOU WANT YOUR AUDIENCE TO**
**CONNECT WITH THE MOOD?**

Though by far the most important to answer, the difficulty of this question is that there's no limit to the possible ways in which one might answer. No matter what you decide, keep in mind, there's no right or wrong answer here.

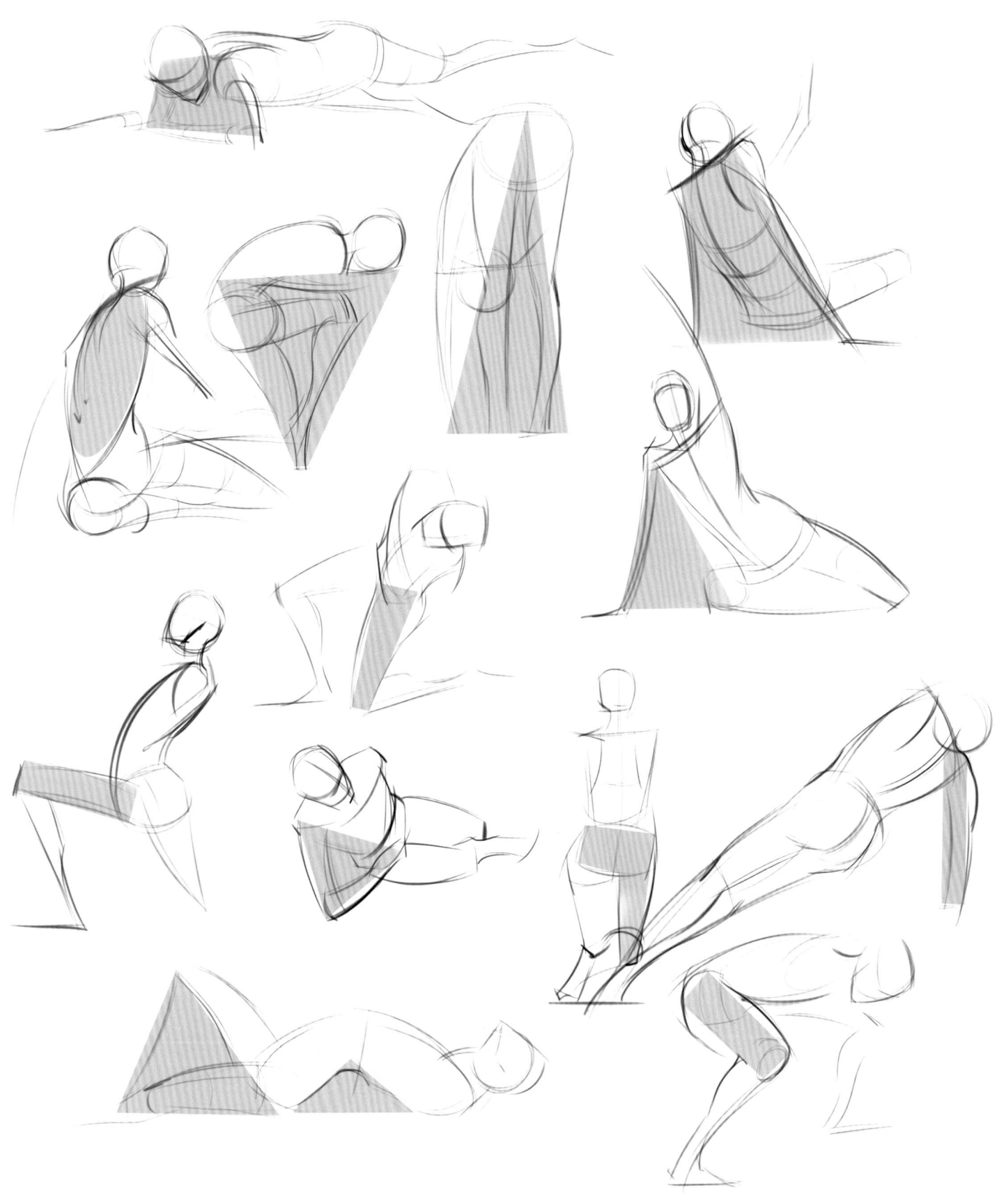

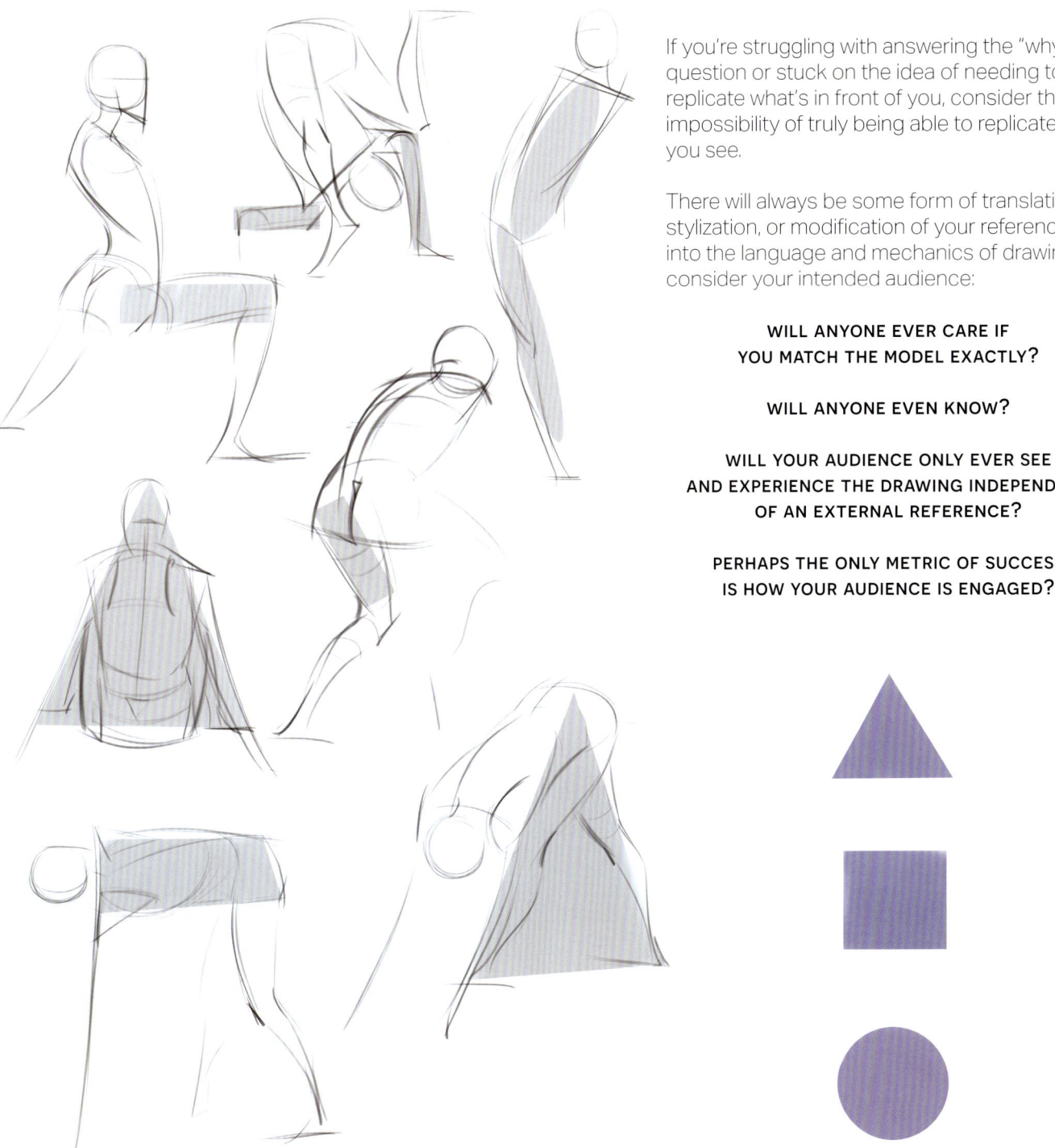

If you're struggling with answering the "why" question or stuck on the idea of needing to replicate what's in front of you, consider the impossibility of truly being able to replicate what you see.

There will always be some form of translation, stylization, or modification of your reference into the language and mechanics of drawing. Or consider your intended audience:

**WILL ANYONE EVER CARE IF
YOU MATCH THE MODEL EXACTLY?**

**WILL ANYONE EVEN KNOW?**

**WILL YOUR AUDIENCE ONLY EVER SEE
AND EXPERIENCE THE DRAWING INDEPENDENT
OF AN EXTERNAL REFERENCE?**

**PERHAPS THE ONLY METRIC OF SUCCESS
IS HOW YOUR AUDIENCE IS ENGAGED?**

*Tip: This application of shape and design can be a powerful tool for creating characters or for pushing an abstract feeling in the context of a gestural study. For example, exaggerating a box-like angularity in a shoulder or hip may increase the sense of weight or importance in a pose. Meanwhile, the passive elongation of a torso using curves enhances the feeling of stretching or lengthening of a body.*

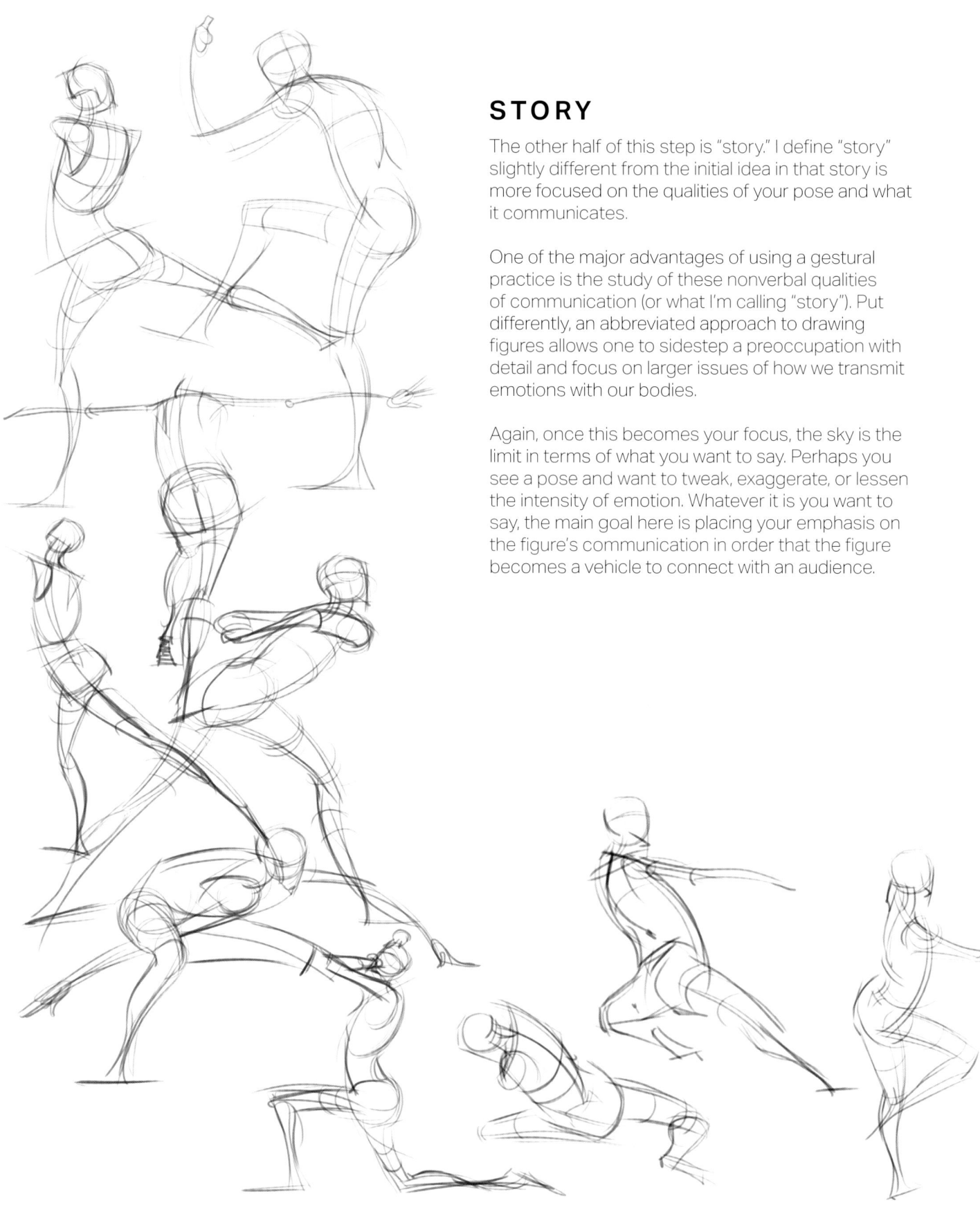

## STORY

The other half of this step is "story." I define "story" slightly different from the initial idea in that story is more focused on the qualities of your pose and what it communicates.

One of the major advantages of using a gestural practice is the study of these nonverbal qualities of communication (or what I'm calling "story"). Put differently, an abbreviated approach to drawing figures allows one to sidestep a preoccupation with detail and focus on larger issues of how we transmit emotions with our bodies.

Again, once this becomes your focus, the sky is the limit in terms of what you want to say. Perhaps you see a pose and want to tweak, exaggerate, or lessen the intensity of emotion. Whatever it is you want to say, the main goal here is placing your emphasis on the figure's communication in order that the figure becomes a vehicle to connect with an audience.

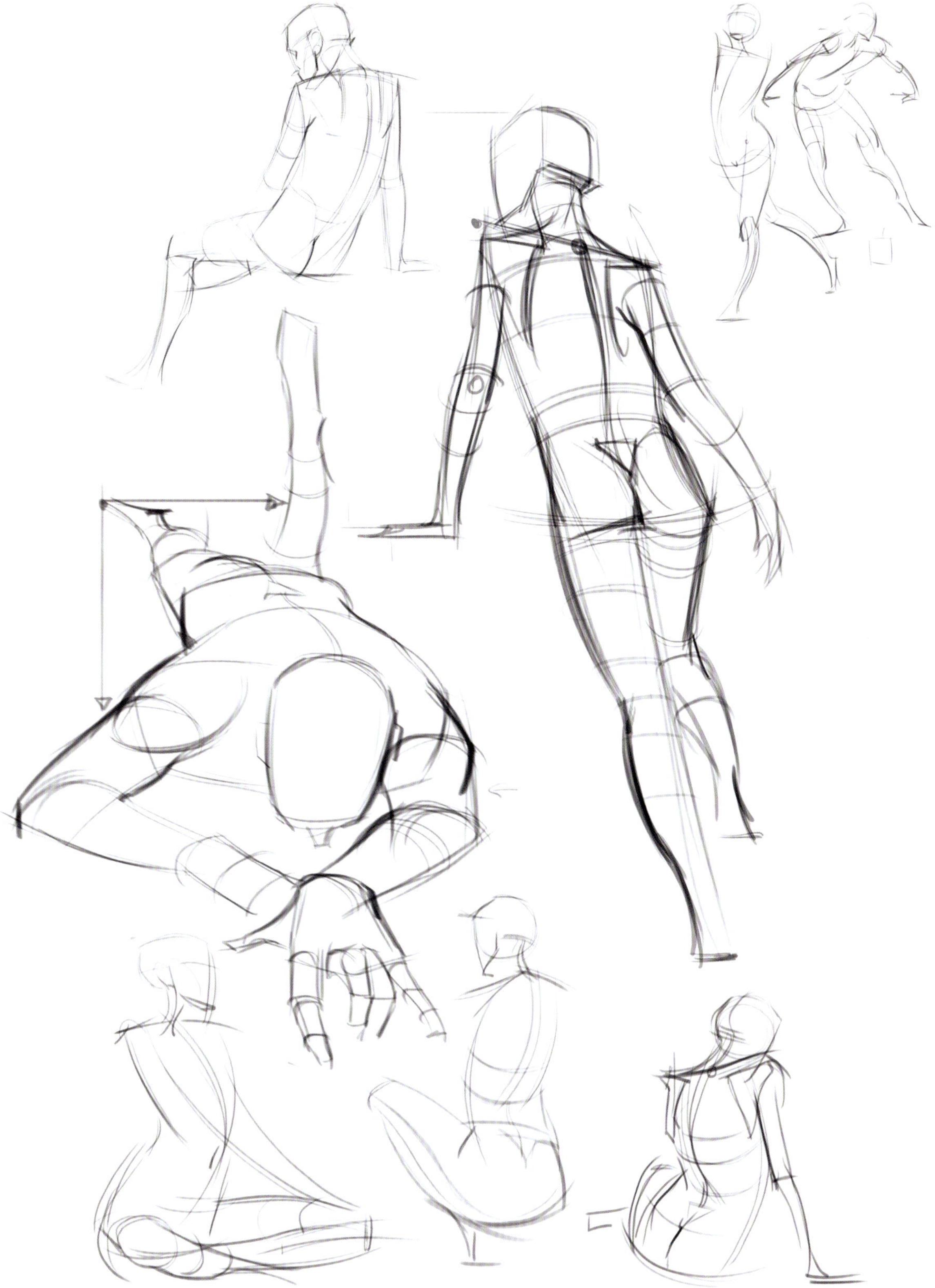

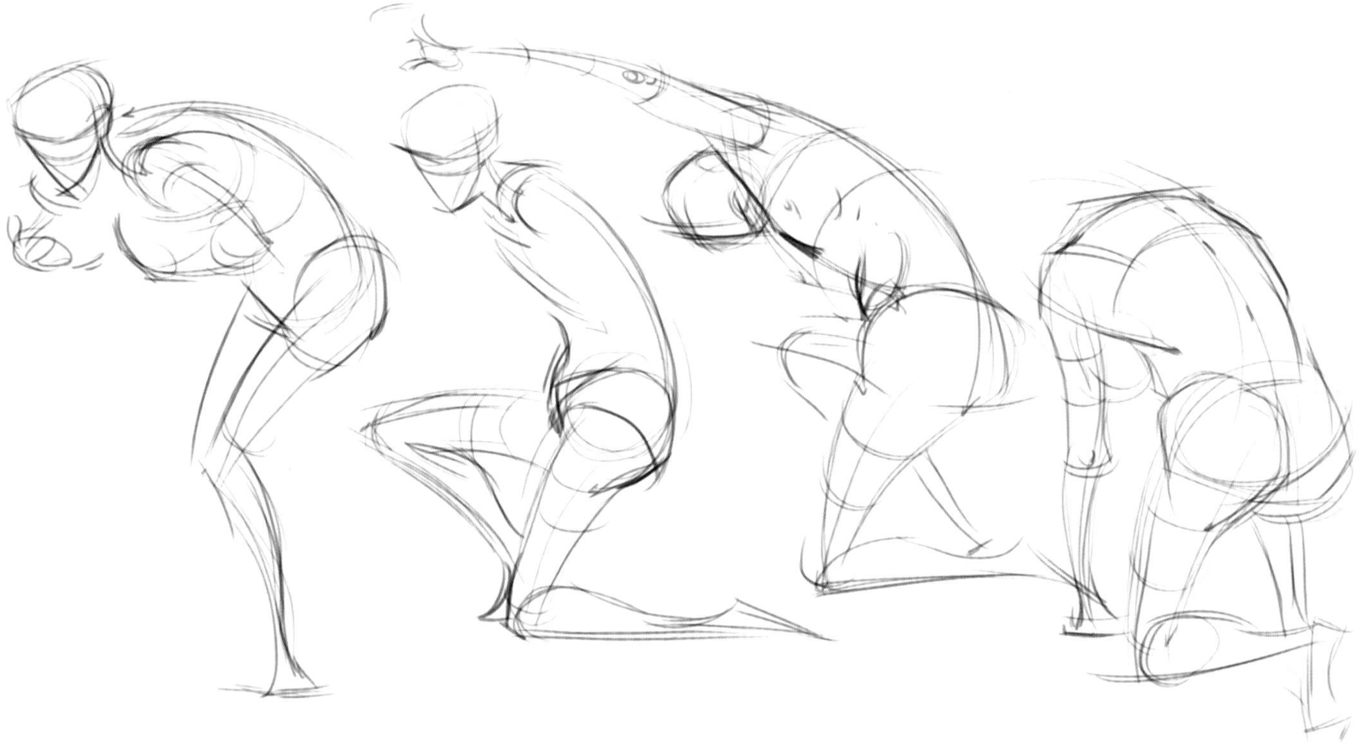

## BODY LANGUAGE

The observation of the body is a fascinating and complex subject. However, it can also be a little daunting to begin with as the human body can give off thousands of nonverbal messages. For this reason, some research or an informal study into body language is incredibly useful to pair with a study of gesture.

According to Joe Navarro and Marvin Karlins, author of the book *What Every Body is Saying: An Ex-FBI Agent's Guide to Speed-Reading People*, nonverbal behaviors make up approximately 60 to 65 percent of interpersonal communication. Navarro and Karlins describe the limbic brain as the catalyst of nonverbal communication and categorize our nonverbal responses into 3 Fs: freeze, flight, and fight.

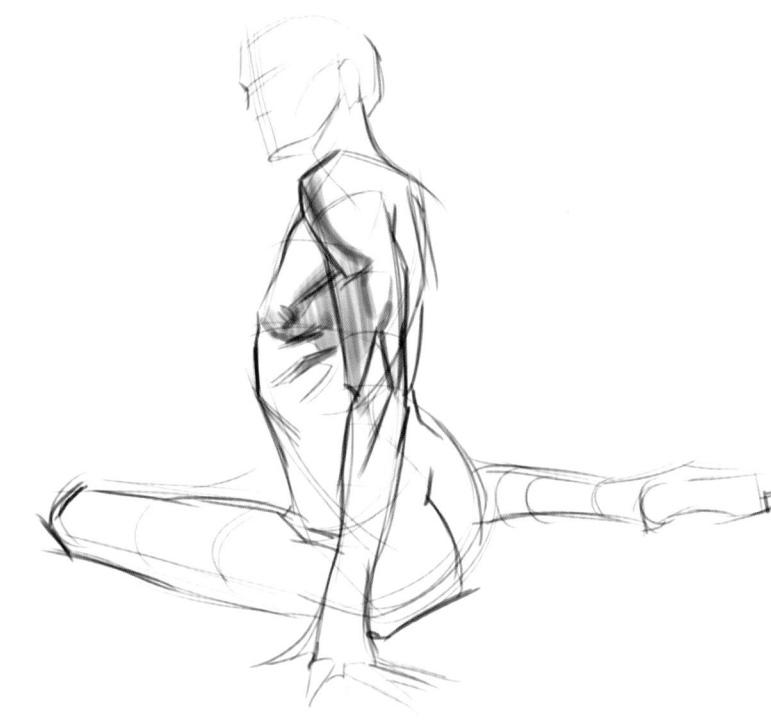

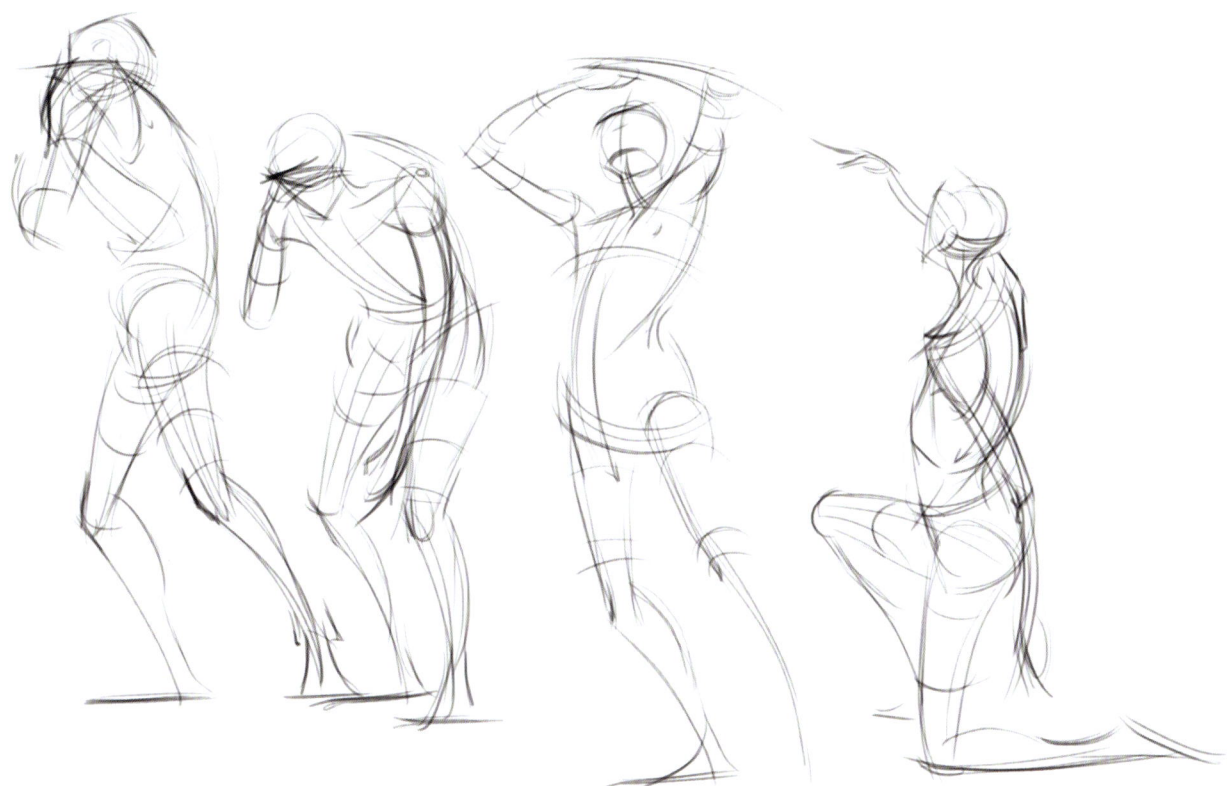

From here, the authors move to reading comfort vs discomfort cues to refine their interpretation of what people are truly saying with body language. Some examples they provide for how the body may transmit the 3 Fs include:

freeze – in the face of a perceived threat we pause, abruptly halt, or hold a static or fixed position. Navarro and Karlins suggest that part of the freeze response may manifest in diminishing our exposure by hiding one's physical presence, including hunching or limiting head exposure.

flight – includes evasive or defensive actions to achieve distance. This might result in blocking behaviors, turning, leaning away, closing the eyes, or any other physical act of establishing distance from a perceived threat.

fight—aggressive survival response (verbal or physical). This might be overt and obvious such as punching or kicking but may also include puffing one's chest, moving into another's space, or an intense stare.

When making gesture drawings, an awareness of body language can help identify patterns to how the body transmits information. One approach for its practice could be looking for variations of the 3 Fs or for behaviors matching comfort (e.g., happiness or contentment) vs discomfort (e.g., anxiety or tension).

Once you establish familiarity with more general emotions and how they manifest as positions, then move to smaller more specific nonverbals.

**SCAN THE QR CODE TO WATCH**
a demo utilizing this concept:
**Life Drawing Session.**

One of my favorite examples of gesture with this in mind can be found in *Comics and Sequential Art: Principles & Practice of the World's Most Popular Art Form*, by Will Eisner.

Specifically, I'm always struck by how effective Eisner's microdictionary of gestures is at communicating complex emotional states with so little. In each row, Eisner catalogs postures and positions that signal specific categories of emotion. This is achieved through a deliberate arrangement of the body into patterns of which we have an intuitive understanding. Eisner's silhouettes are a clear and concise example of the body projecting a mood, emotion, or psychological state. In the context of appreciating the value of gesture and its relationship to the story of the body, it's worth considering how endless attempts at rendering couldn't substitute for this setup.

Eisner's s mirodictionary includes bold and dramatic examples of nonverbal communication. However, gestures may also aim for more subtlety in their treatment of the figure and its nonverbal communi-cation strategies. Examples of subtlety in nonverbal communication might be the pacifying behavior of touching the sternal notch, neck, or underside of our jaw when

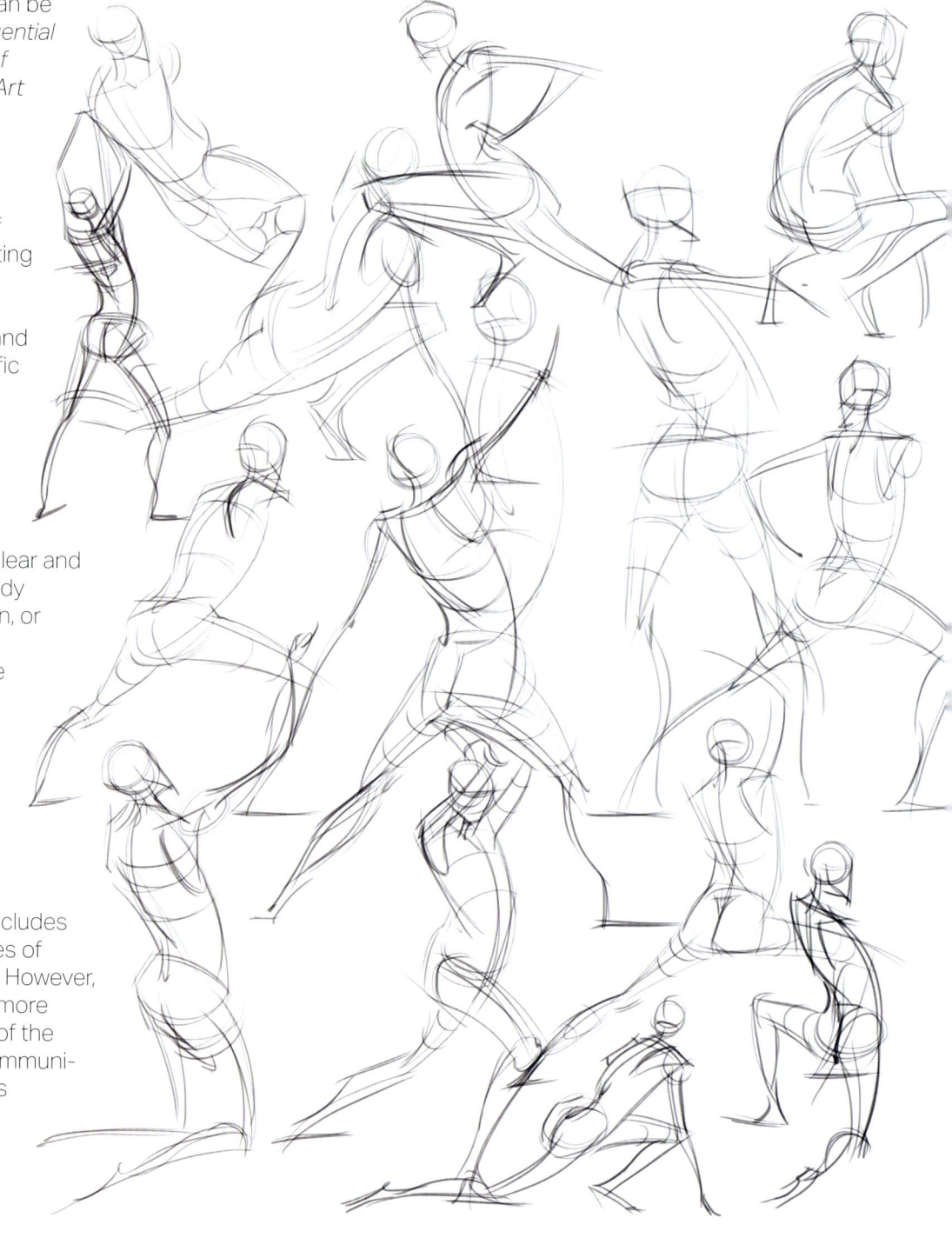

uncomfortable, or how you might recognize your best friend/family member from 50 feet away.

Imagine stripping out all our details and instead seeing unique qualities of positioning, balance, weight, or posture.

To conclude, with all of this I am suggesting that we shift our thinking from the "observation" of a figure to instead an emphasis on interpretation. As artists, we're primarily dealing with the image, often without type or verbal pronouncements. As such, the importance of understanding nonverbal communication is crucial as it allows our audience an avenue to understand our communicative intention. Remember, there's no right or wrong answer here.

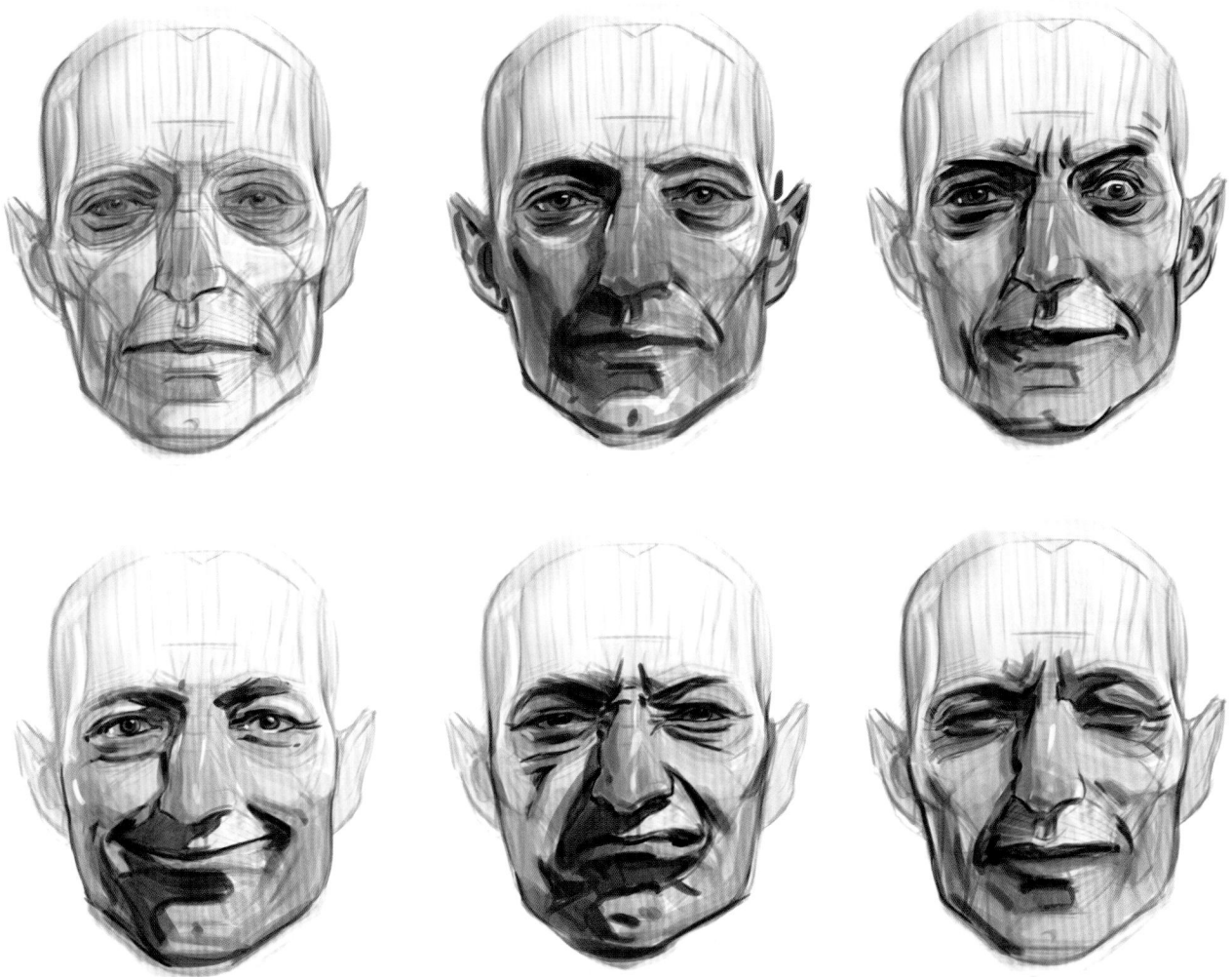

*Tip: If you're anything like me, you've found yourself wishing you could go back to the start of your drawing and fix proportions, the pose, or make your figures feel more compelling.*

*One exercise that may help with this is to jot down whatever comes to mind about the pose first. Perhaps it's one word, "sad," "exciting," "depressing," or whatever else comes to you. Now make the intention of your drawing to communicate this quality using the figure. In other words, arrange the parts to communicate the expression.*

# WEIGHT AND BALANCE

Having addressed some thoughts on "story," let's turn to ideas of "weight and balance." If the story is about the larger conceptual framing behind your gesture, then concerns of weight and balance are more specific to the "actual" design of the skeleton or anatomy.

Put differently, thinking about the weight and balance of the figure brings us out of a subjective interpretation and into a study of the mechanics of the body.

These qualities of weight and balance are the best opportunity to capture certain designs which can evoke an underlying feeling of realism. In this section, I'll go through certain features which illustrate these designs, what to look for, and how we can digest this information back into our practice.

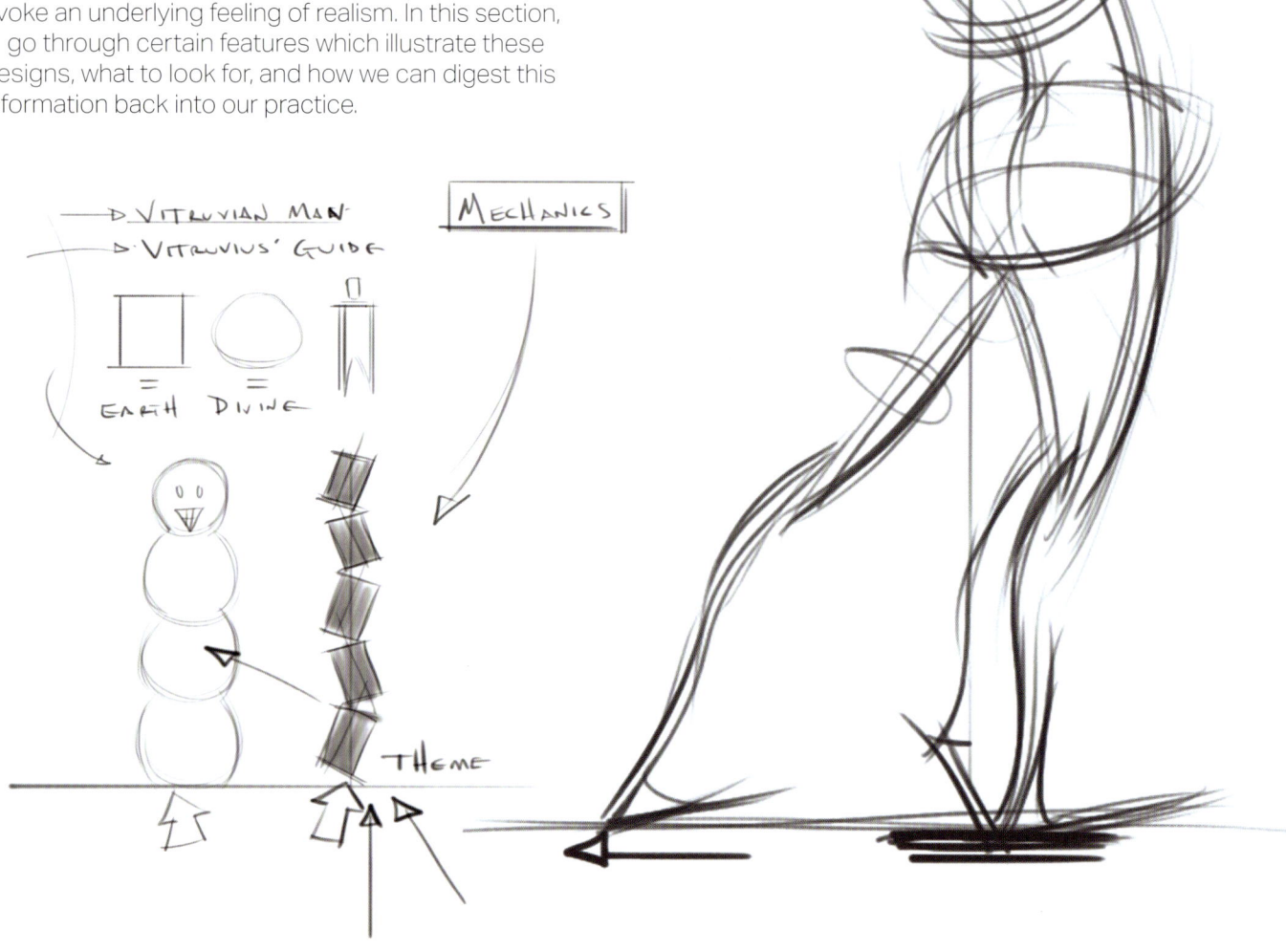

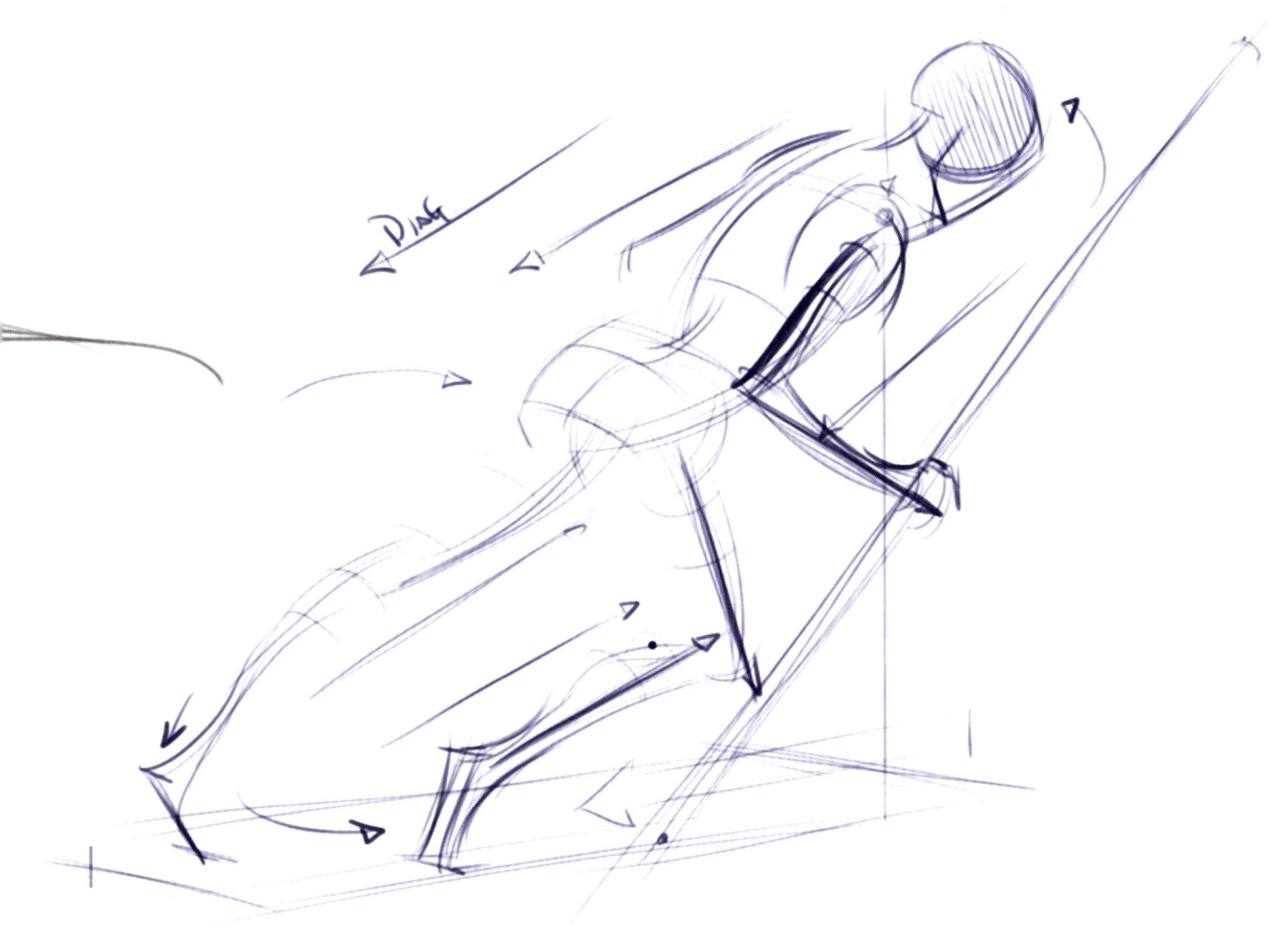

Let's start this section by pointing out a common mistake I see many artists make with gesture (I'm including myself here). I affectionately refer to this style of drawing as "Mr. Hankey," as it looks like the bizarre *South Park* character. Alternatively, I've heard this design referred to as a Michelin tire man or Popeye figure.

The preceding characterizations all refer to an awkwardness that results from an over reliance on symmetry. My best guess is that this comes from a sincere focus and concentrated effort placed on observing the outside of the figure. However, with too much focus here it becomes easy to neglect the whole, or a study of the interior forms. While there's nothing wrong with contour drawing, creating a "Mr. Hanky" is the complete antithesis of what we're after

at this point as it detracts from a believable sense of realism or underlying anatomy in your drawings.

Again, the issue here is the symmetry, which causes a stiffness or static feeling. Used intentionally, there's nothing wrong with this. It's perhaps just not the most effective abstract design to match the rhythmic qualities of the human body. Symmetry is caused by the mirrored-like paralleling of lines, which effectively creates a trap for the eye and impedes any natural sense of movement.

To avoid this, let's look at a few areas in the body which exhibit this natural quality of weight and balance. The goal here is to learn, through an investigative analysis, design alternatives that might be more in line with the body.

# WHAT?

I begin this analysis by simplifying the figure into eight parts. This naturally leads us to our second category of study, which is "What."

"What" is in reference to the subject you're drawing. In this case, the eight parts of the body. It may sound strange to phrase it like this, but I'll also use this approach to draw animals, which would entail a different organization or thinking of the eight parts.

The eight parts of the body include the head, rib cage, pelvis, legs, arms, and most importantly, the spine. In brief, you can think of the goal of your gesture as the purposeful summary of these eight parts.

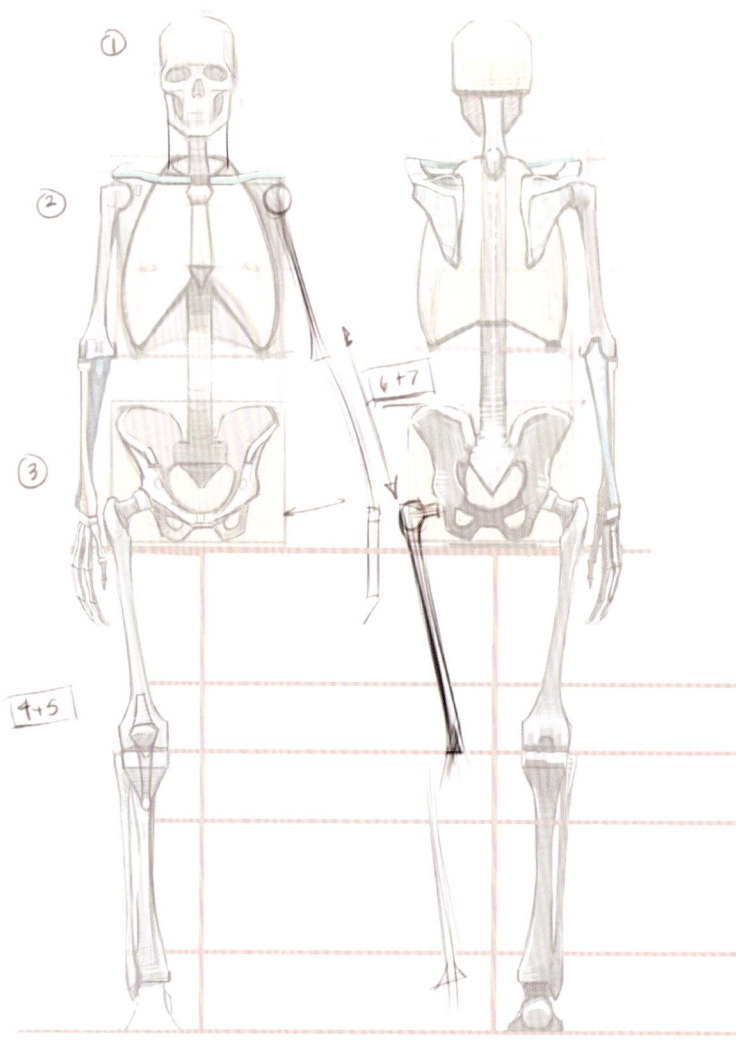

# EIGHT PARTS

### SPINE
The spine is the most important of part as it ties together all others. The spine is composed of three distinct areas, the cervical, thoracic, and lumbar areas.

### HEAD
The cranial mass and mandible combine to create the head shape. Connected to the diagonal of the cervical spine, the head sits out and over the rib cage.

### RIB CAGE
The rib cage is made of 12 ribs (5 true, 5 false, and 2 floating). I position the rib cage as an egg shape set at a counter diagonal to the cervical column and head above.

### PELVIS
The last of our core masses, the pelvis angles with the lumbar section and will sit at another counter diagonal to the thoracic section and rib cage above.

### TWO LEGS
The femur, tibia, and fibula support and balance the core masses above. From the front, I push a dynamic feeling to the legs in a lighting bolt design. From the side, a long sweeping "S."

### TWO ARMS
The humerus, radius, and ulna will always project away from the rib cage in a diagonal. Often, this angle will be greater in women.

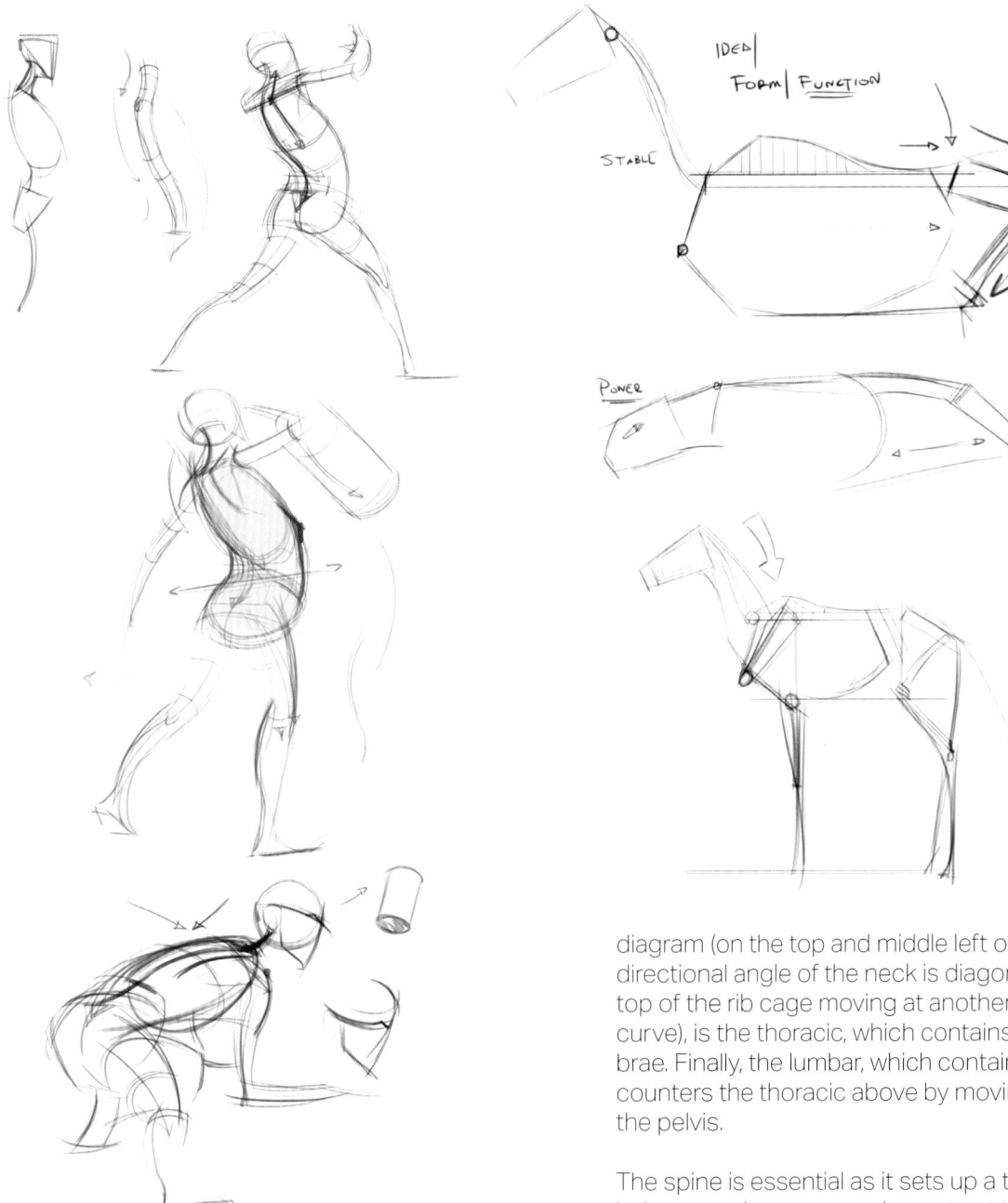

To start, let's begin with the spine, as I consider it the most important design for unraveling the complexity of the body.

The spine is composed of three distinct areas, the cervical, thoracic, and lumbar areas. The cervical, leading from the back of the head down into the ribcage, consists of seven vertebrae. Notice in the diagram (on the top and middle left on 29) that the directional angle of the neck is diagonal. From the top of the rib cage moving at another diagonal (or "C" curve), is the thoracic, which contains twelve vertebrae. Finally, the lumbar, which contains five vertebrae, counters the thoracic above by moving away toward the pelvis.

The spine is essential as it sets up a theme of radical balance and asymmetry. In contrast to the stable and stacked symmetry of a "Mr. Hankey" drawing, notice instead that the design of the spine organizes the eight parts of our body into a chaotic tower. This is an essential tension to highlight when creating gestures.

I realize this isn't immediately obvious when observing the shape of the figure. However, once understood, you'll begin to see its impact everywhere, and your drawings will take on a more dynamic quality in the torso area.

To move one step further, notice how the spine organizes the three core masses (head, rib cage, and pelvis) into an echo of its asymmetry. This is visible in the way the core masses counterbalance in a way that is not symmetrical or suggestive of a stacked symmetry.

Specifically, when looking at the profile, notice that the head is farther out over the ribcage. So, while the head is pushed forward by the cervical column, the thoracic column positions the rib cage at a counter angle to the neck and head above. Lastly, the lumbar column sets the angle of the pelvis at a counter angle to the rib cage.

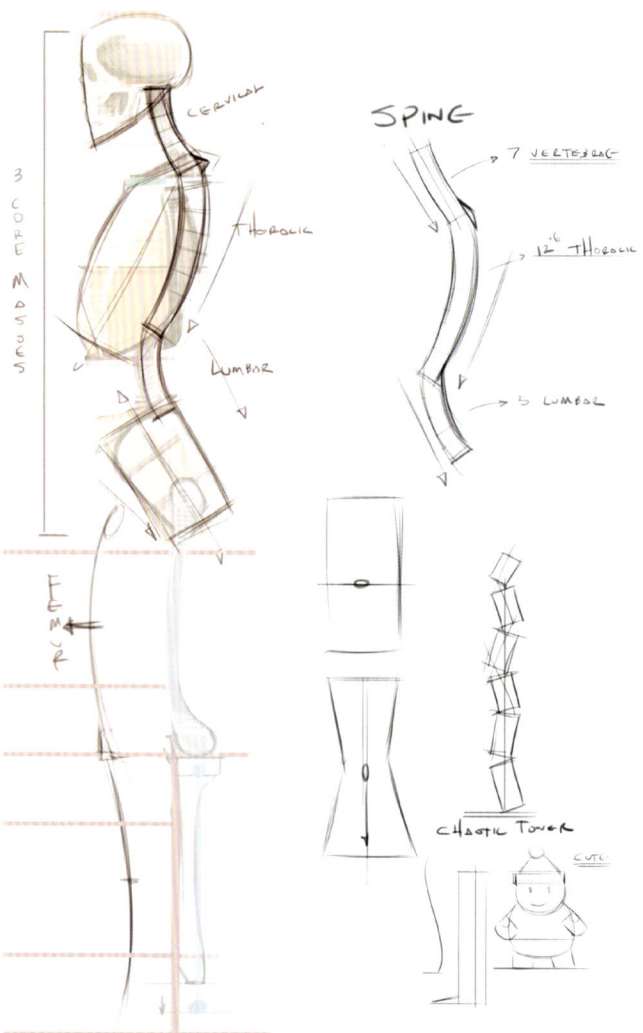

The effect of this is an upright, vertical posture created through the counter positioning of the three main masses. This is an excellent design to emulate if we're looking to embrace natural qualities of "weight and balance" in our drawings.

This theme of asymmetry is further found in areas outside of the spine and core masses. Consider the design of the legs (femur, tibia, and fibula). Notice from the profile view, that the femur has a large bow or curvature to it.

This curvature finds an opposite in the lower leg giving an overall "S" curve to the legs (upper and lower). An important design allowing for an absorption of weight/impact.

In contrast, imagine for a moment how ineffective it would be if the legs were perfectly vertical or sym-metrical. Though it may sound ridiculous, this is the default design suggested by most contoured figure drawings that fall victim to the "Mr. Hankey" effect. If our legs did have that design, again, imagine how painful jumping or impact of any kind would be. We'd likely just snap a bone or fall over.

Further, consider the design of the legs from the front and back views. I'm fond of referencing this design as a lightning bolt due to the natural diagonal trajectory of the femur toward the inside of the body (this is stereotypically a more dramatic angle in women), the knee with a slight counter out, and the lower leg back in again.

Another example of balance in the figure might be the distribution of texture, specifically, hard vs soft forms. Notice how every hard bony mass is always transi-tioned by a soft area (neck, waist, hip, and so on).

Though this list isn't exhaustive, I hope it draws your attention to the underlying designs of the body and their common thread of weight/balance and asymmetry. I am constantly looking at these qualities when deciding on the important aspects to abstract when making gestures. I might even take this a step further and say the attributes of weight/balance pointed out thus far are the most important to help push a "realistic" quality in figures.

While this may be a controversial opinion, paying attention to inherent design principles has always struck me as more realistic when compared to translating the outside contour of the figure.

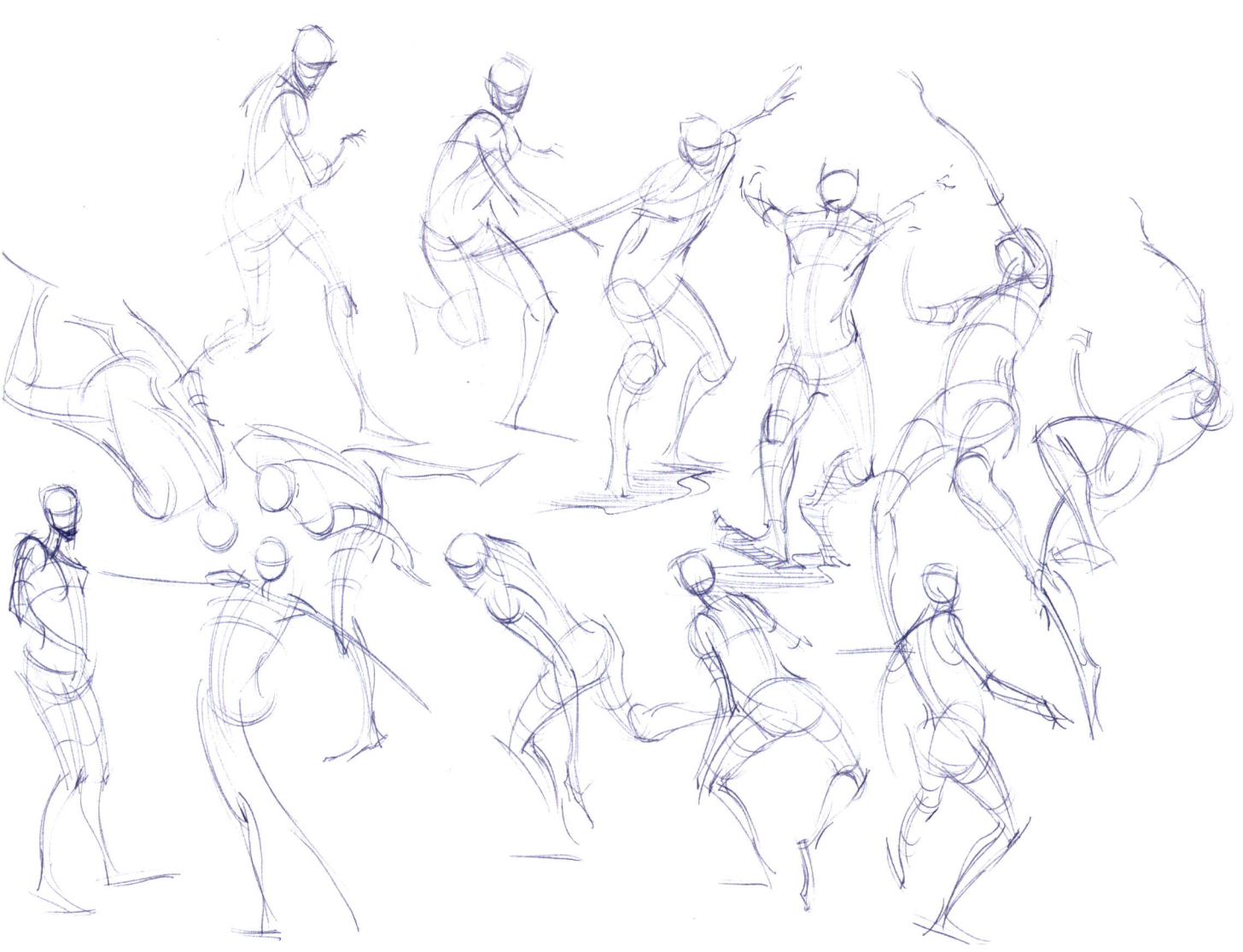

*Tip: Making simple studies or sketches like the ones shown on this page may be helpful to begin thinking about the important directional angles that the spine takes.*

# HOW?

Before moving on, let's do a quick summary of what I've set up so far. Remember that my goal continues to be to tie my list of essential qualities in gesture together with one overall design theme.

We began with story, which is tied to the why of your drawing and its making. This is where you decide what's important to say with your work. From there we stepped into the mechanics of the figure by looking at principles of weight and balance. We did so by looking at the eight parts (or what) of the figure. Our discussion "now" shifts to movement, which is connected to the how or "how to" of the drawing. Said differently, our how is best defined as the clearest use of abstract/formal elements to communicate the total of concerns outlined previously.

A bit more now on the third essential "movement."

## MOVEMENT

I think an expectation many of us have when looking at a figure drawing is a sense of realistic motion. The question becomes, how does one create this in a static image? If we want to suggest that our figure has the capacity for dynamic movement, I need to choose a technique that highlights visual qualities of motion.

The most obvious way *not* to depict motion into your gesture drawing is, again, the symmetry of the "Mr. Hankey" design mentioned previously. That static symmetry is without any visual expression conducive to movement.

Ask yourself instead, what type of line conveys all the outlined concerns, including the summary of the eight parts (connecting parts to a whole), the tension of naturalistic weight and the body's natural balance, anticipation of movement, and so on.

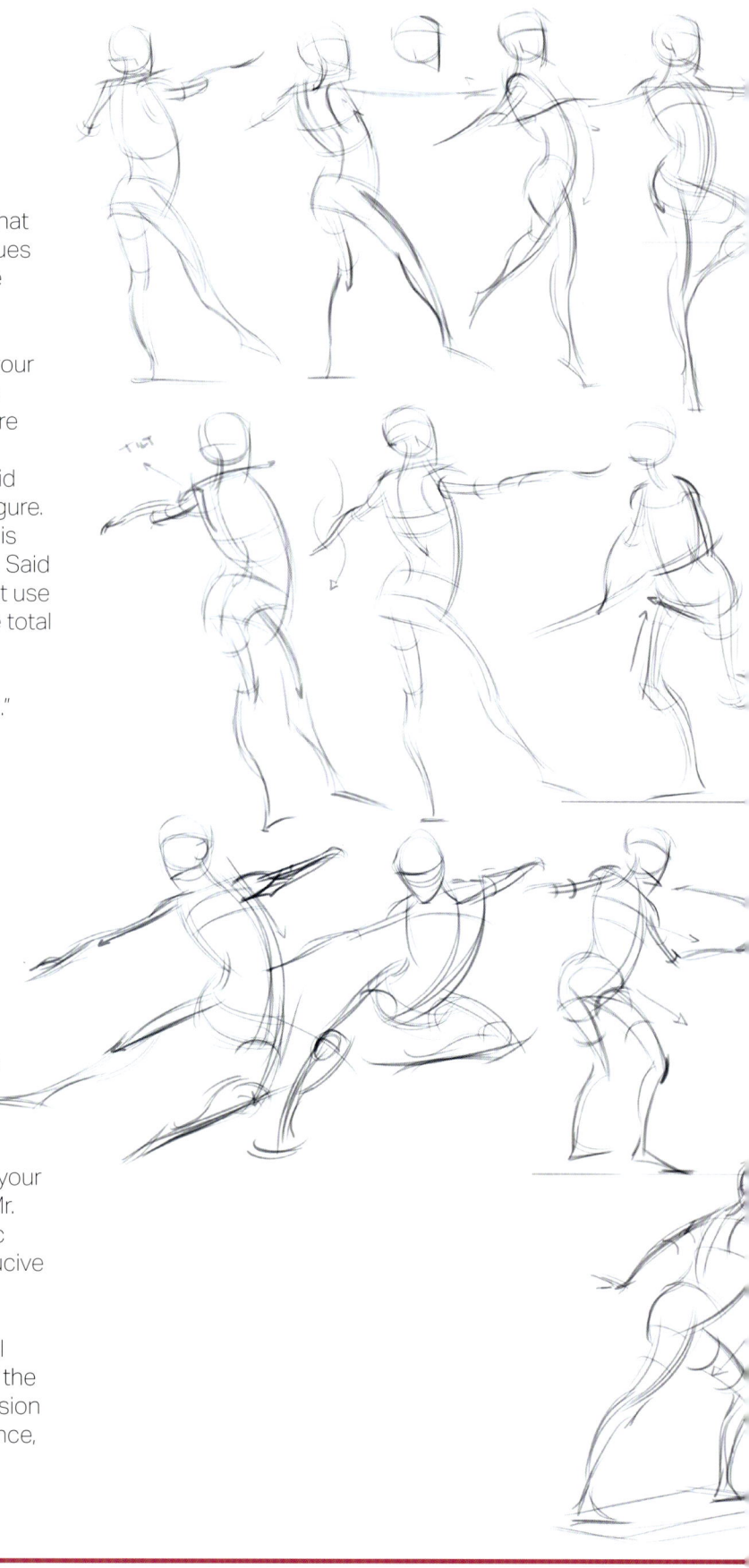

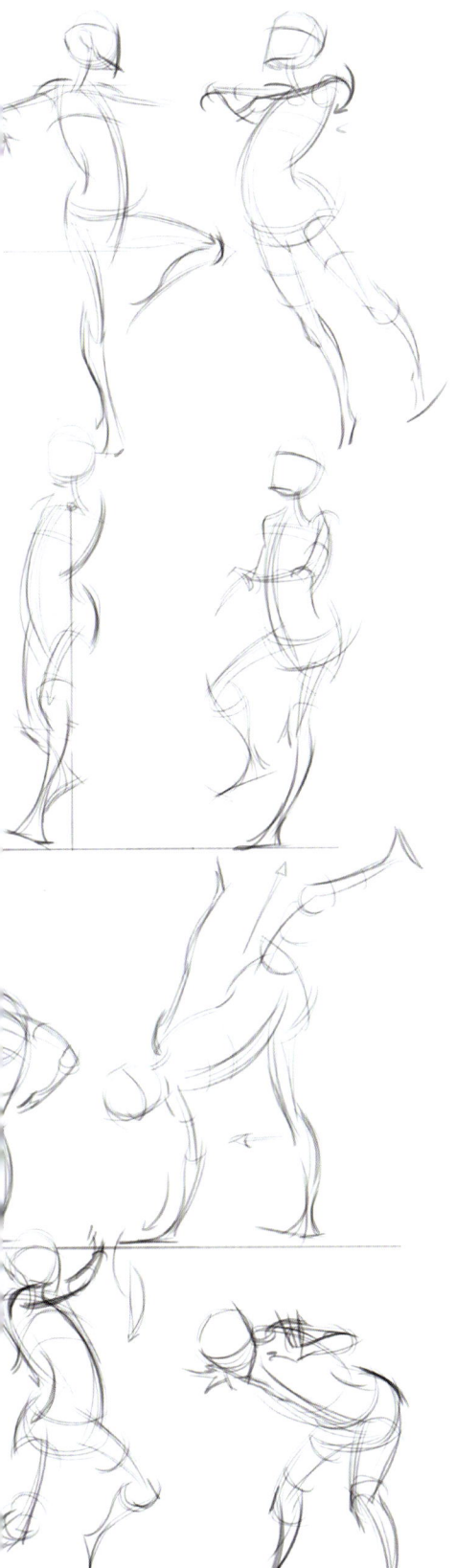

Your "how" should say all these qualities. In other words, I'm attempting to share my own thought process when abstracting a figure.

While I understand this may read as overly redundant, this is consistent with how I am defining gesture, the abstraction of the figure into the most important formal qualities. My emphasis on conveying this definition and process is to pull back the curtain on my formula or thought process. The benefit in doing so is that you might be able to create gestures more personalized to your own concerns and not just copy my technique.

The most effective approach for showcasing movement, maintaining a sense of fluidity, and all the other design themes touched on so far is asymmetry. However, before making our own gestures, let's look at a few examples from artists that have employed the same technique. The use of asymmetry to produce a figure filled with motion is not unique to me or any other artist writing on the topic of gesture. One of my favorite sketches by Michelangelo shows a graceful yet simple figure indication (Fig. 2). This sketch accompanies a sonnet describing the difficulties of painting the Sistine Chapel ceiling.

What we can see here in Michelangelo's sketch are the parts of the body summarized through curves all in an asymmetrical relationship to the one below and above. There is a story (painting the Sistine Chapel ceiling sucks and is uncomfortable), a showcasing of weight and balance (notice how the description of parts feels like the chaotic tower mentioned prior), and an accompanying sense of movement generated through that active asymmetrical positioning of curves.

*Fig. 2*

*Fig. 2 – Michelangelo, sketch illustrating a sonnet describing the painting of the Sistine Chapel, 1508*

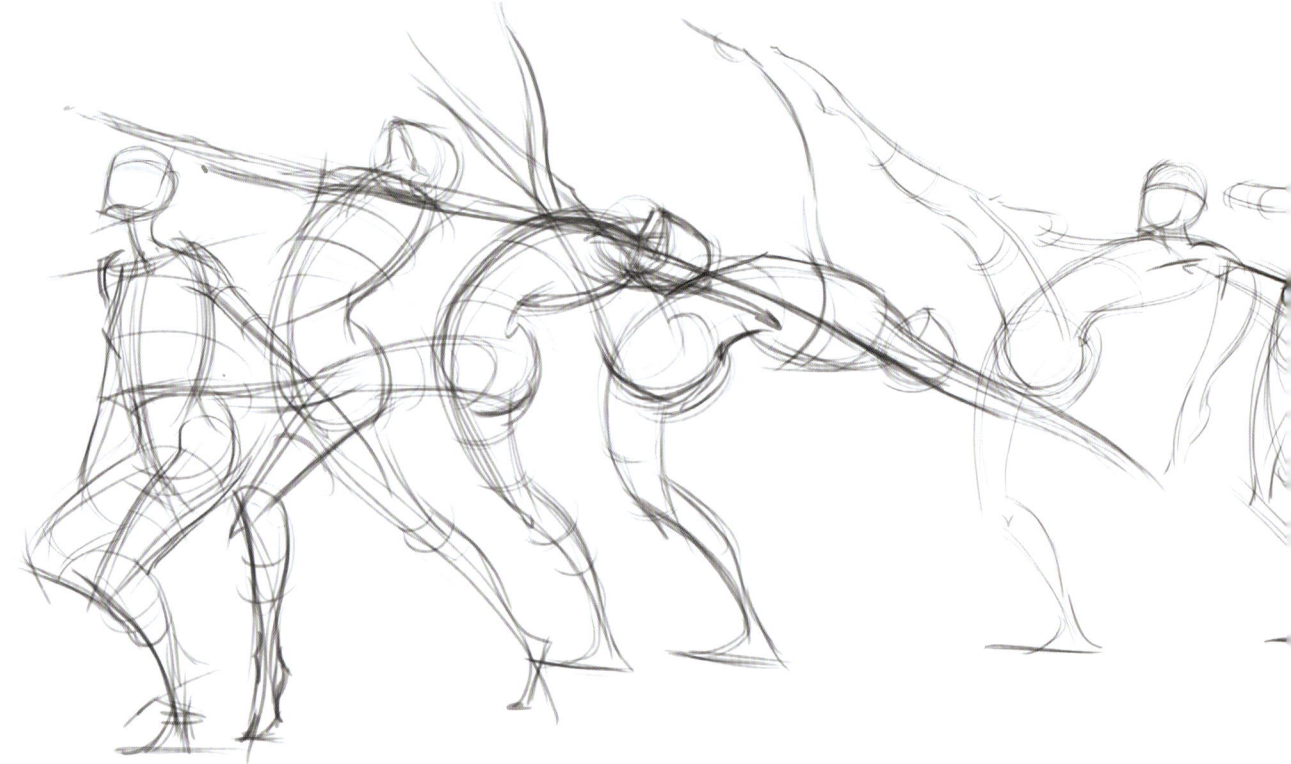

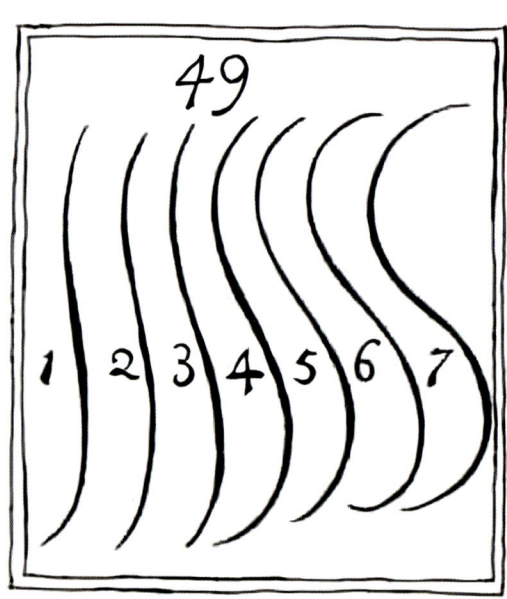

*Fig. 3*

A staple and invaluable reference in the teaching/learning of figurative drawing is Andrew Loomis's, *Figure Drawing for All It's Worth*. In his book, Loomis describes rhythm as "flow" and a "continuous line resulting in a sense of unity and grace." Loomis's description and philosophy of rhythm (unified plan/purpose) is referenced as being indebted to the work of William Hogarth and his thinking developed in his *The Analysis of Beauty* from 1753. Within, Hogarth describes the serpentine line, which gives play to imagination, delighting the eye, and furthers the idea of the human body as being composed of waving/winding forms (Fig. 3).

In a final example from *The Illusion of Life*, the 500-page text on the history and evolution of Disney studios, I'm specifically interested in the section on "Appeal" where we can see the progression of Disney's early aesthetic as an evolution from symmetry to asymmetry. We can see in the book (not pictured here) how the symmetrical designs are described as ineffective for supporting a sense of movement and solidity, while the asymmetrical designs are celebrated for their depiction of naturalism. Relative to the aesthetic of Disney, think of this difference as that between *Steamboat Willie* and *Snow White*.

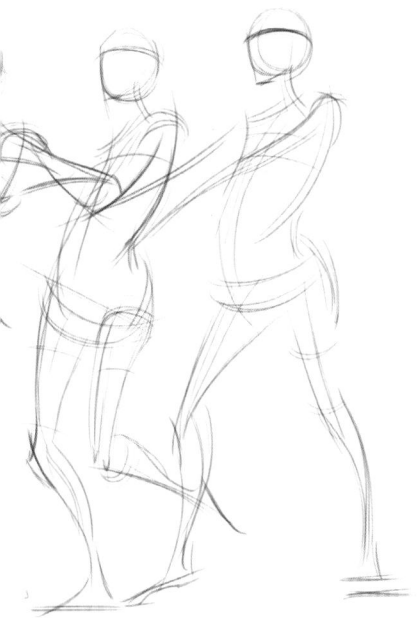

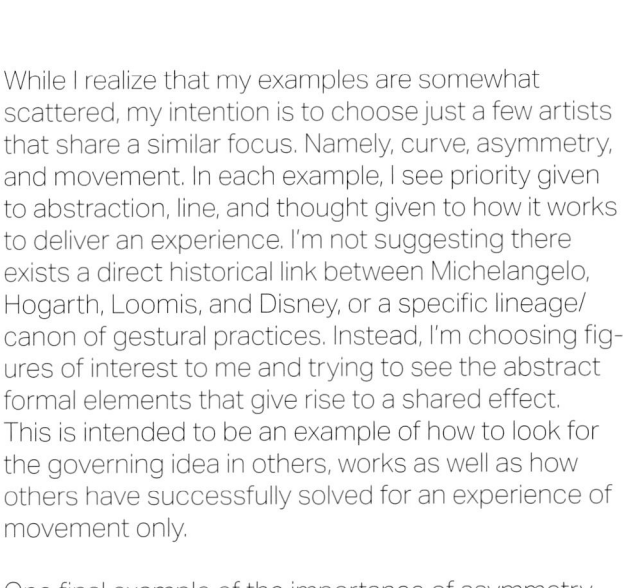

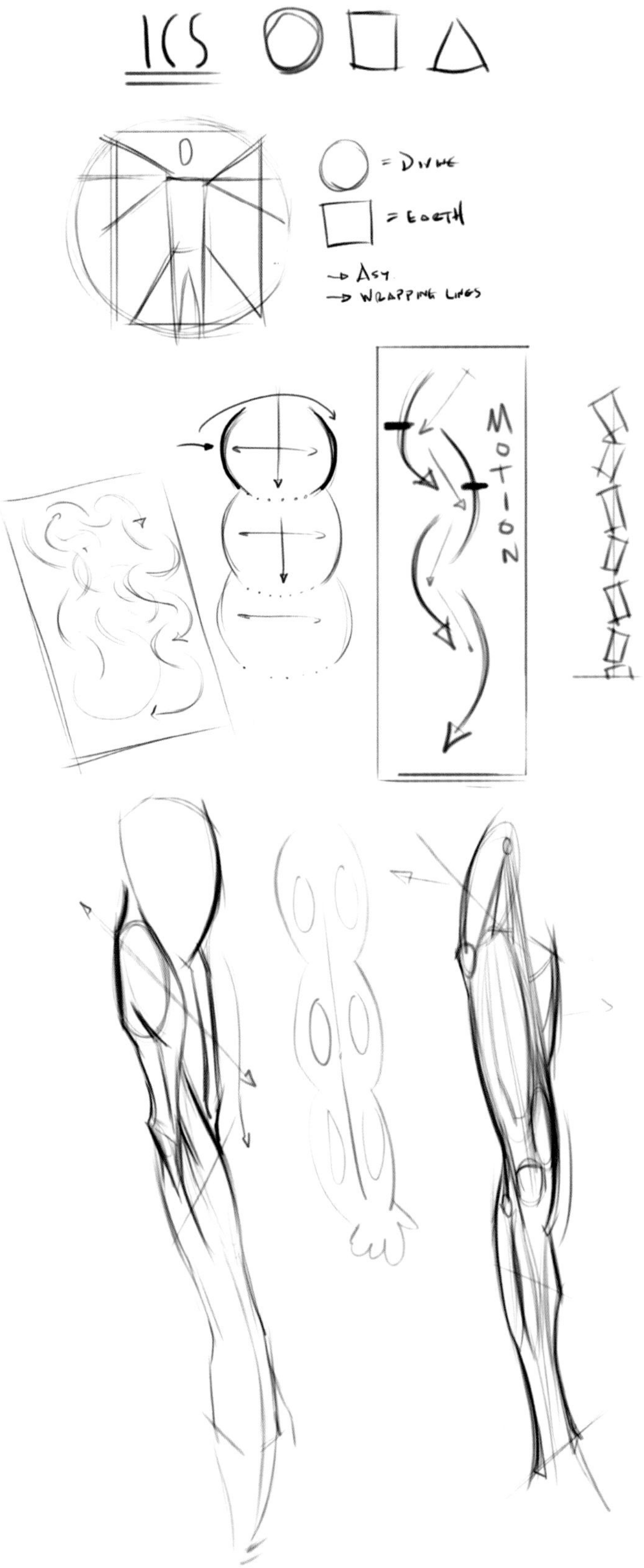

While I realize that my examples are somewhat scattered, my intention is to choose just a few artists that share a similar focus. Namely, curve, asymmetry, and movement. In each example, I see priority given to abstraction, line, and thought given to how it works to deliver an experience. I'm not suggesting there exists a direct historical link between Michelangelo, Hogarth, Loomis, and Disney, or a specific lineage/canon of gestural practices. Instead, I'm choosing figures of interest to me and trying to see the abstract formal elements that give rise to a shared effect. This is intended to be an example of how to look for the governing idea in others, works as well as how others have successfully solved for an experience of movement only.

One final example of the importance of asymmetry can be seen by paying close attention to the contour of an arm or leg. In these forms we might notice the passive and active positioning of muscle groups and the way they resemble the same asymmetry I'm attempting to describe. This is largely the reason I prefer this method of gesture when teaching or studying anatomy as it sensitizes students early on to the actual surface design of anatomy from the start of the drawing.

*Fig. 3 – William Hogarth,* The Analysis of Beauty, *plate 16, 1753*

Let's take a closer look now at the abstract ideas behind this way of composing our lines. First, if we're to draw figures with even the suggestion of symmetry, the effect is to produce closure. In other words, the use of symmetry suggests to us a completed form or shape (see Mr. Hankey). Closing a form off in this way is counterproductive to movement. More generously, we might say it creates a broken, staccato-like motion as using line in this way separates and closes off the rhythmic transition from one area of a drawing to another. Good or bad (I'm not assigning judgment as this is really an issue of your intention or style), this creates a start–stop design for the viewer.

In contrast, I try and maintain constant fluidity throughout the figure. If it's helpful, try and think of your drawings at this stage as abstract diagrams of motion rather than being figures. This is even a helpful way to practice this technique. Though this may sound odd, I find that this helps offset our need to make a figure and allows for a more objective emphasis on the technique.

To connect with this technique, consider the following: each of the eight parts of the body can be broken down into and summarized by a curve. So, if each part of the body is simplified into a curve, and the goal of creating movement is the asymmetrical placement of the next curve, then consider the narrow area of negative shape between them as a joint.

The goal of moving from one part of the body to the next is that we maintain a complete sense of fluidity between all the parts.

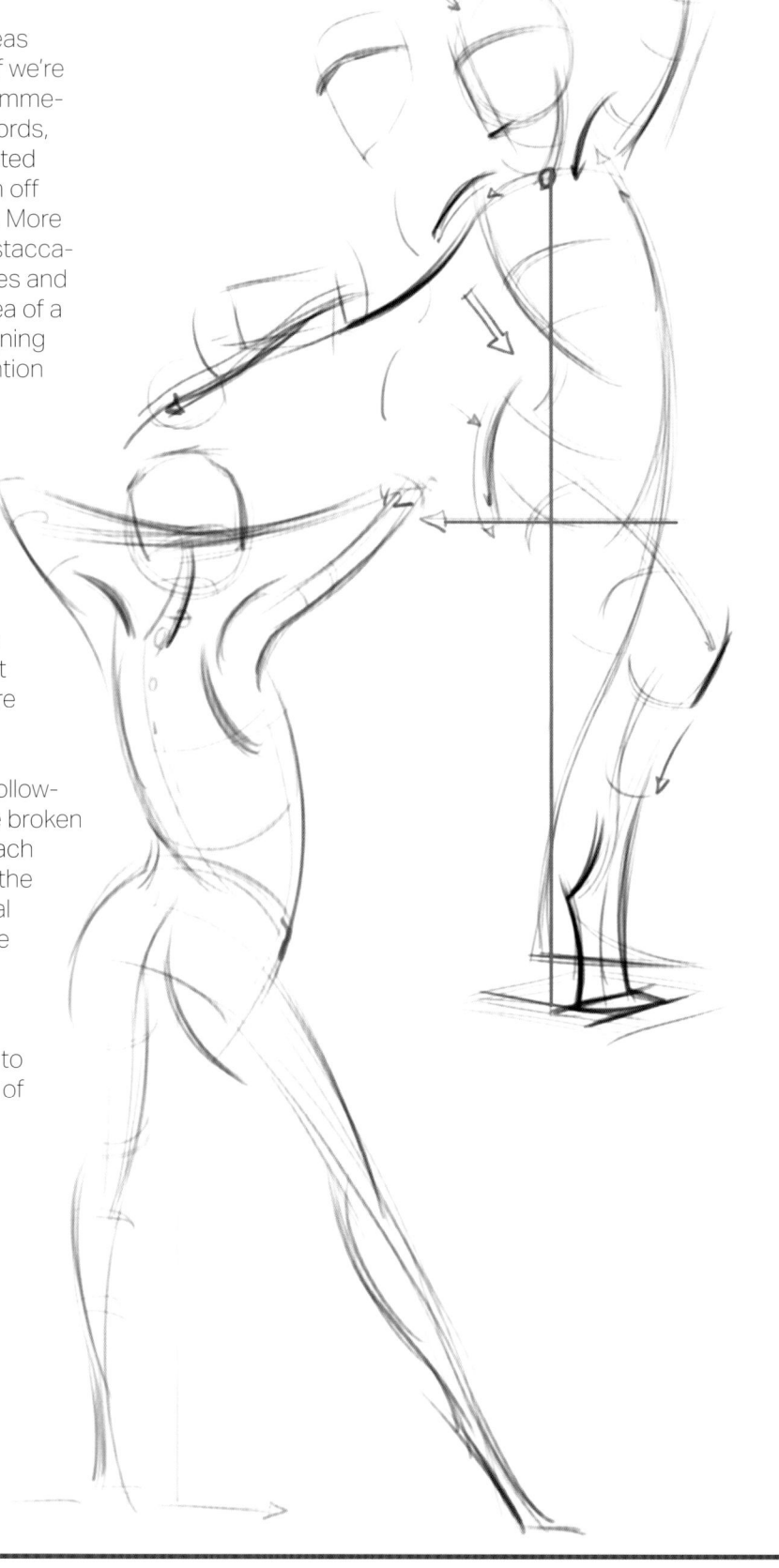

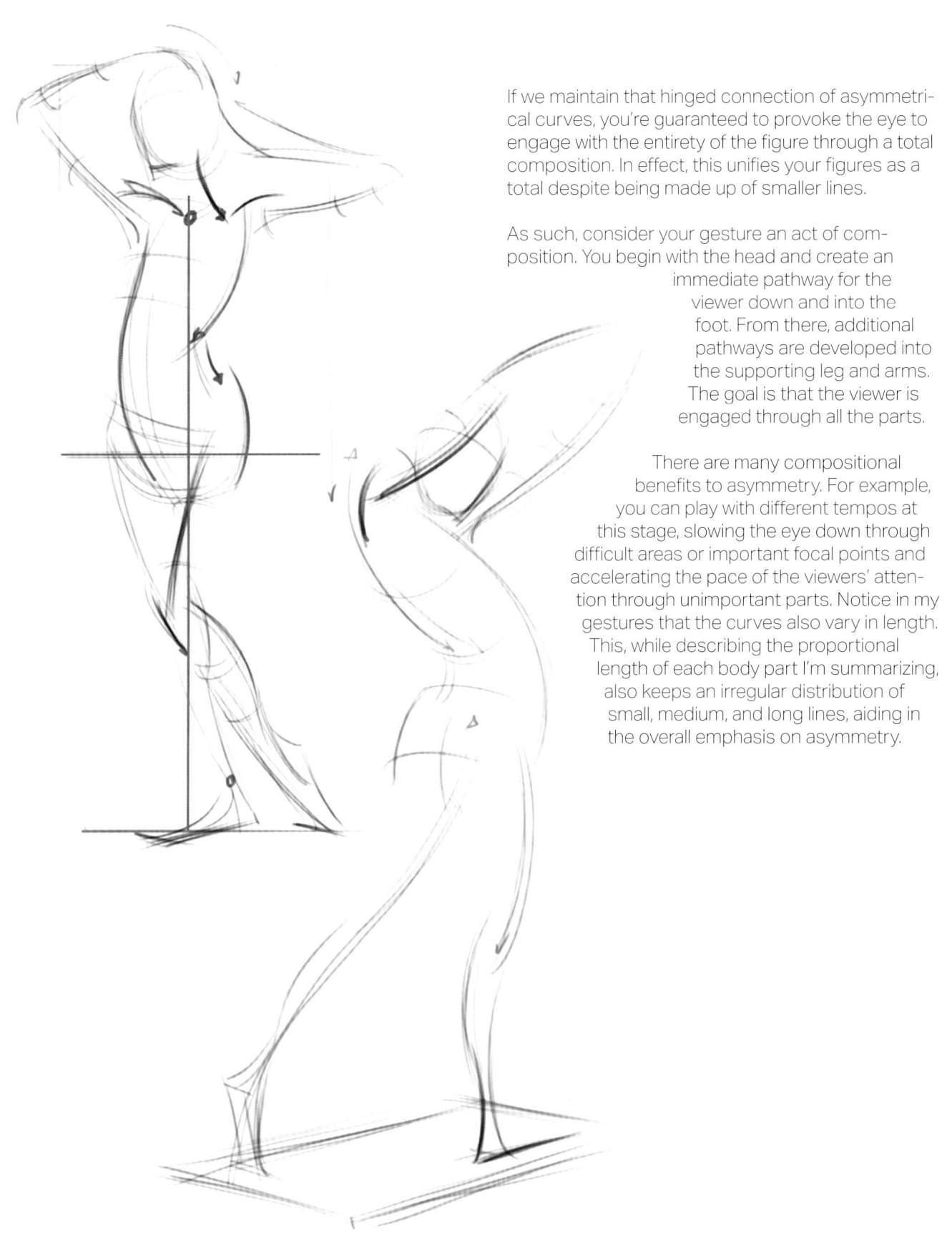

If we maintain that hinged connection of asymmetrical curves, you're guaranteed to provoke the eye to engage with the entirety of the figure through a total composition. In effect, this unifies your figures as a total despite being made up of smaller lines.

As such, consider your gesture an act of composition. You begin with the head and create an immediate pathway for the viewer down and into the foot. From there, additional pathways are developed into the supporting leg and arms. The goal is that the viewer is engaged through all the parts.

There are many compositional benefits to asymmetry. For example, you can play with different tempos at this stage, slowing the eye down through difficult areas or important focal points and accelerating the pace of the viewers' attention through unimportant parts. Notice in my gestures that the curves also vary in length. This, while describing the proportional length of each body part I'm summarizing, also keeps an irregular distribution of small, medium, and long lines, aiding in the overall emphasis on asymmetry.

# PROPORTION

The fourth and final element on my list for gestures is "proportions." Proportions are, of course, important in figure drawing; however, I often downplay their importance during this stage. My thinking is that too much emphasis placed on proportions can often suffocate a more exaggerated and expressive drawing. Basically, the story or idea stage can be compromised with too much attention to getting the figure "right" proportionally.

In your own drawings, see if you can first understand proportions as connected to your larger idea. Throughout art history, artists have manipulated proportion to this end. For example, Michelangelo would lengthen his figures to nearly 13 heads tall during his Mannerist phase. Rodin would exaggerate the size of the hands and feet to push a feeling of heroism in his sculpture. I grew up a fan of comics in the 90s. While the proportions of the figures in those comics were not academically correct, their distortions added a certain dynamic appeal that would have been be lost if drawn "correctly." Consider too that popular drawing manuals, such as those by Andrew Loomis, suggest a proportion chart with variable heights assigning a better and worse size based on his preference for idealism. Loomis's female proportion chart even describes the ideal female as being necessitated through the inclusion of high heels (!?).

My point is, try to not let academic proportions dictate your idea. Don't get me wrong, proportions are crucial, but with gesture we can always come back and correct or allow for a more careful consideration of proportions in subsequent stages. Early on, my preference is to make communication of an idea and movement a priority.

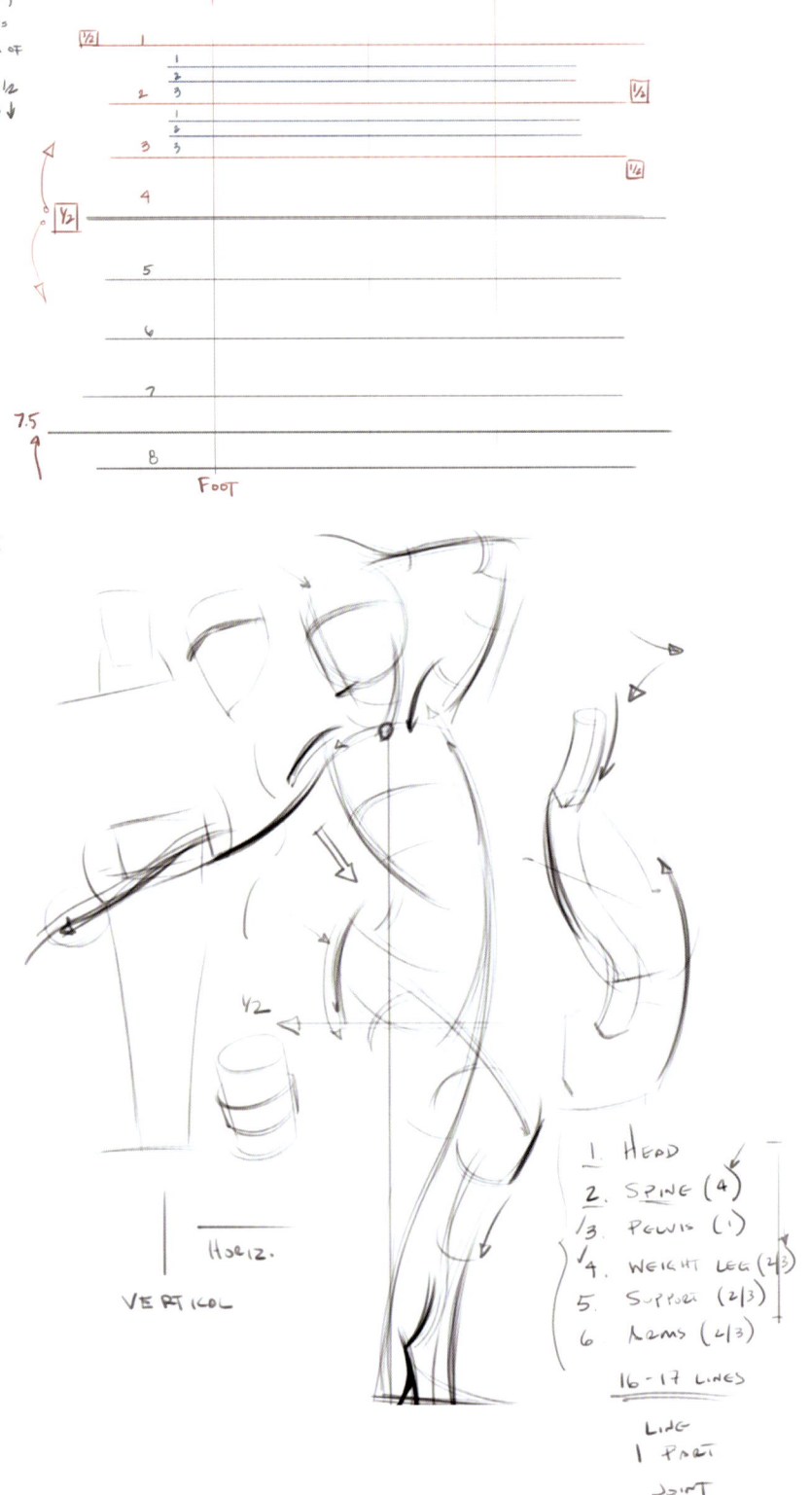

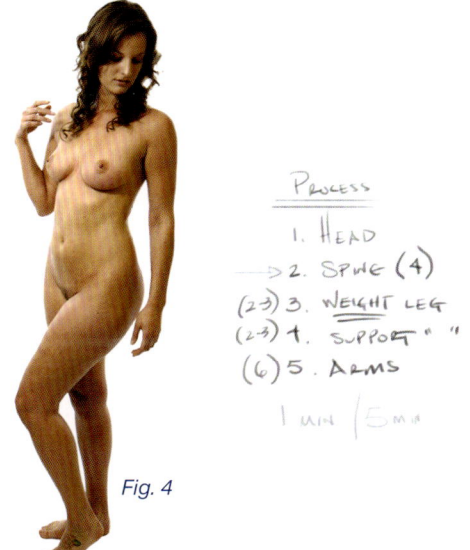

*Fig. 4*

Handwritten notes (Fig. 4):

PROCESS
1. HEAD
2. SPINE (4)
(2-3) 3. WEIGHT LEG
(2-3) 4. SUPPORT " "
(6) 5. ARMS

1 MIN / 5 MIN

## GESTURE AND PROPORTION HALVES

Here are a couple recommendations for ways to approach your proportions.

First, begin by establishing your scale. Place one line for the top of the head and another for where your foot will be.

Divide this space in half. This line marks a halfway point on the figure and represents the bottom of your pelvis.

Within the halves (top and bottom alike) separate these spaces into another half, and then two more (3 lines total). This creates an eight-head chart (see chart on top of page 38). This would present an idealized height. To move this closer to academic proportions just raise the foot/ ground line by a half head. This creates a seven-and-a-half-head tall chart by shortening the leg length.

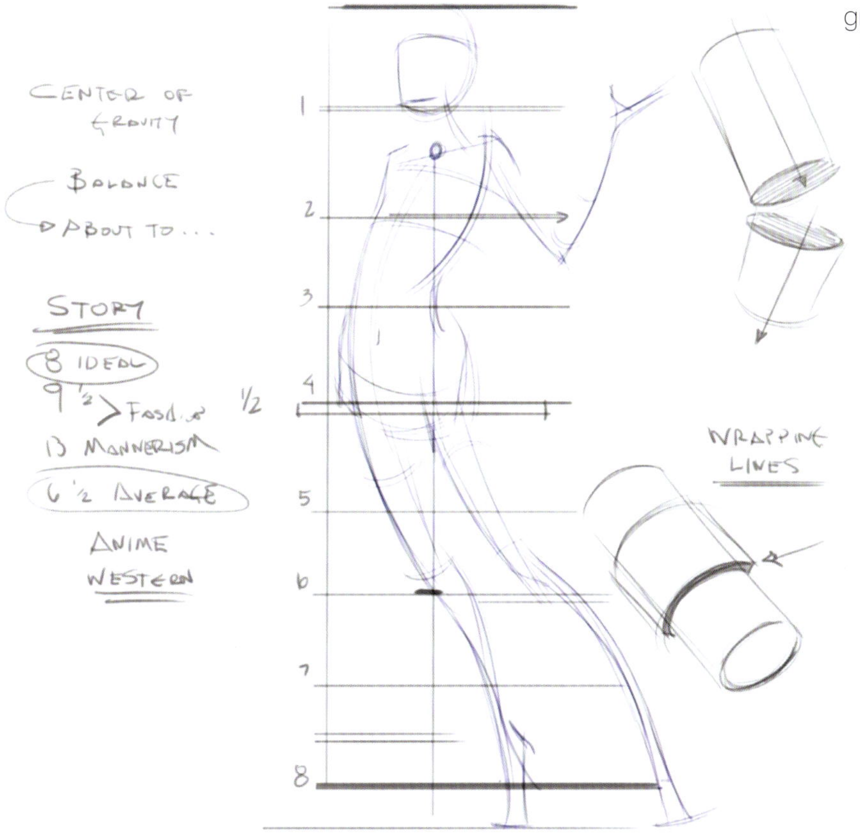

## GESTURE AND PROPORTION THIRDS

Divide the area between spaces 2 and 3 into thirds. Notice in the left illustration, on the far-right side, how consistently I can fit my gesture lines in the proportional breakup. In other words, the same measurements correspond to the approximate lengths of my gesture lines which are, again, simplifications of those parts. This might be a helpful reminder for anyone still confused by gesture as a process without structure and expressive.

Handwritten notes (left illustration):

CENTER OF GRAVITY
BALANCE
ABOUT TO...

STORY
8 IDEAL
9 ½ FASHION  ½
13 MANNERISM
6 ½ AVERAGE
ANIME
WESTERN

WRAPPING LINES

*Tip: Remember, gesture is an early blueprint to get your ideas down on paper. You will continue to tweak, build, and bring more resolution to the specifics of the figure as your drawings progress. This is important to keep in mind, so you don't make your gestures something they're not. In other words, this is not the time for rendering or any detail work. I also love that stage, but instead I'm advocating for a more patient setup to allow us the best possible results once the drawing is ready for that level of focus and resolve.*

*Fig. 4 – Courtesy of Proko™*                                                                 39

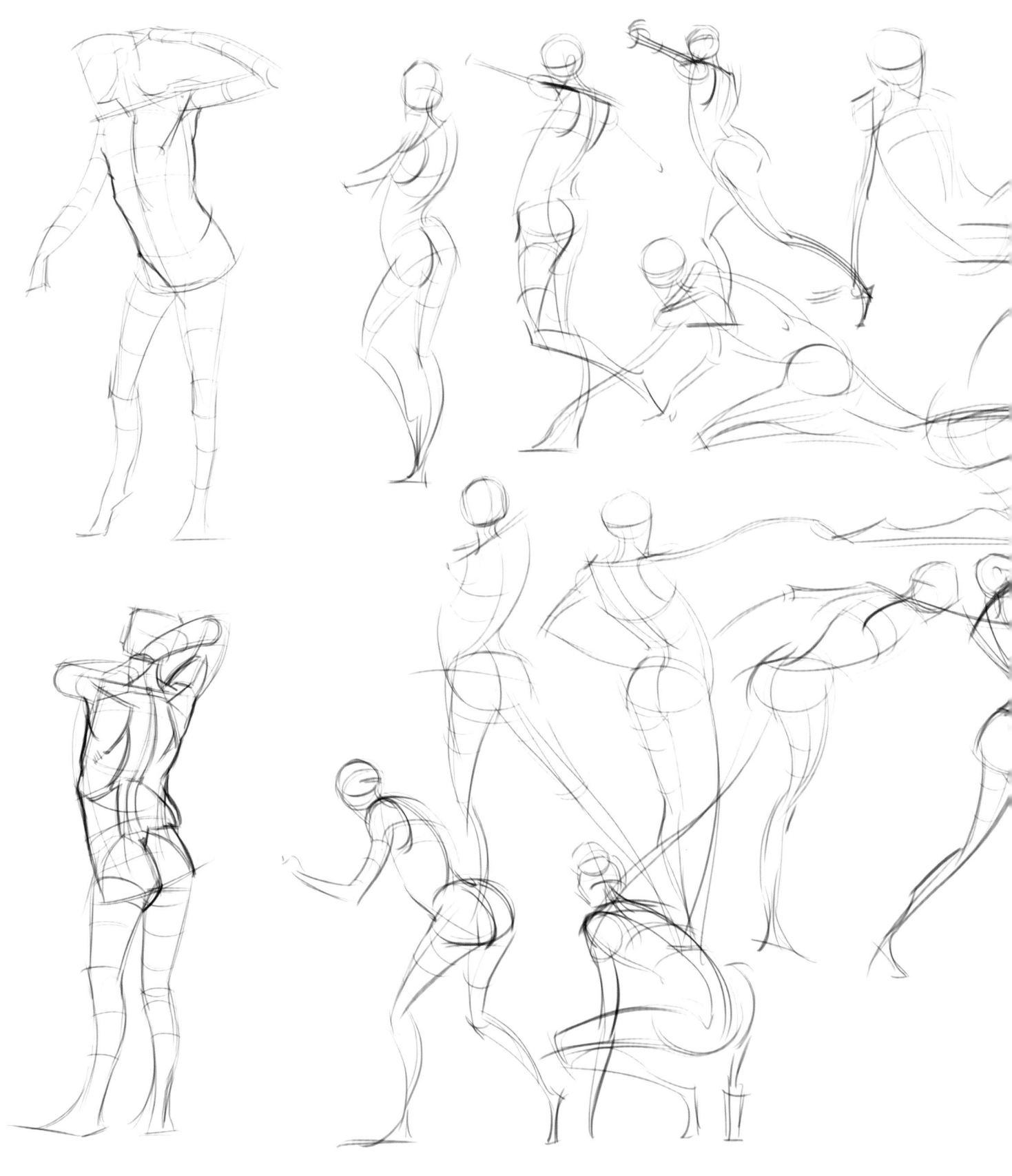

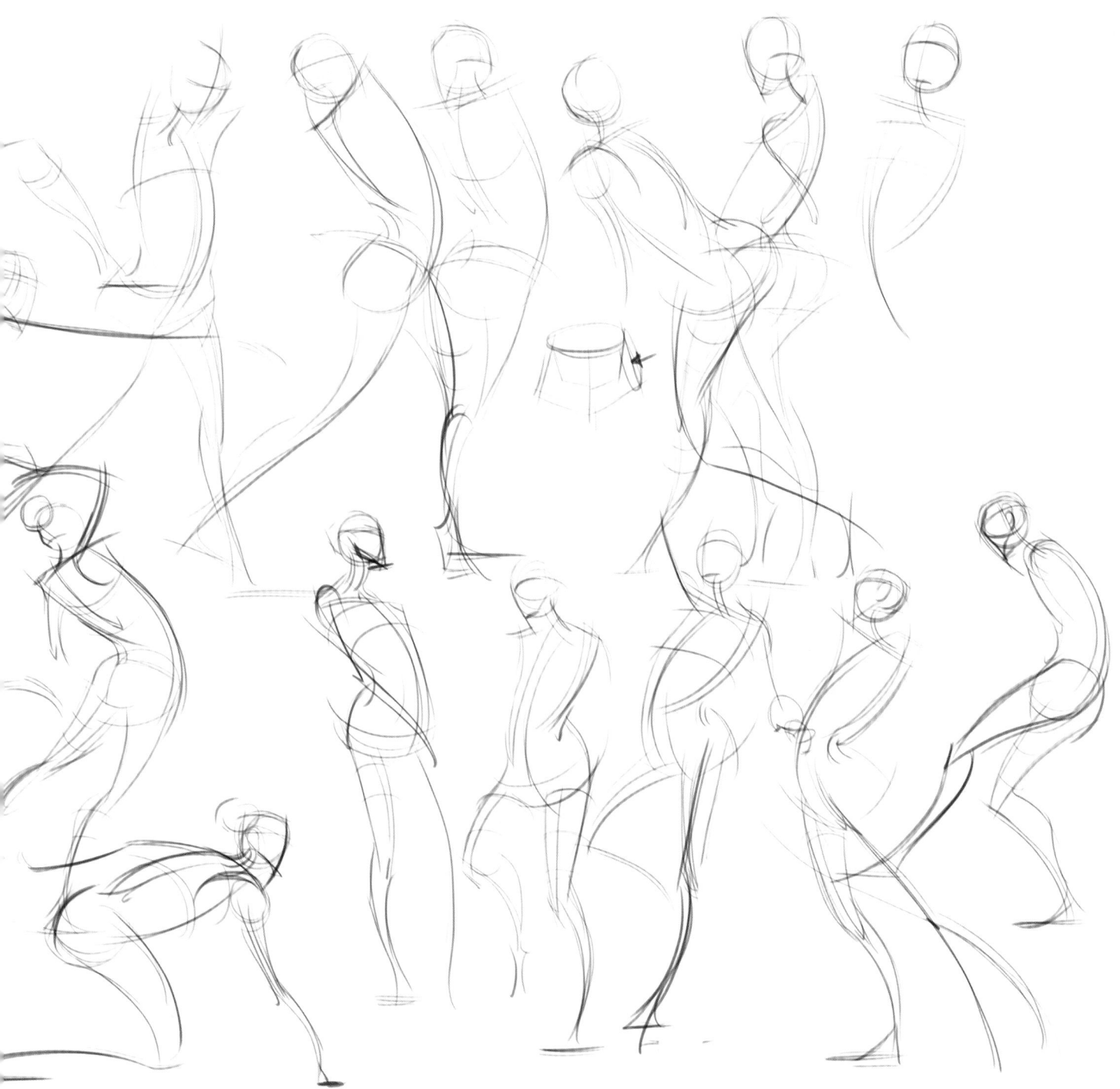

# EXAMPLES

Now that the thinking behind a gesture has been covered, let's move into a discussion of the practical "how-to" of its making. At this stage, I am limiting myself to only a few formal elements, including a straight line, a "C" curve, and an "S" curve to create the previously discussed asymmetry.

In total, my drawings never exceed six elements. A straight line, "C" curve, "S" curve, ellipses, boxes, and spheres (all of which are generated by a line).

Keep in mind, at this stage we are not drawing what we see, rather, we are analyzing and interpreting.

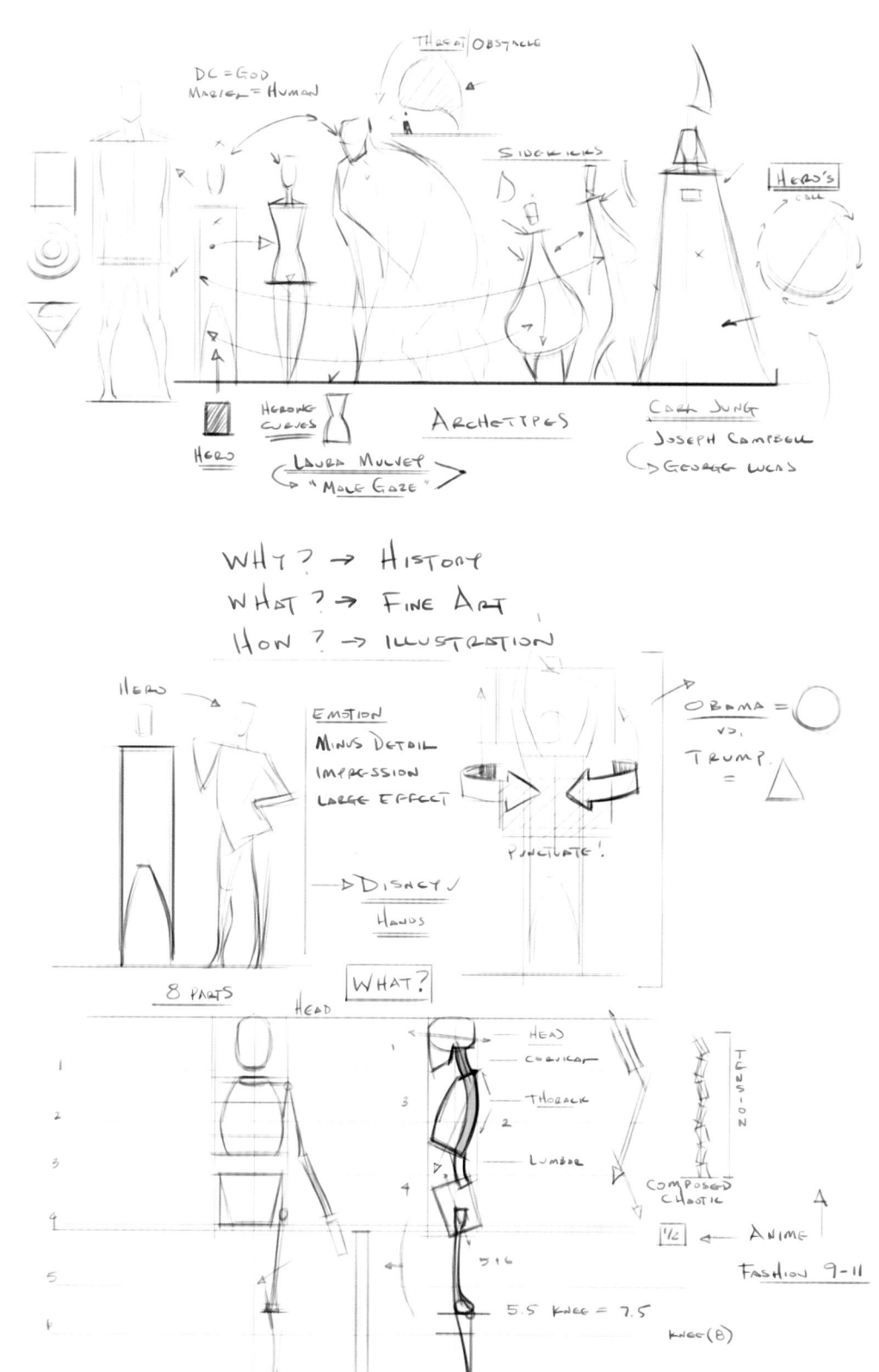

WHY? → HISTORY
WHAT? → FINE ART
HOW? → ILLUSTRATION

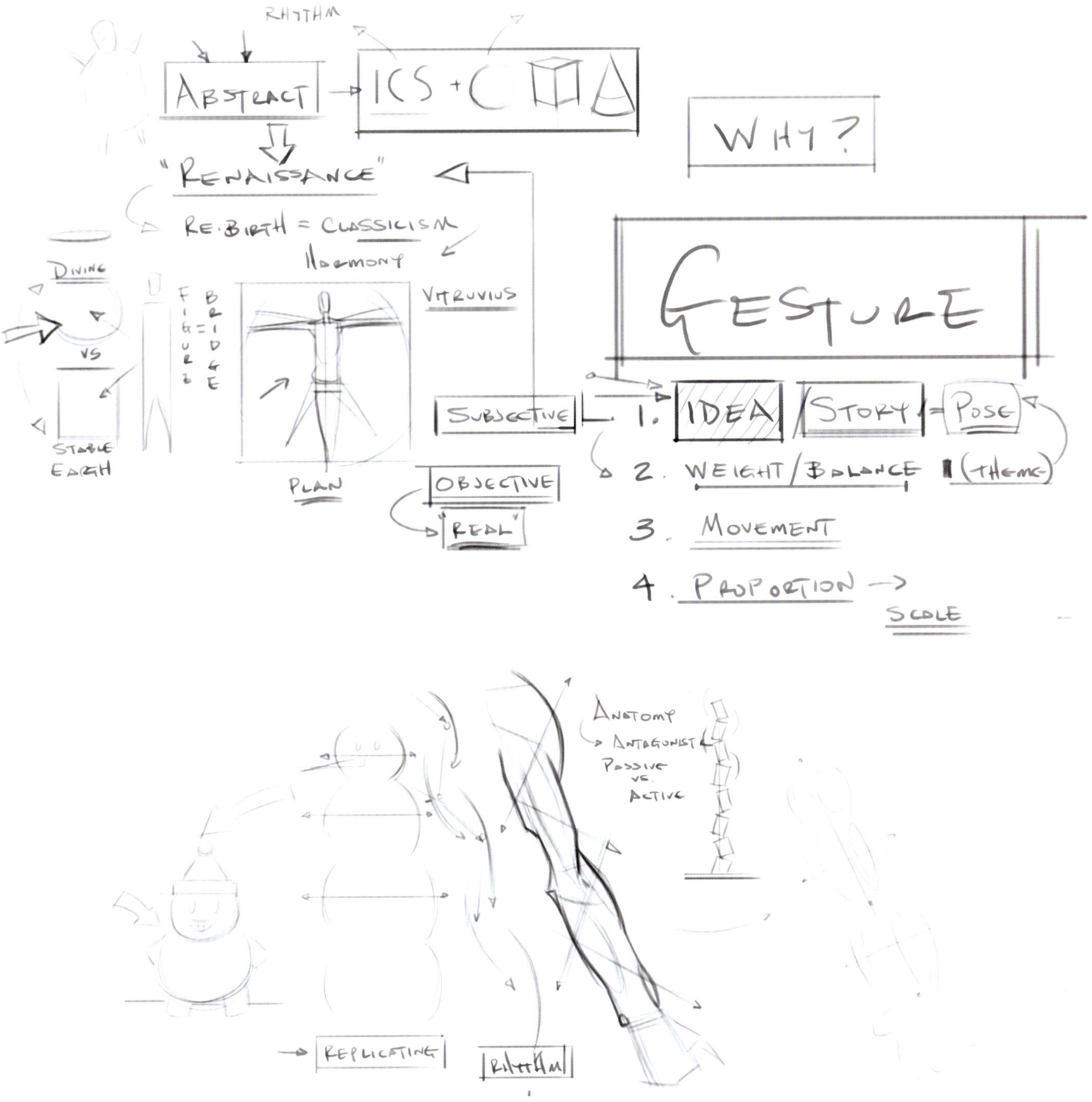

RHYTHM

ABSTRACT → ICS + C ▢ △

⇩

"RENAISSANCE"

RE·BIRTH = CLASSICISM
HARMONY

DIVING

VS

STABLE
EARTH

F B
I R
G = I
U D
R G
E E

VITRUVIUS

PLAN

SUBJECTIVE

OBJECTIVE
"REAL"

WHY?

GESTURE

1. IDEA | STORY = POSE

2. WEIGHT / BALANCE (THEME)

3. MOVEMENT

4. PROPORTION →
SCALE

ANATOMY
ANTAGONIST
PASSIVE
VS.
ACTIVE

REPLICATING   RHYTHM

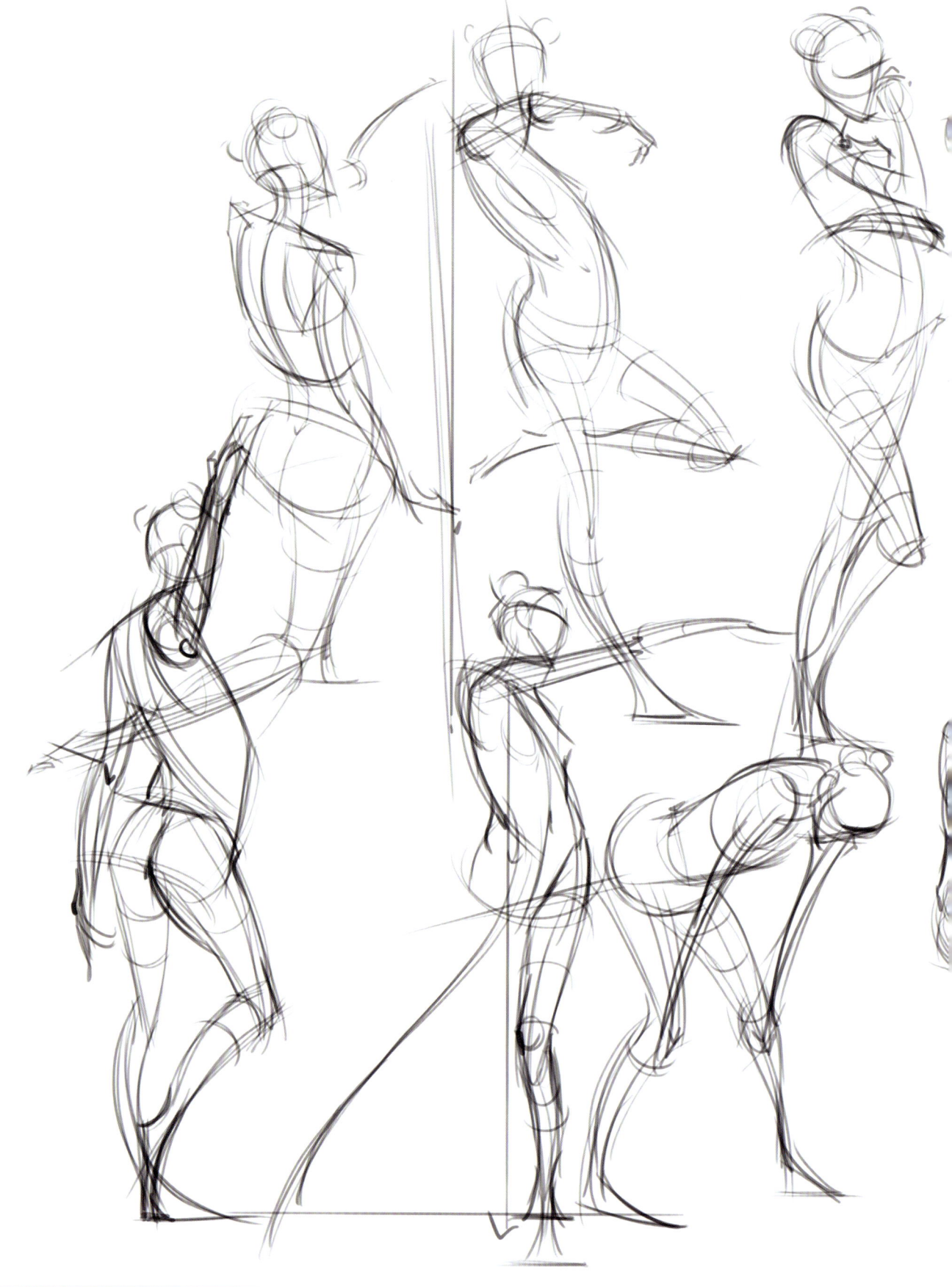

# APPLICATION

This section will focus on the technical challenges of creating gestures in multiple positions. I'll begin by describing my approach, which uses 16–17 lines. This doesn't have to be exact, just a suggestion to help focus our attention.

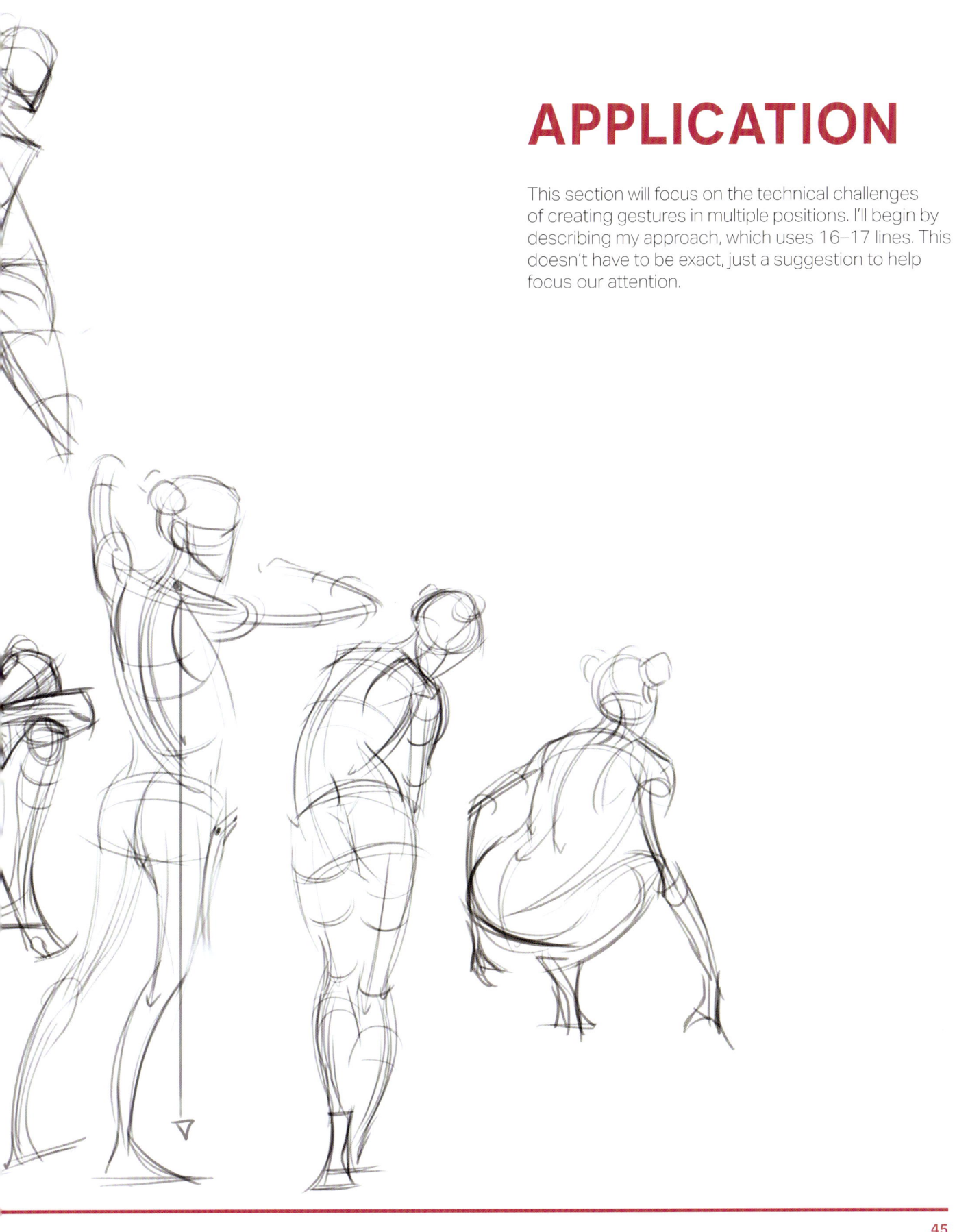

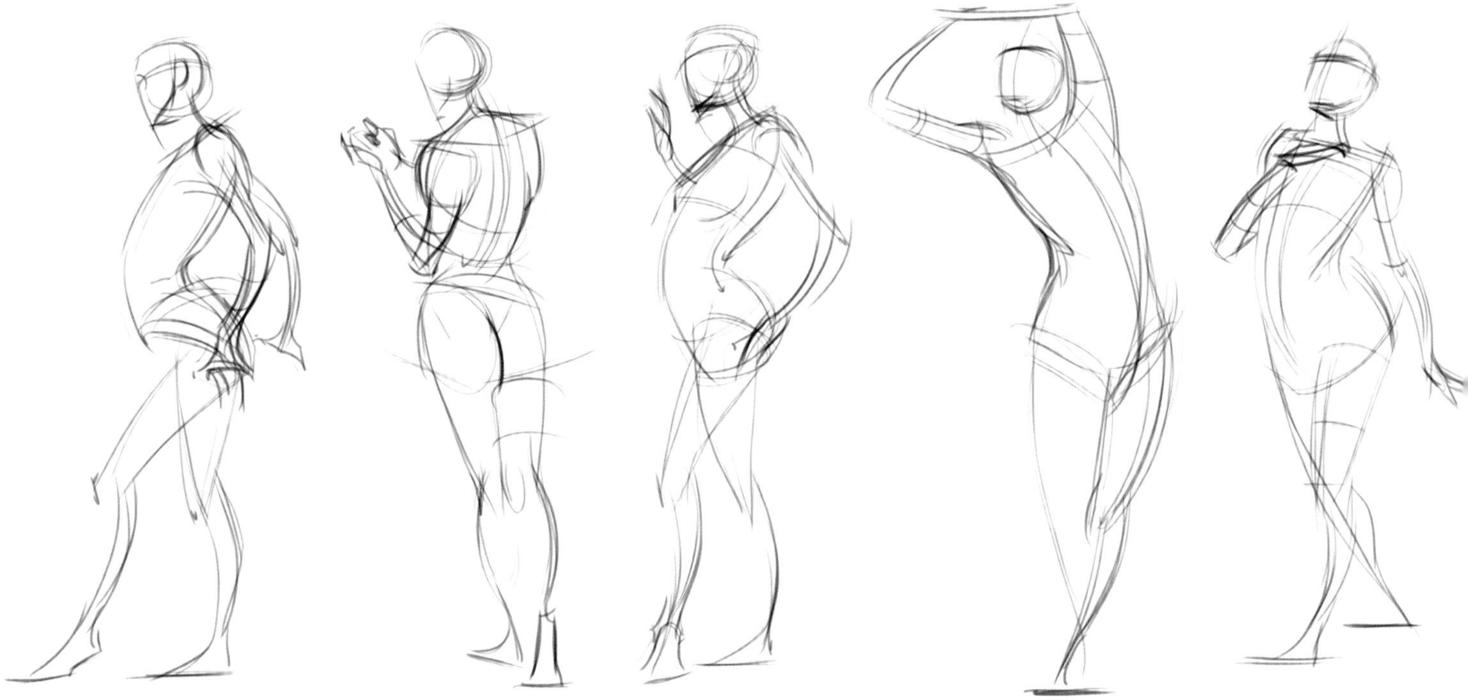

I will start this section by showing my approach to standing poses from different angles (i.e., front, side, back, and so on). From there, I move to more challenging positions such as crouching, and leaning, and then, lastly, to foreshortened poses. Throughout this section, both in the diagrams and gallery images, try comparing and looking for the 16 minimum lines I describe. Notice that each position, regardless of its complexity, uses these lines alone (with modifications).

Remember, for me, gestures are always an abstraction of the important elements described in the Foreword and Part 1. If my pose doesn't exactly copy the reference, try and remember that I'm more concerned with analyzing/interpreting than I am a strict observation. Personally, the finish of a drawing at this stage doesn't interest me nearly as much as the reasons for and mechanics of its making.

I do realize that trying to understand a drawing process using static images can be frustrating. For this reason, I have also included links to video demonstrations throughout so you can easily see this process demonstrated.

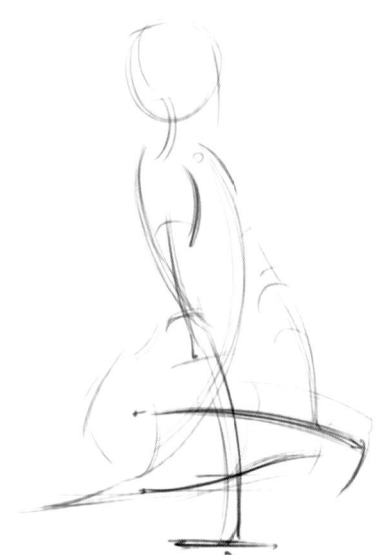
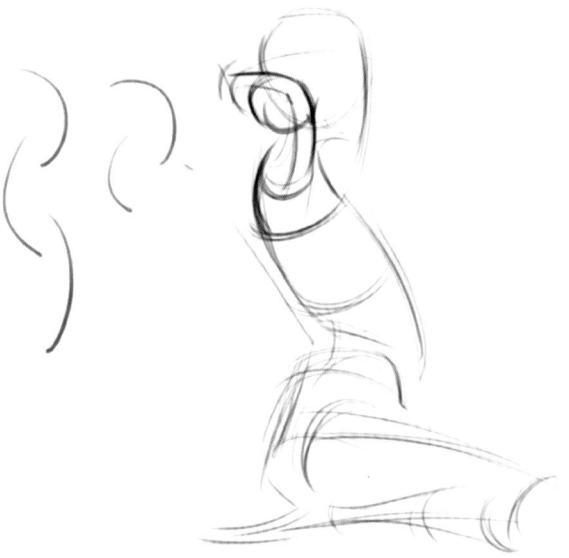

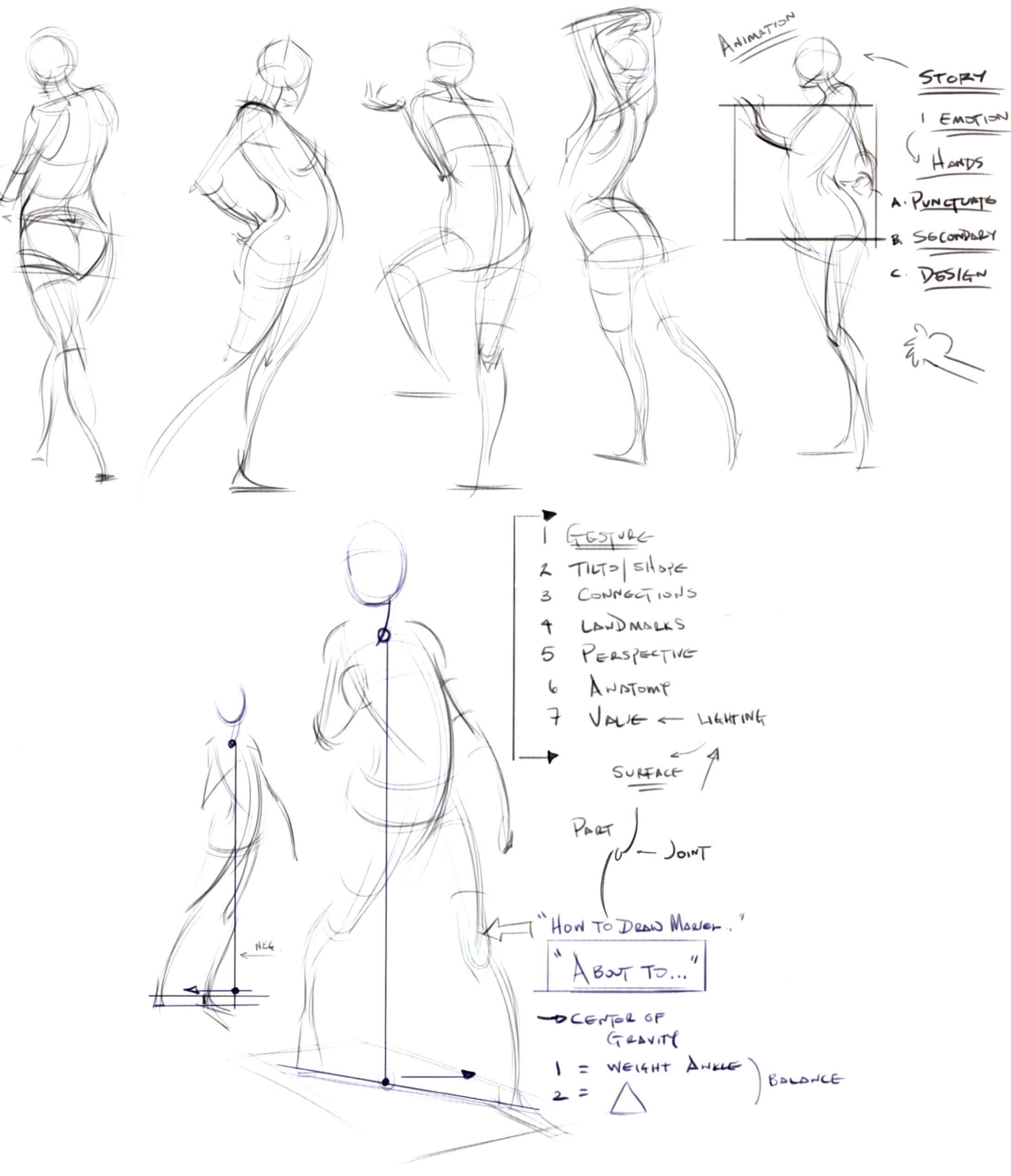

ANIMATION

STORY

1 EMOTION

HANDS

A. PUNCTUATE

B. SECONDARY

C. DESIGN

1 GESTURE
2 TILTS/SHAPE
3 CONNECTIONS
4 LANDMARKS
5 PERSPECTIVE
6 ANATOMY
7 VALUE ← LIGHTING

SURFACE

PART ⌐ JOINT

"HOW TO DRAW MARVEL.."

"ABOUT TO..."

CENTER OF GRAVITY

1 = WEIGHT ANKLE
2 = △ } BALANCE

NEG.

*Tip: Remember that my gesture lines always represent a simplified part and that their spacing can be thought of as the joint.*

# THE 16-LINE APPROACH

**CIRCLE OR OVAL FOR THE HEAD**
**SPINE: 4 LINES**
**PELVIS: 1 LINE**
**WEIGHT BEARING LEG: 2–3 LINES**
**SUPPORTING LEG: 2–3 LINES**
**ARMS: 2–3 LINES EACH**

To begin this approach, I always start with a shape for the head (this will be the only shape I include in the gesture). Though starting with the head isn't mandatory, I choose it because it functions as an obvious focal point for our audience. I anticipate the viewer will begin here initiating a compositional starting point. Additionally, having a set head size allows me to gauge the length and proportion of the body relative to it. Once done, I move into analyzing the spine. Remember, the curves you are using here are an abstract analysis of the neck and spine. At no point am I intentionally copying the outside of the neck or any other contour for that matter.

Take your time and decide on an exaggerated angle. Do your best to avoid getting sucked into a static copying of the neck as a shape. Lastly, notice how all the "C" and "S" curves I use are set on a diagonal orientation or tilt.

In the diagram at right, notice the difference between the curves placed vertically in the upper right and the diagonal positioning in the drawing of the figure (center). The curves drawn in the upper right feel flatter and more static. This is the result of the curves not sitting on a diagonal trajectory. Even though they are curved and asymmetric they still look somewhat lifeless.

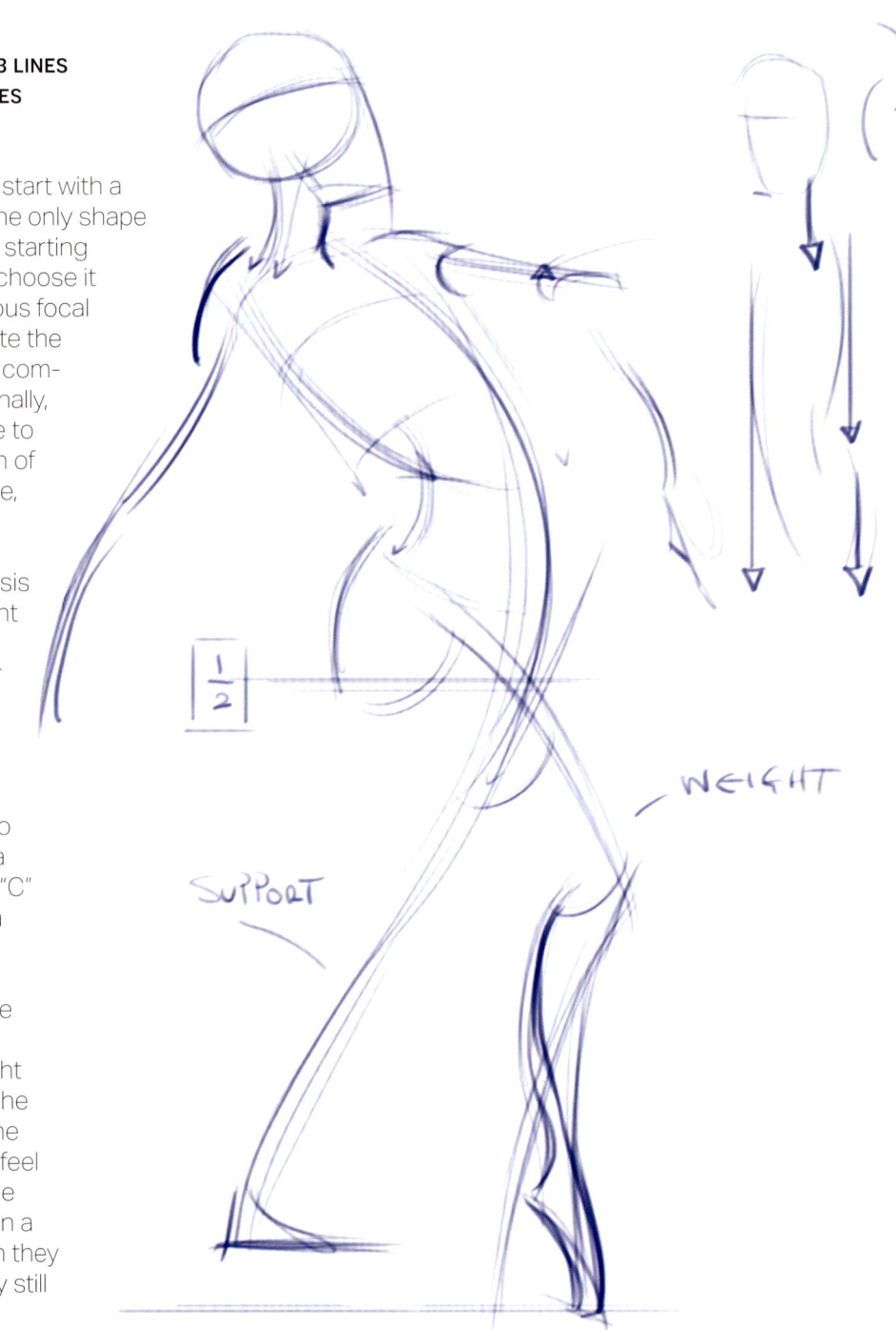

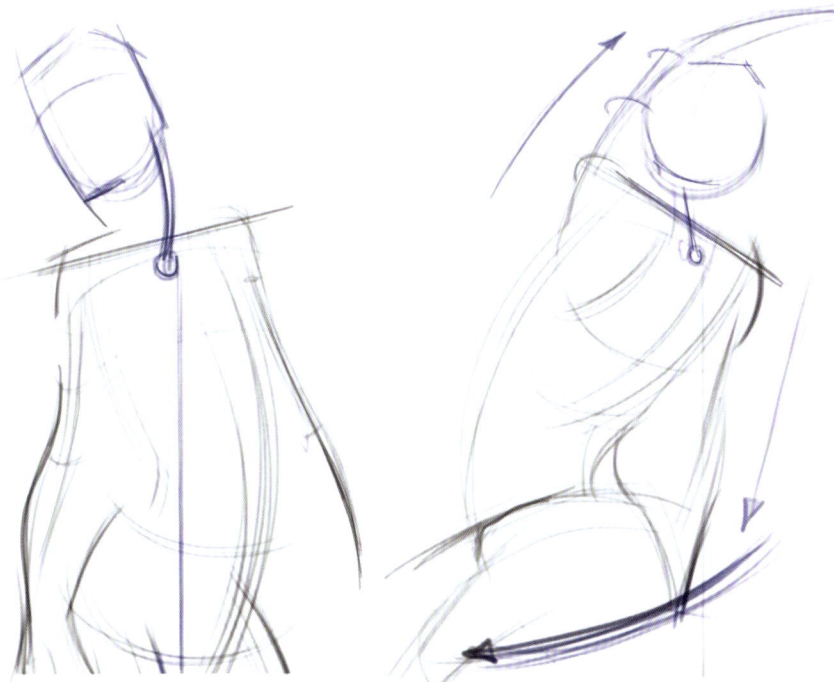

My fourth line represents the lumbar, which should continue the motion of the stretch and counter the diagonal of the thoracic above. Pause and study the relationships described in the in the diagrams on this page. Notice how each line anticipates the next in the development of rhythm.

From the lumbar, I make one curve to represent the angle of the pelvis. Though not a requirement, I generally place this curve on the weight-bearing side of the pelvis. When trying to decide which side is holding weight you might look for the tilt of the pelvis, the leg with more active muscle shapes, or any other visual clue you're familiar with.

I've now made it from the head, through the spine, and into the pelvis. To help solidify your understanding, look at the diagrams on this page. See if you can identify the pathway I've described. Further, notice that I can use the exact same cadence and order of line for any view of the figure. Front, three-quarter, back, and side are all indicated the same way.

For my first line of the cervical spine, I always imagine leading the viewer's eye out and away from the oval of the head and toward some diagonal direction reflective of the neck's position. Once I've drawn the curve of the cervical, I catch that motion and counter it with a curve for the thoracic spine.

See if you can find this initial relationship in the images on this page. What I'm doing here is emulating the design effects of the spine, cradling the curve of the cervical into a counter curve of the thoracic. Once you find this initial connection, look for it in the other example gesture drawings included in this section. I guarantee that once you begin to see these initial moves, the mechanics of every drawing included will become obvious.

The third line of the spine is a curve representing the stretch of the abdomen starting at the pit of the neck and ending at the bottom of the pelvis. This is not a direct abstraction of the spine, instead I use this curve to keep the motion between the thoracic and lumbar below. Think of this line as a stretch between the rib cage and pelvis, or an abstraction of the abdomen.

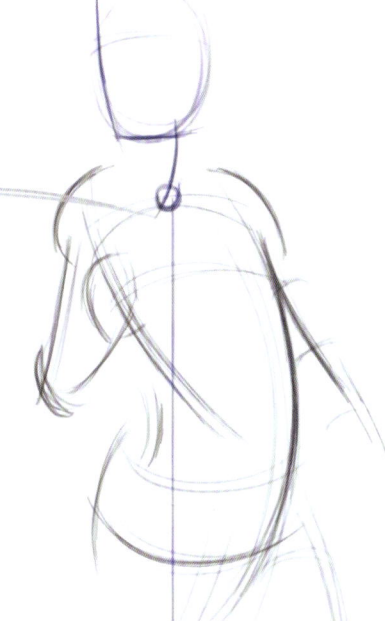

Connecting to the pelvis, my gestural path will now move into the leg on the weight-bearing side. On this weight-bearing leg, I use one curve for the femur then catch and counter that movement into the lower leg.

This creates my initial pathway, leading the viewer from the head into the foot. Once this is established, I look to the supporting leg, using the same two curves

or, at times, one long curve. I reserve longer curves for the supporting or passive areas of the body. This, while still contributing to the overall sense of rhythm and motion, emphasizes a different feel from the active weight-bearing areas. A longer curve helps the supporting leg feel lengthened, less of a focal point, and more relaxed. In my thinking, this is a summary of the muscles moving down a form and covering

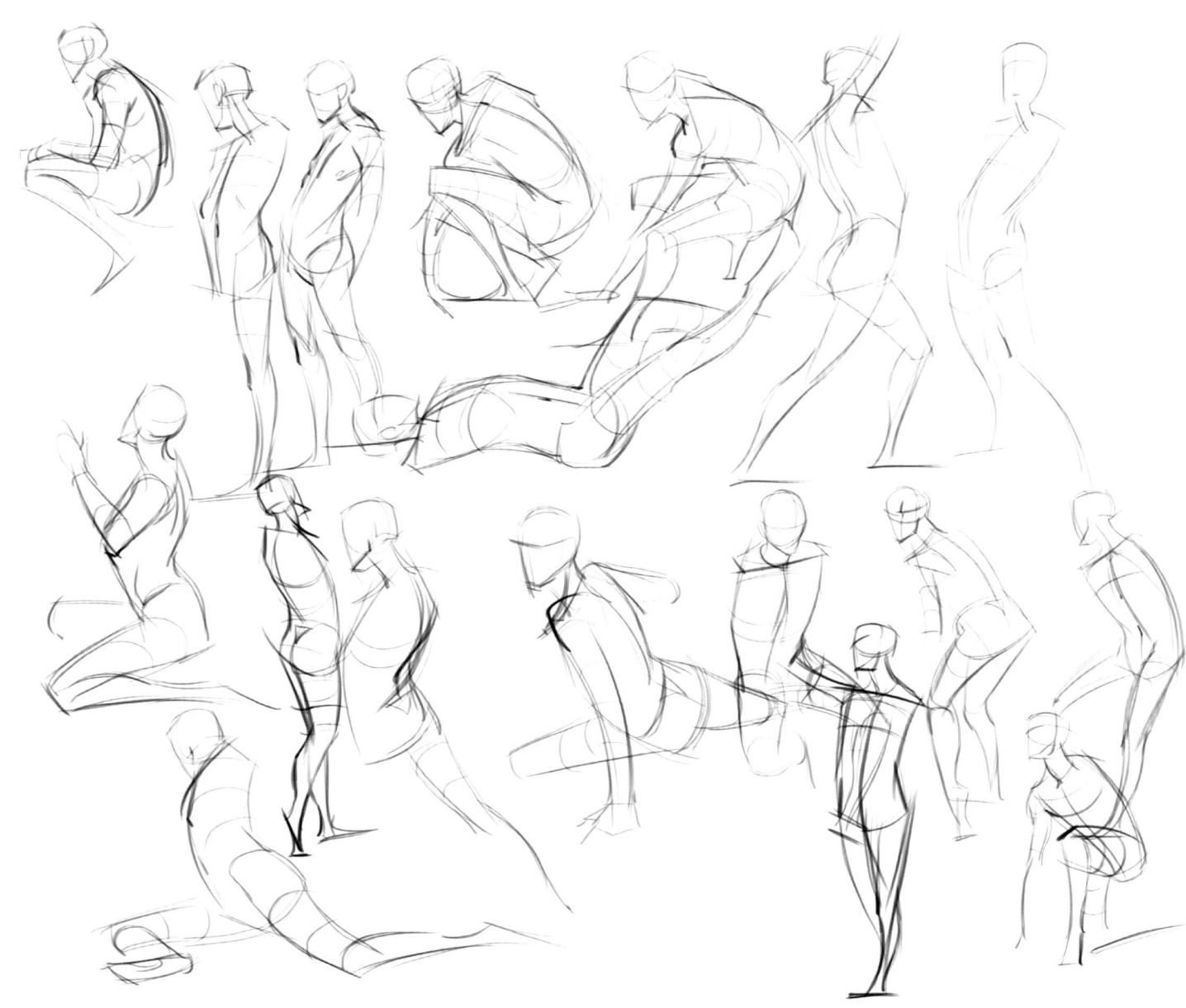

the hard surface area of the knee. In contrast, active muscles will raise and tighten creating greater visual alignment with shorter more truncated asymmetries.

Examine the diagram shown here for this principle. Compare the gesture to the contour study of the leg anatomy next to it to help in explaining my point.

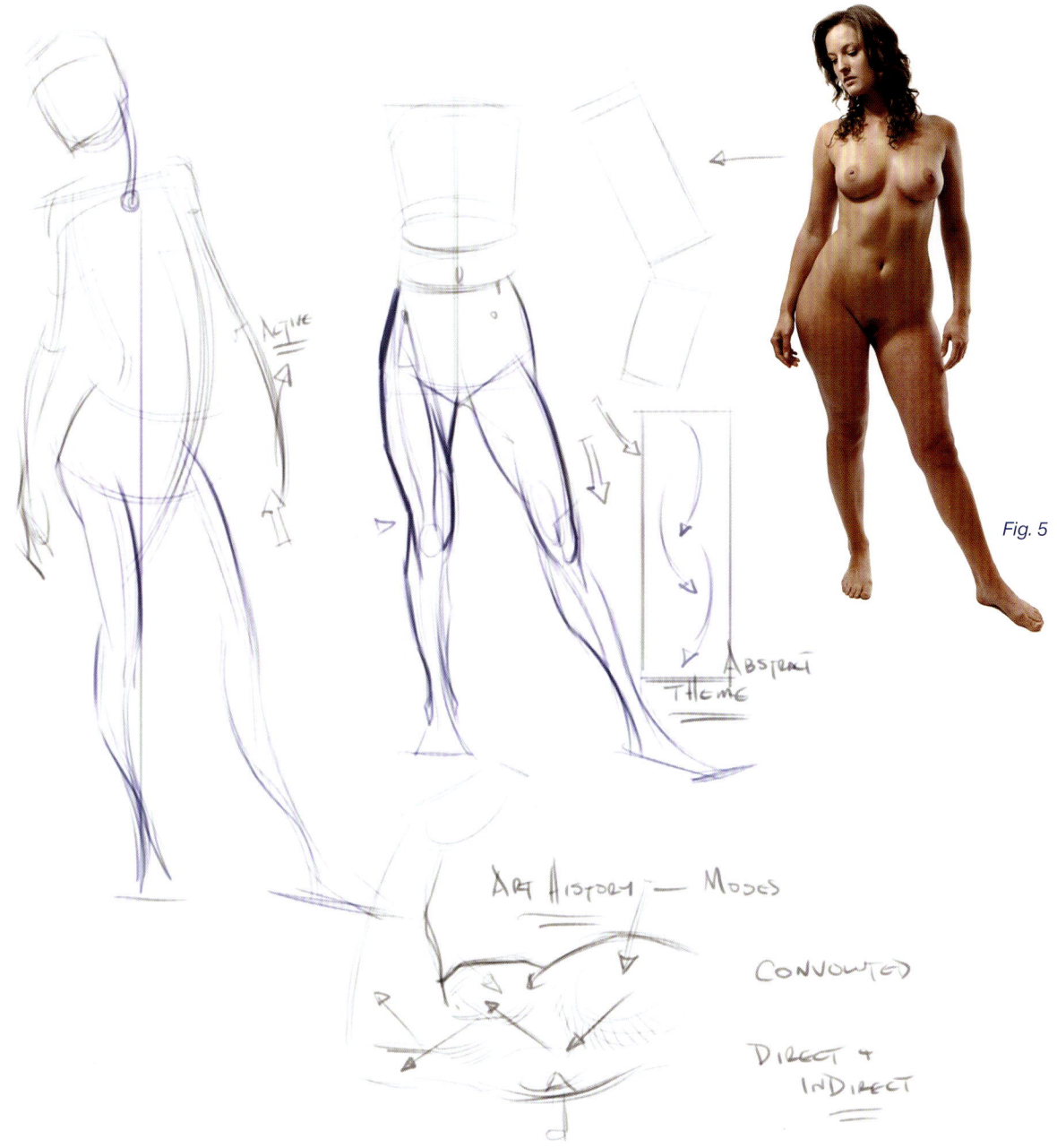

Fig. 5

*Tip: In a standing pose, you can use the bottom of your pelvis as the halfway point. Though this is a rough estimate for an idealized figure, take the upper half and project that height down by copying the same distance (note this is marked in blue in the diagram on page 52). This is where you can aim to have your foot or ground plane. Alternatively, you can lay in the proportion chart described in Part 1 and train yourself with more accuracy to describe the gesture lines as stricter approximations of the spine and skeleton.*

*Fig. 5 – Courtesy of Proko™*

51

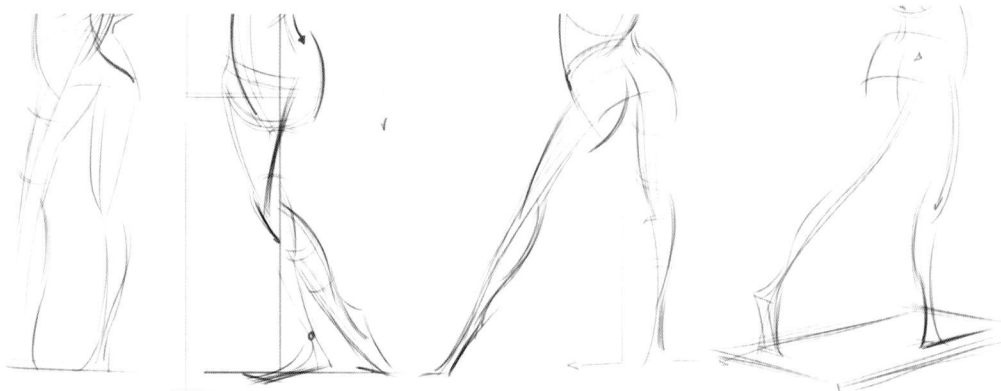

While there is certainly no right or wrong answer to gesture drawing, what I constantly look for is a unifying quality of curves and asymmetry in which each curve leads to and connects with another. My drawing aims for a seamless visual movement in which all parts lead to the rest of the image. Pay special attention throughout to my focus on the creation of rhythm and movement and not on drawing a leg or contoured representation of an object.

In the following pages, study the examples provided to see if you can track how rhythm is carried throughout all parts of the figures. Remember to look for the juxtaposition of asymmetrical curves.

Having worked from the head to feet I'll then return to the top and establish the arms. Like the legs, I'll use 2 to 3 lines for the arms, relating their tether to the body with an asymmetrical connection. Usually the cervical or thoracic curve works best to integrate

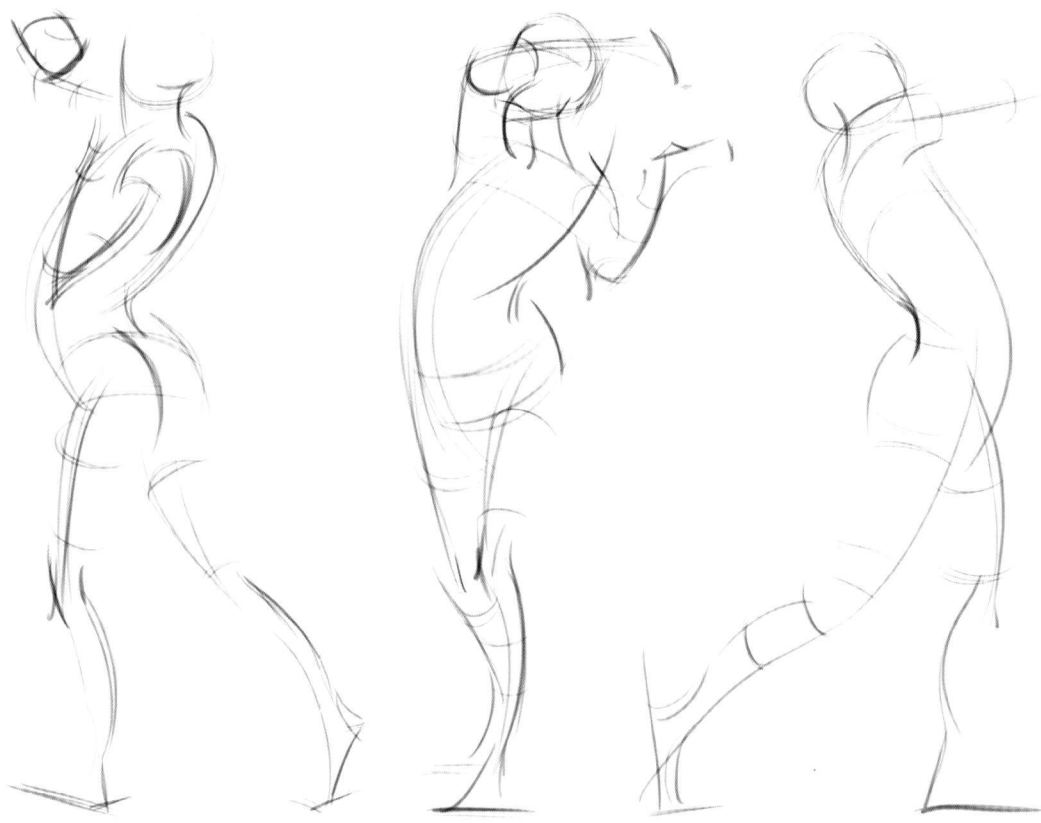

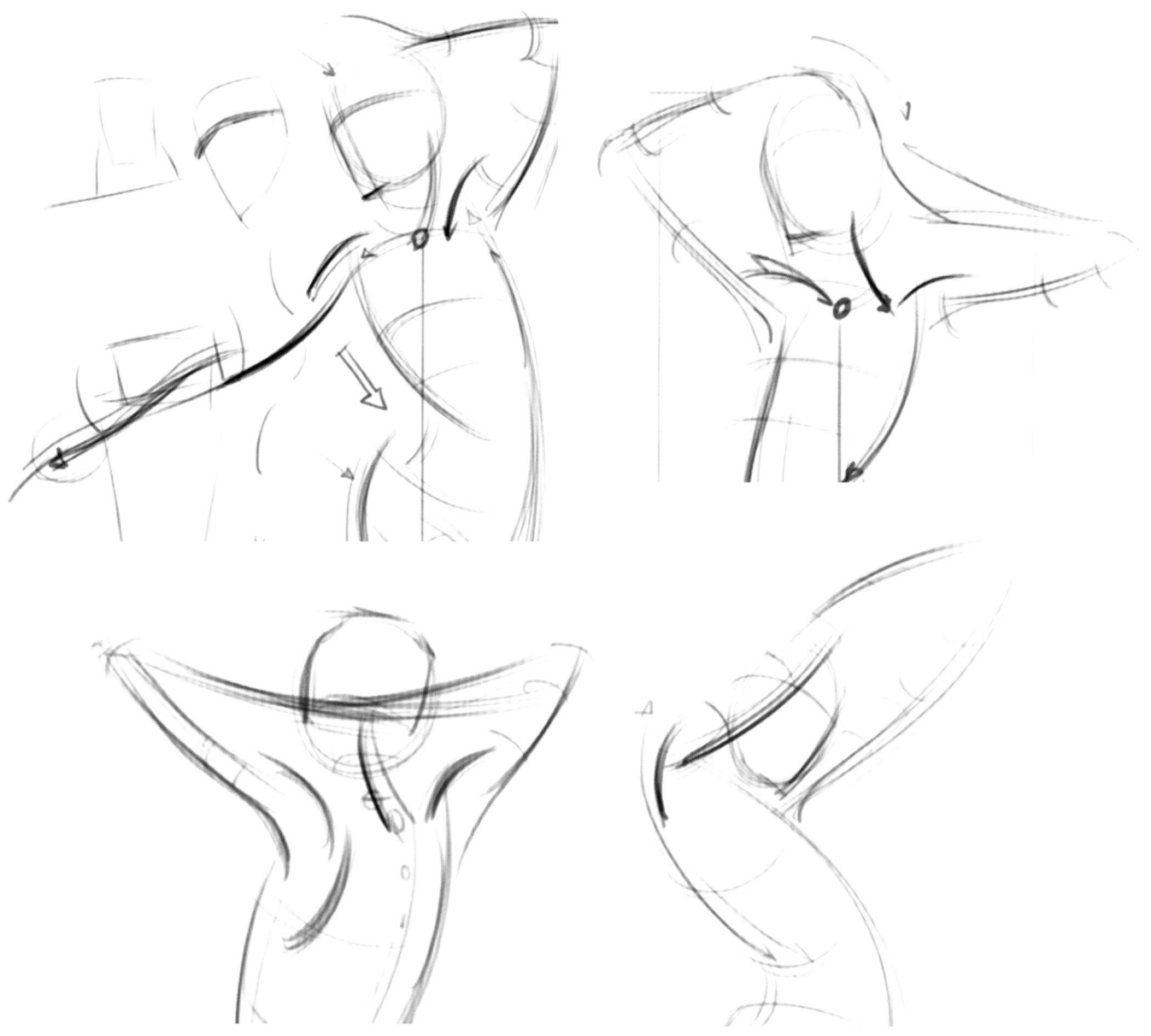

the shoulder. Each arm, at most, breaks the shoulder, humerus, and forearm/hand into one curve each.

In the diagrams shown here notice that the top two images show the front and front three-quarter positions, while the bottom two show back and back three-quarter (profile). As mentioned, for the top two I form the shoulder connection/rhythm by relating my lines to the curve of the cervical, thoracic, or stretch.

For the bottom two (back views), I add an extra line representing the scapula, which can be integrated by relating a curve to any existing lines in the torso. With this curve for the scapula in place I can build a connecting curve for the deltoid/shoulder, then humerus, radius/ulna, and hand.

When looking at my gesture studies of arms and legs, notice the difference between how I treat the straight vs bent arm/leg. I more often use two curves for a straight arm or leg and three for the bent. This additional line represents the knee or elbow and acts as a redirect to the more abrupt transition into the bent lower leg or forearm.

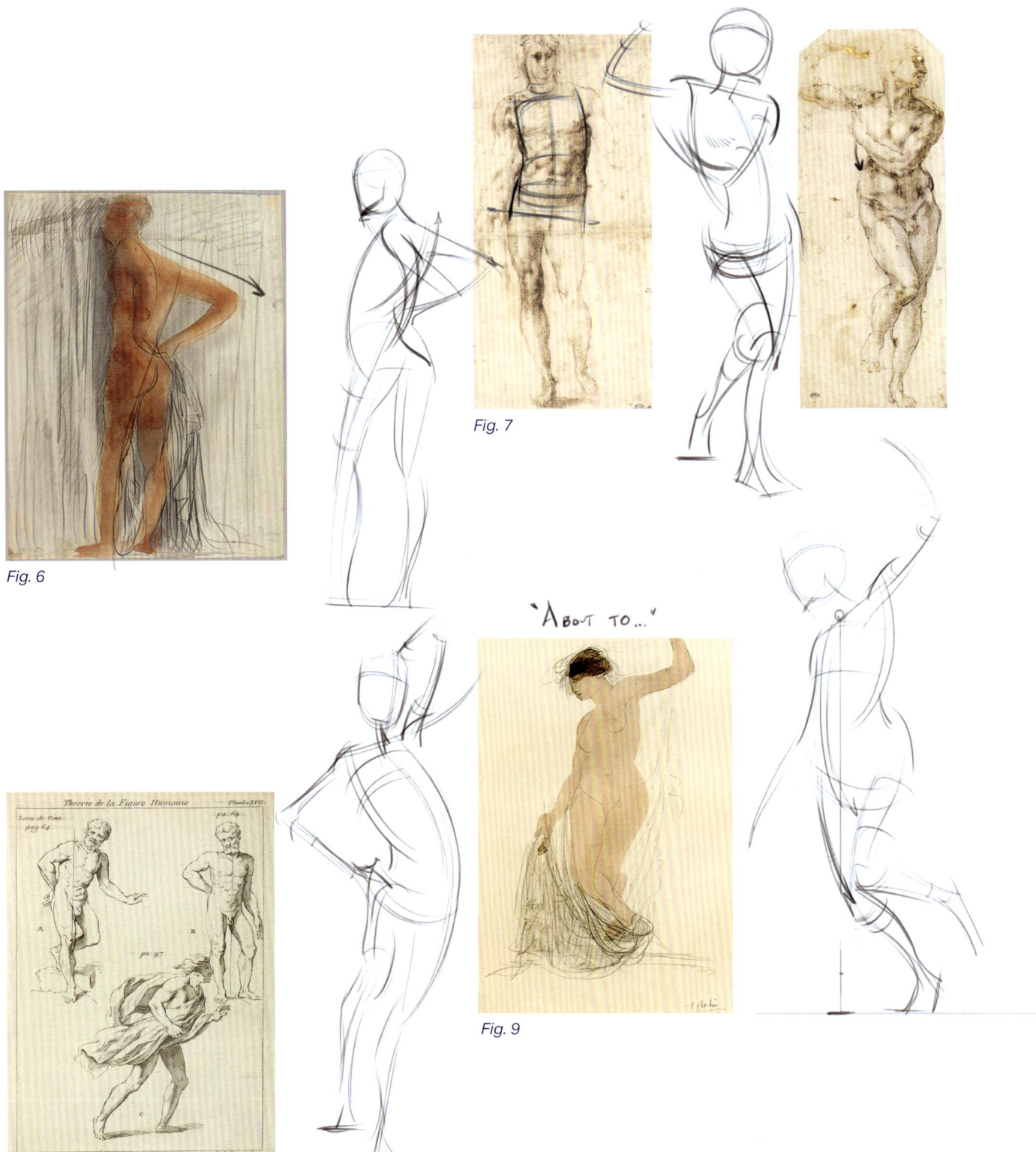

Fig. 6

Fig. 7

"ABOUT TO..."

Fig. 9

Fig. 8

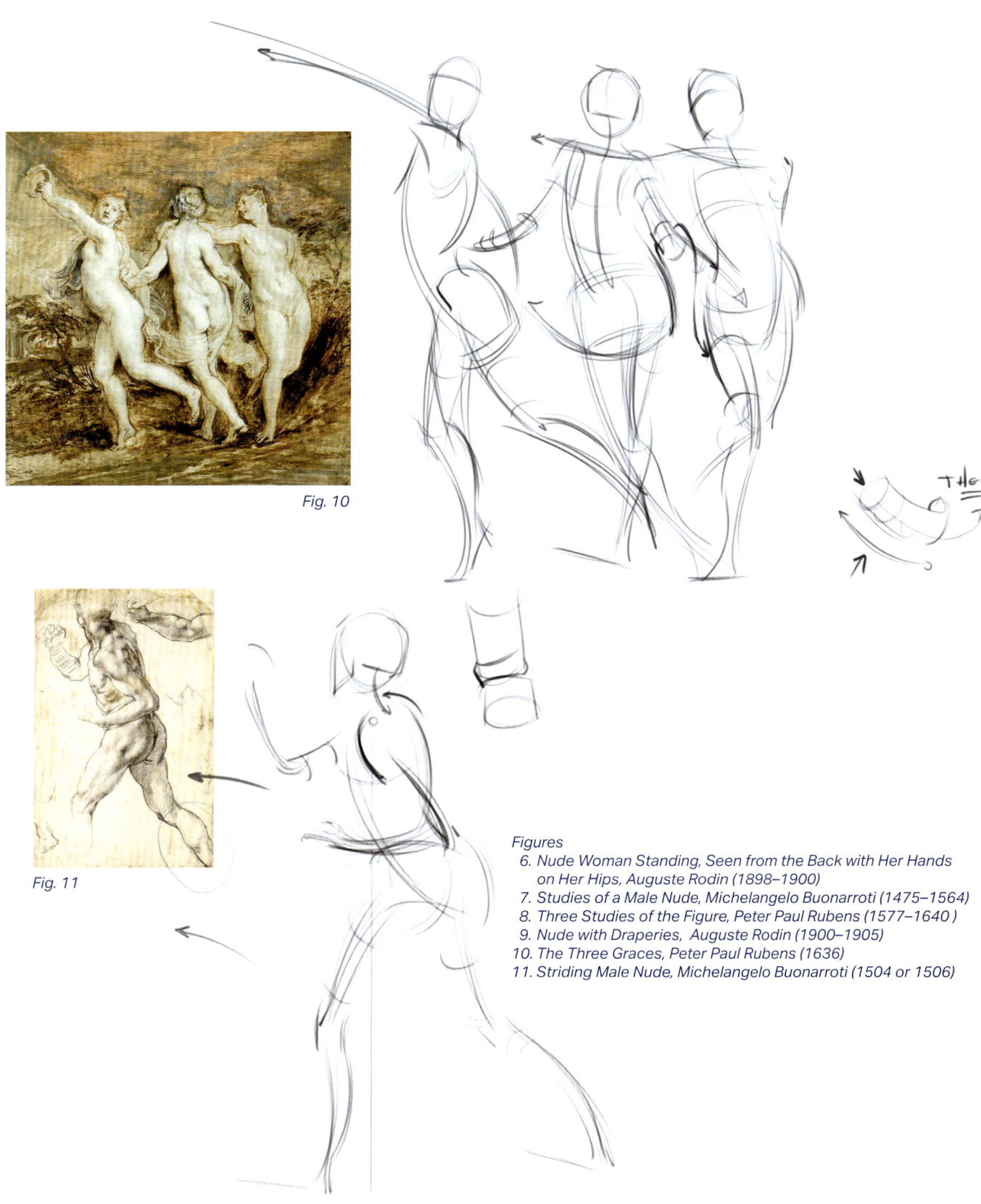

Fig. 10

Fig. 11

Figures
6. Nude Woman Standing, Seen from the Back with Her Hands on Her Hips, Auguste Rodin (1898–1900)
7. Studies of a Male Nude, Michelangelo Buonarroti (1475–1564)
8. Three Studies of the Figure, Peter Paul Rubens (1577–1640 )
9. Nude with Draperies, Auguste Rodin (1900–1905)
10. The Three Graces, Peter Paul Rubens (1636)
11. Striding Male Nude, Michelangelo Buonarroti (1504 or 1506)

# WRAPPING LINES

In addition to the use of asymmetrical curves, notice that I am also including lines across the figures. Commonly referred to as "wrapping lines" these are used to abbreviate the perspective direction of the eight parts of the body. Wrapping lines, also described as cross contours, are an economical way to suggest a cylinder's perspective when making gestures.

At this stage, I don't want to take the time to lay in an entire cylinder. Wrapping lines gives the same summary impression by laying ellipses around these imagined perspective directions. Imagine the wrapping lines are rubber bands, traversing the surface of the projected cylinder.

This gives a sense of the three-dimensional direction a form is leaning. I generally place two or three wrapping lines per part. If I'm happy with the gesture, my following stages invest more time in building out the perspective.

Look at the figures on this page and the next for examples of how I use wrapping lines. Next to each of the wrapping lines on the figure on page 57, I created a cylinder to demonstrate my thinking. From each cylinder,. I'm using the ellipse of different turns and angles to depict a part of the body coming toward or away from me.

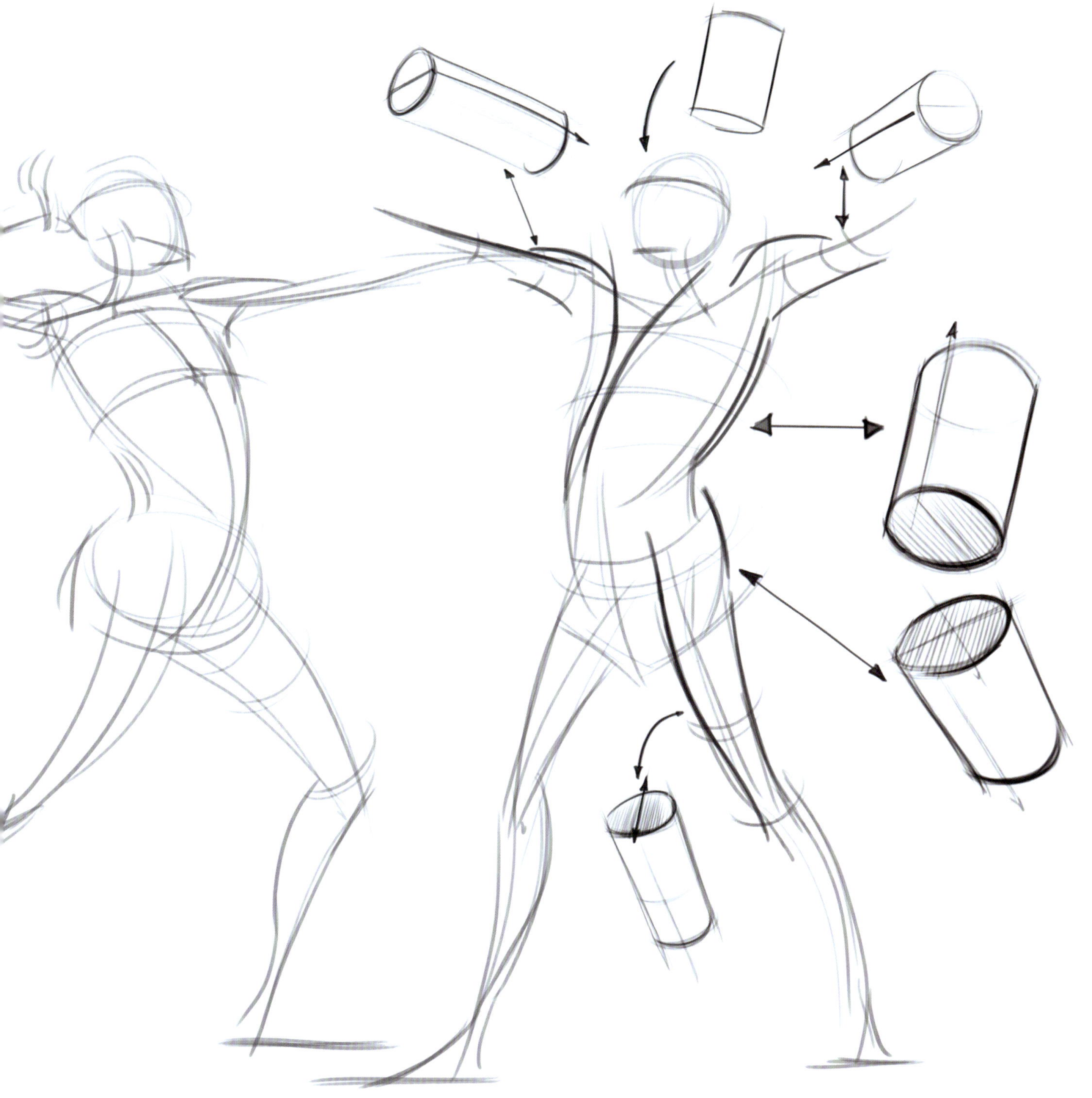

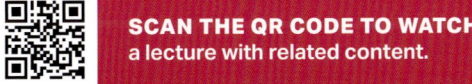

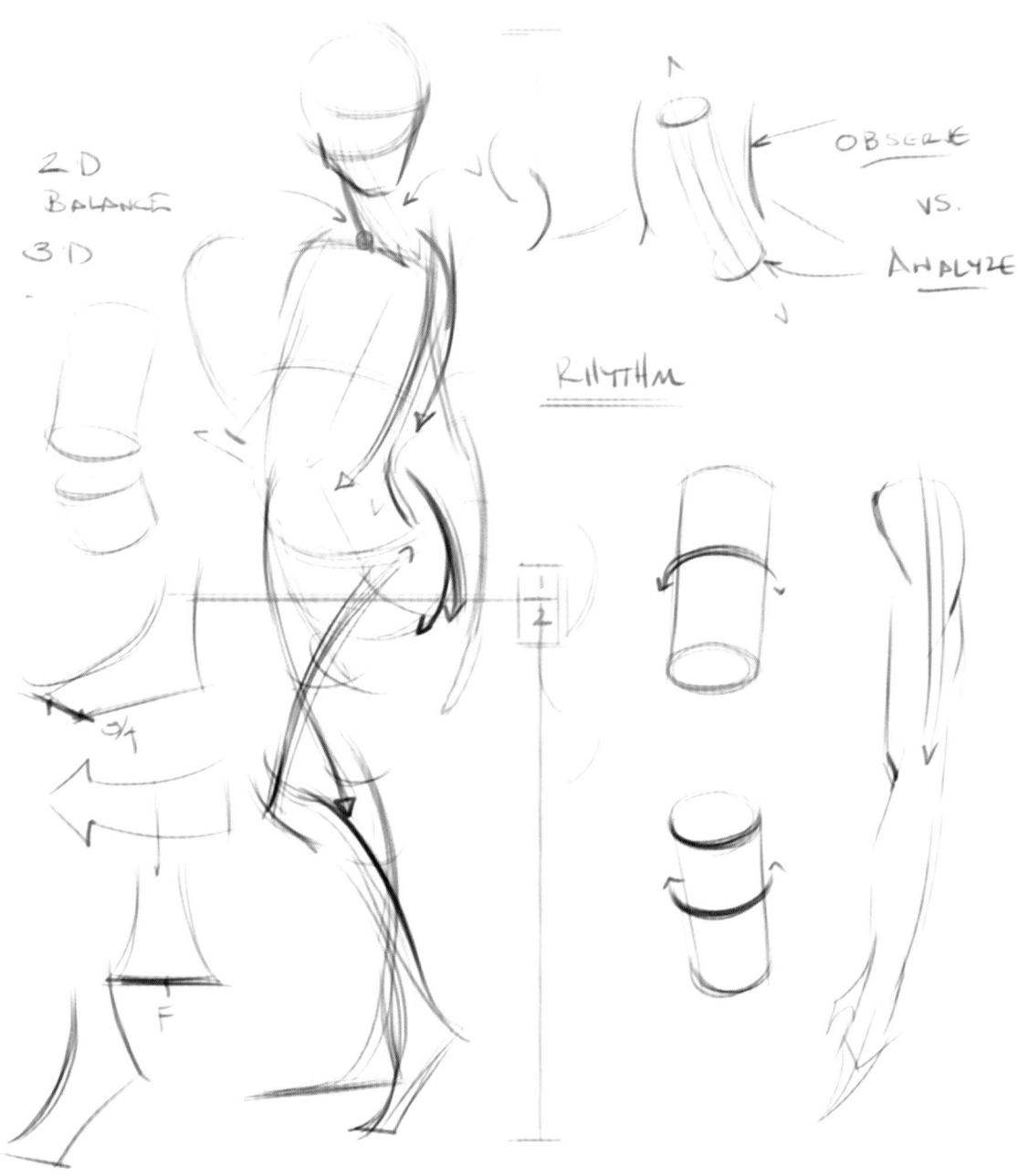

2 D
BALANCE
3 D

OBSERVE
VS.
ANALYZE

RHYTHM

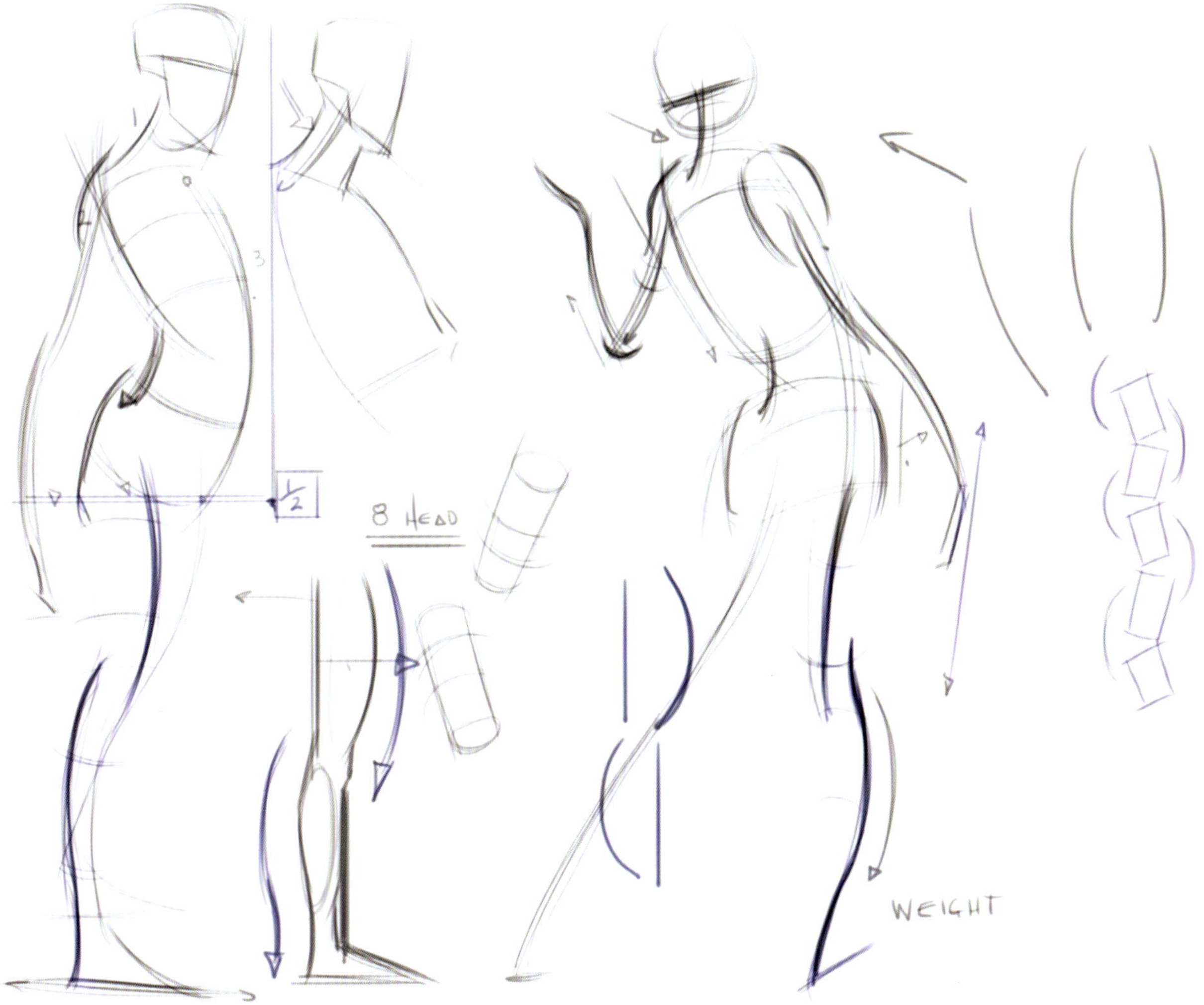

8 HEAD

WEIGHT

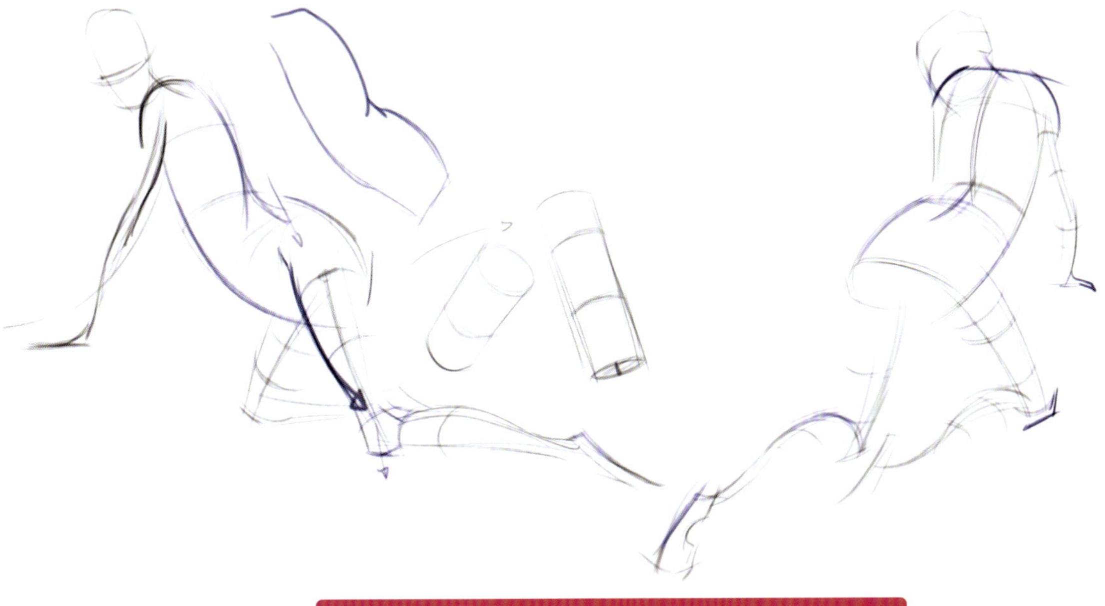

**SCAN THE QR CODE TO WATCH**
a lecture with related content.

59

# COMMON QUESTIONS

Before moving into a discussion of how I summarize the head, hands, or feet in gesture, I'd like to pause and address some common questions. Some of these might reinforce points I've already brought up; however, my hope is that what follows helps to alleviate any confusion, questions, or problems you may be encountering at this point.

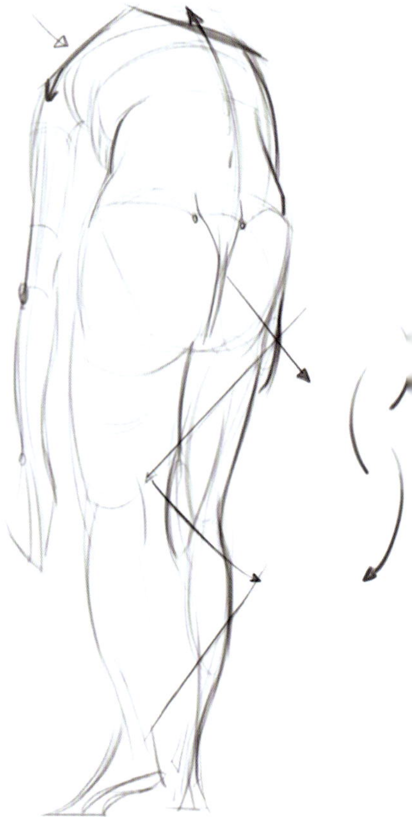

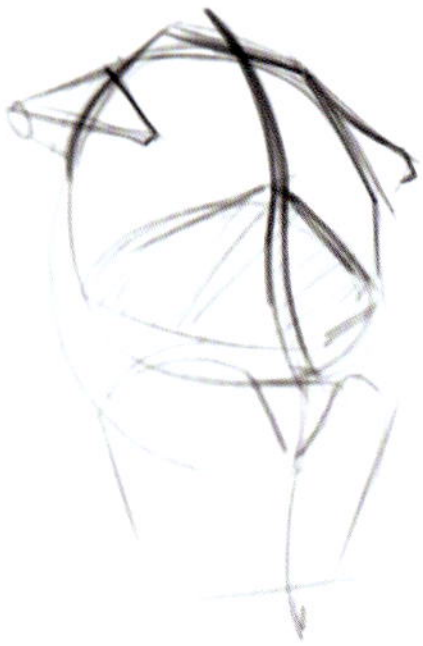

### "WHEN MAKING GESTURES ARE YOUR LINES DESCRIBING THE CONTOURS?"

No, not intentionally. I find that sticking to contours at this point stiffens a drawing through too much attention to the outside detail (remember Mr. Hankey). While there's nothing wrong with contour, my gesture lines aim for the center of a form and exaggerate based on the spine/movement of the figure.

Using contours as clues as to what is happening is more in line with my mindset. If a line happens to land near a contour, fine. Otherwise, by starting at the center of a form my approach will gradually build toward the contour.

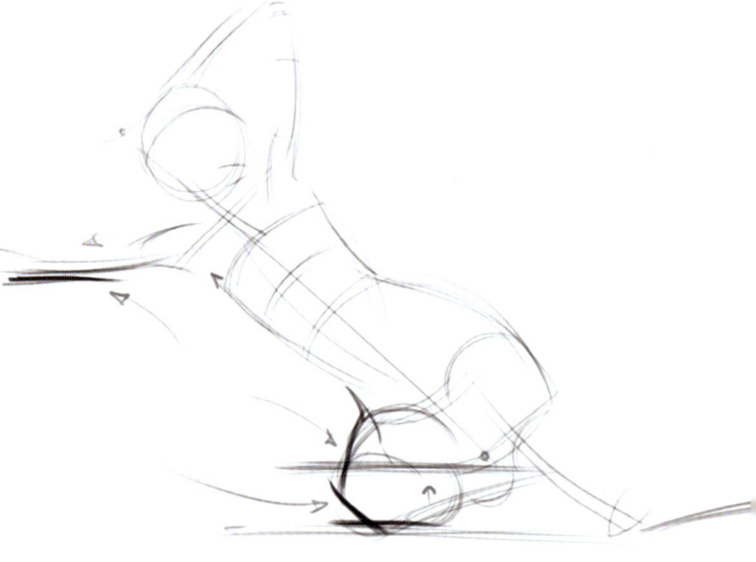

For example, if I'm looking at a neck, I may be tempted to draw the outside as a vertical line, tracing the curvature of the trapezius or sterno-mastoid. When doing this, unless I'm very careful and conscious of the underlying form, I run the risk of flattening that form by reducing the silhouette of muscles to being squared and static. Instead, I want to train myself to be aware of the muscle's natural quality of movement.

Placing my emphasis on the gesture at this stage helps build a stronger appreciation for the internal design mechanics of the figure and spine.

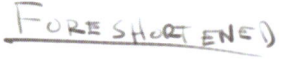

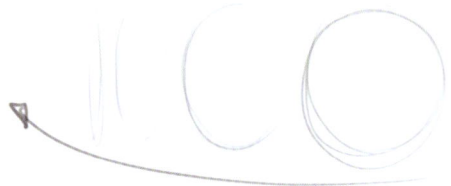

FORESHORTENED

---

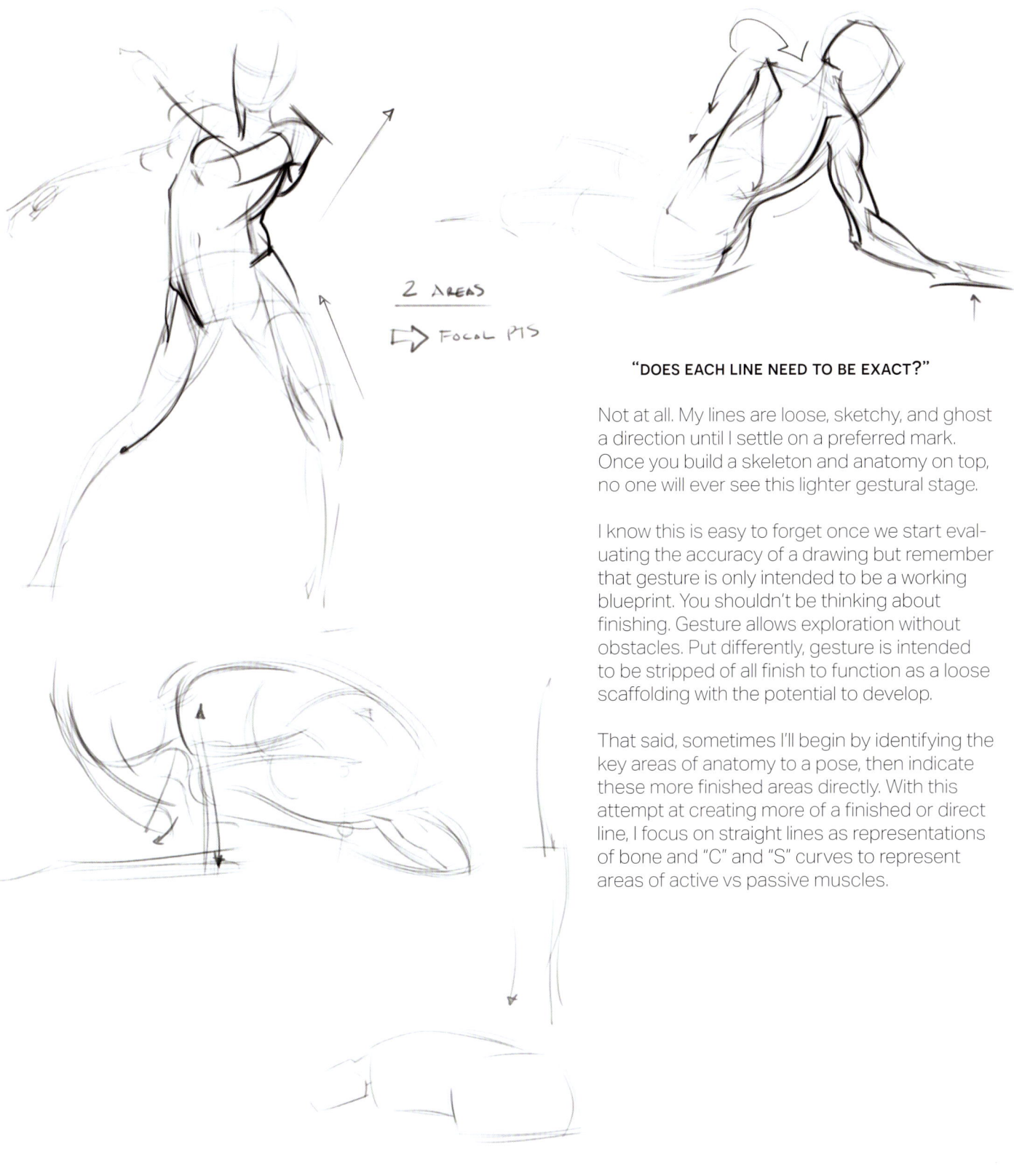

2 AREAS

⟹ FOCAL PTS

## "DOES EACH LINE NEED TO BE EXACT?"

Not at all. My lines are loose, sketchy, and ghost a direction until I settle on a preferred mark. Once you build a skeleton and anatomy on top, no one will ever see this lighter gestural stage.

I know this is easy to forget once we start evaluating the accuracy of a drawing but remember that gesture is only intended to be a working blueprint. You shouldn't be thinking about finishing. Gesture allows exploration without obstacles. Put differently, gesture is intended to be stripped of all finish to function as a loose scaffolding with the potential to develop.

That said, sometimes I'll begin by identifying the key areas of anatomy to a pose, then indicate these more finished areas directly. With this attempt at creating more of a finished or direct line, I focus on straight lines as representations of bone and "C" and "S" curves to represent areas of active vs passive muscles.

**"HOW DO I HANDLE FORESHORTENED POSES WITH THIS METHOD?"**

This is a tricky question since we are really limited at this stage in the drawing to lines alone. To truly make sense of a foreshortened figure we need shapes and perspectives to create spatial overlaps which in turn allow those diminished distances to be read.

The best way I've found to quickly communicate foreshortening in this method is to adjust the length of your lines to suggest a foreshortening effect. So, for example, the average length of the arm might be cut in half to indicate its foreshortened pull back in space.

In the drawings in this section, compare the length of the limbs. Notice that the limbs parallel to the picture plane have a consistent length more related to the proportion chart discussed previously. Compare these to arms/legs moving away or toward the picture plane. In these examples, I cut the length of the lines down to emphasize a change in proportion based on foreshortening. In addition, I push the degree of ellipses, as discussed in my wrapping lines, to indicate a greater angle of the perspective.

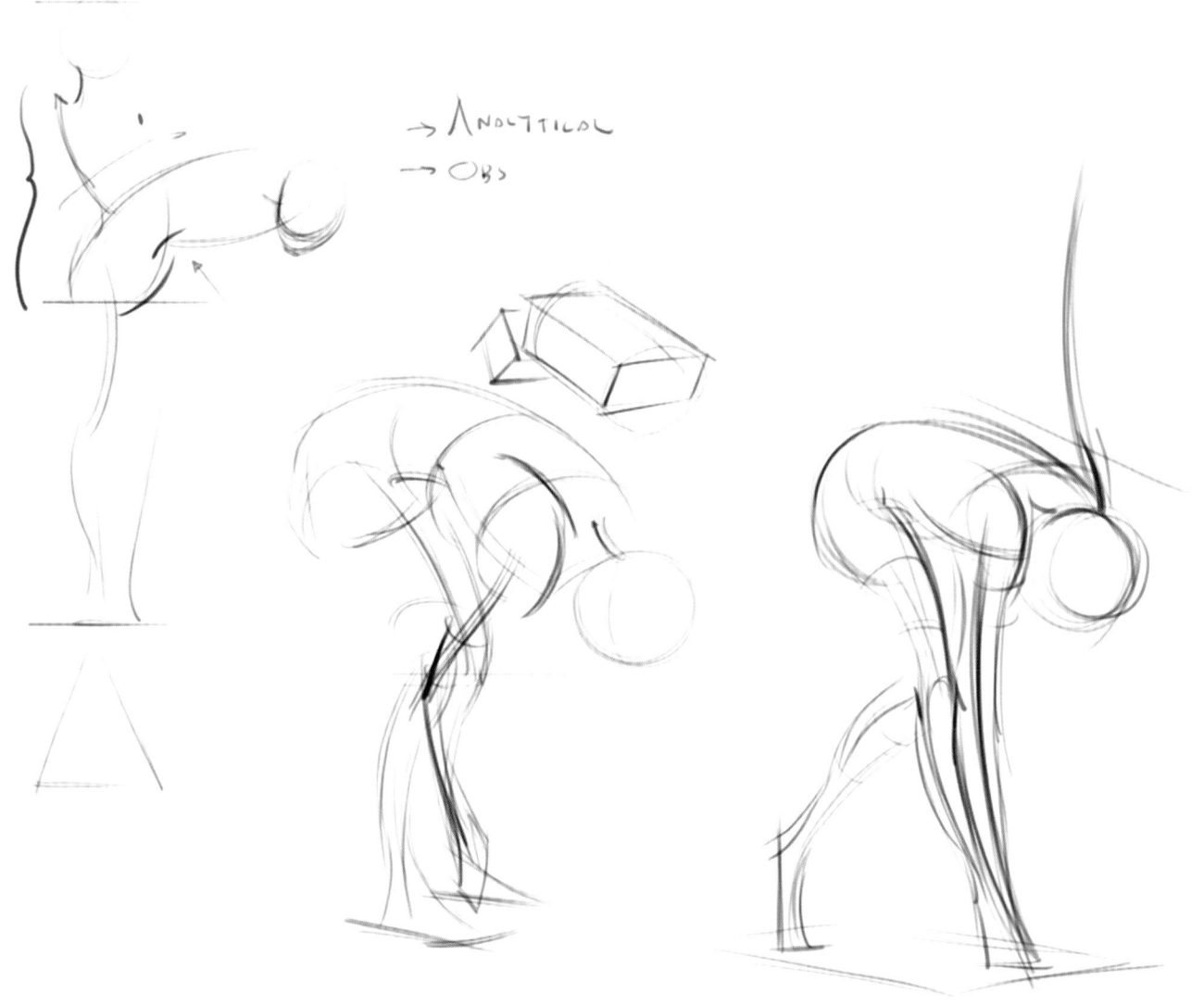

## "HOW WOULD YOU DRAW A FIGURE LEANING FORWARD?"

To indicate the forward bend or flexion of the figure I simply swap the orientation of my spine. To suggest the figure leaning forward move your longer stretch line to the back of the figure and then move your thoracic and lumbar lines to the front to indicate a pinch in the front of the torso. This, combined with changing the overall tilt of the torso, can give you a quick indication of a directional lean. With this variation you can keep your approach consistent but find small modifications to suggest different positions.

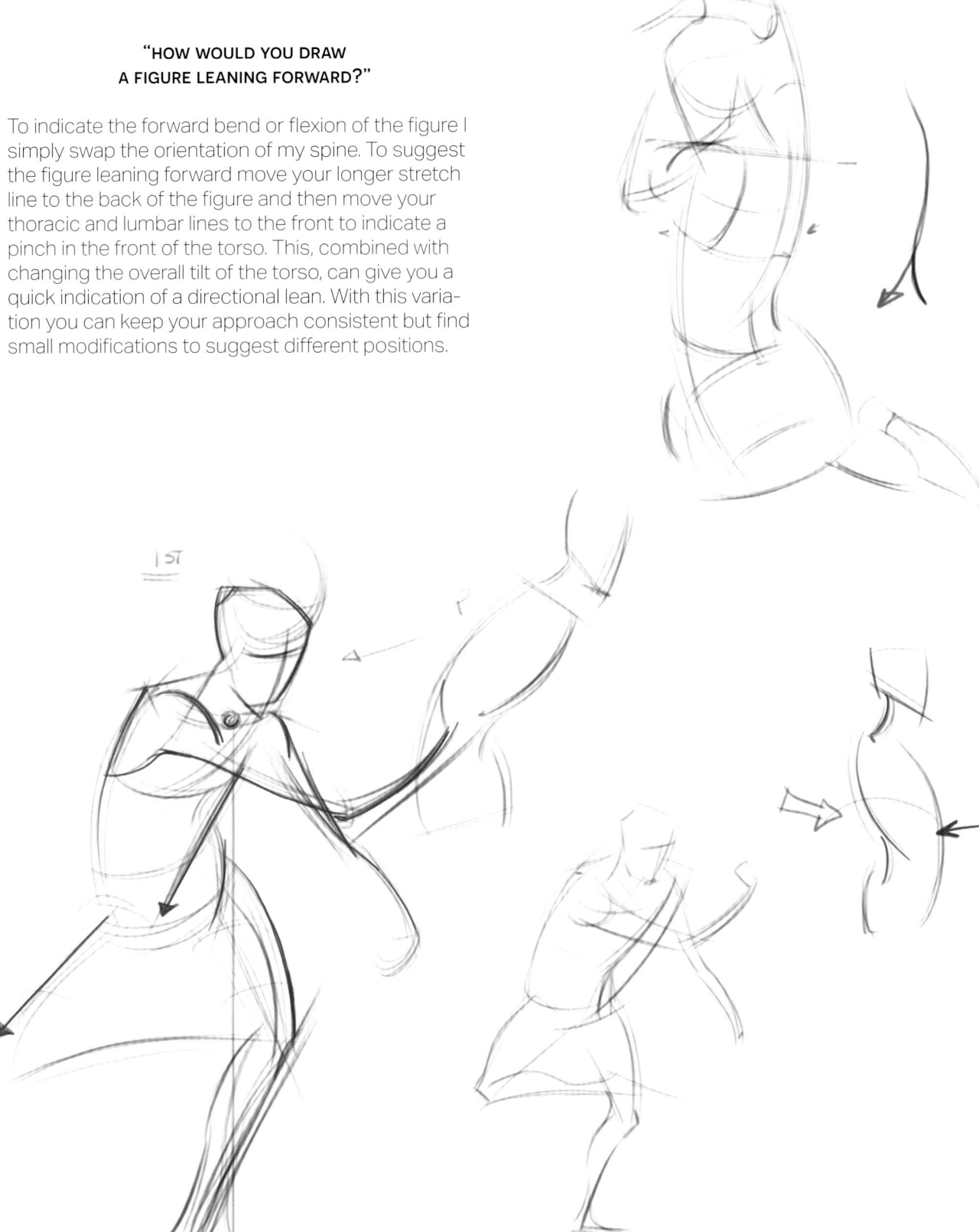

### "HOW CAN I DRAW SEATED POSITIONS USING THIS TECHNIQUE?"

I treat seated poses consistent with the approach described thus far, again, with a few discussed variations. Specifically, with a congested position, I'll use more curves to slow the eye through more difficult transitions (such as the bending of limbs) and focus on the diminishing length of lines to indicate foreshortening. If you keep your emphasis on developing rhythm and building pathways, a seated figure can become a study of movement, be it in a more challenging direction.

### "HOW DO I DRAW A FIGURE FACING DIRECTLY AT ME (FRONT OR BACK)?"

This pose is by far the most difficult. That may be surprising since there isn't much of anything too challenging going on such as foreshortening, a twist, a weird bend, and so on However, the fact that absolutely nothing is going on is what makes the front/back poses uniquely difficult. There's nothing wrong with using this position. In fact, it may be necessary. In any event, here are a few strategies for dealing with this position.

In a straight-on front/back pose, the biggest challenge is the vertical and static positioning of the head, neck, rib cage, and pelvis. The best way that I can maintain themes of asymmetry and movement (described previously) is by pushing the 3D directions of the head, neck, and torso using wrapping lines. The same can be done from the back, however, keep in mind that your perspective directions will be the reverse of those used in the front.

Alternatively, there is always the option in gesture to *not* draw what you see. Remember, no one will ever see your drawing and know that it doesn't resemble the model. Being that no one will likely ever know what your reference is, they will enjoy the drawing on the merits of the drawing alone. What matters most is what you want to communicate to an

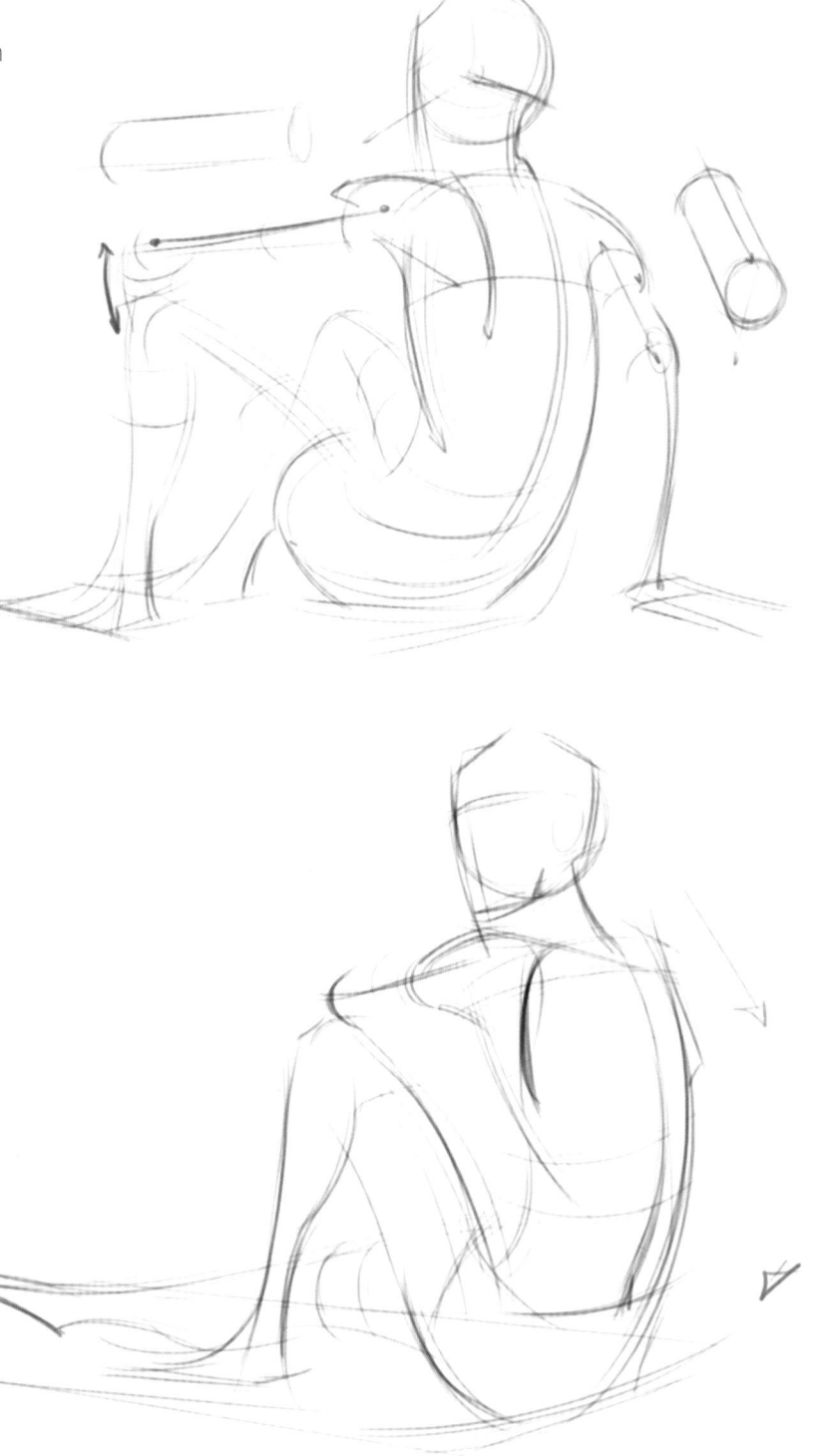

audience, not a misplaced devotion to maintaining adherence to your reference.

In a front/back pose, try and just subtlety shift the weight. If I slightly emphasize weight on one side of the hip that offsets the angle of the pelvis, rib cage, neck, and head, it gives me enough to start introducing some asymmetry and movement into the drawing.

For me, the challenge in this position is really the head, neck, and torso. The arms and legs shouldn't offer the same difficulty as I'm able to introduce an asymmetrical design. I've tried to reinforce this with the anatomical diagrams drawn on this page.

Again, there is no right answer here. Only options. What matters most is that you're exploring and finding the right position that communicates your idea.

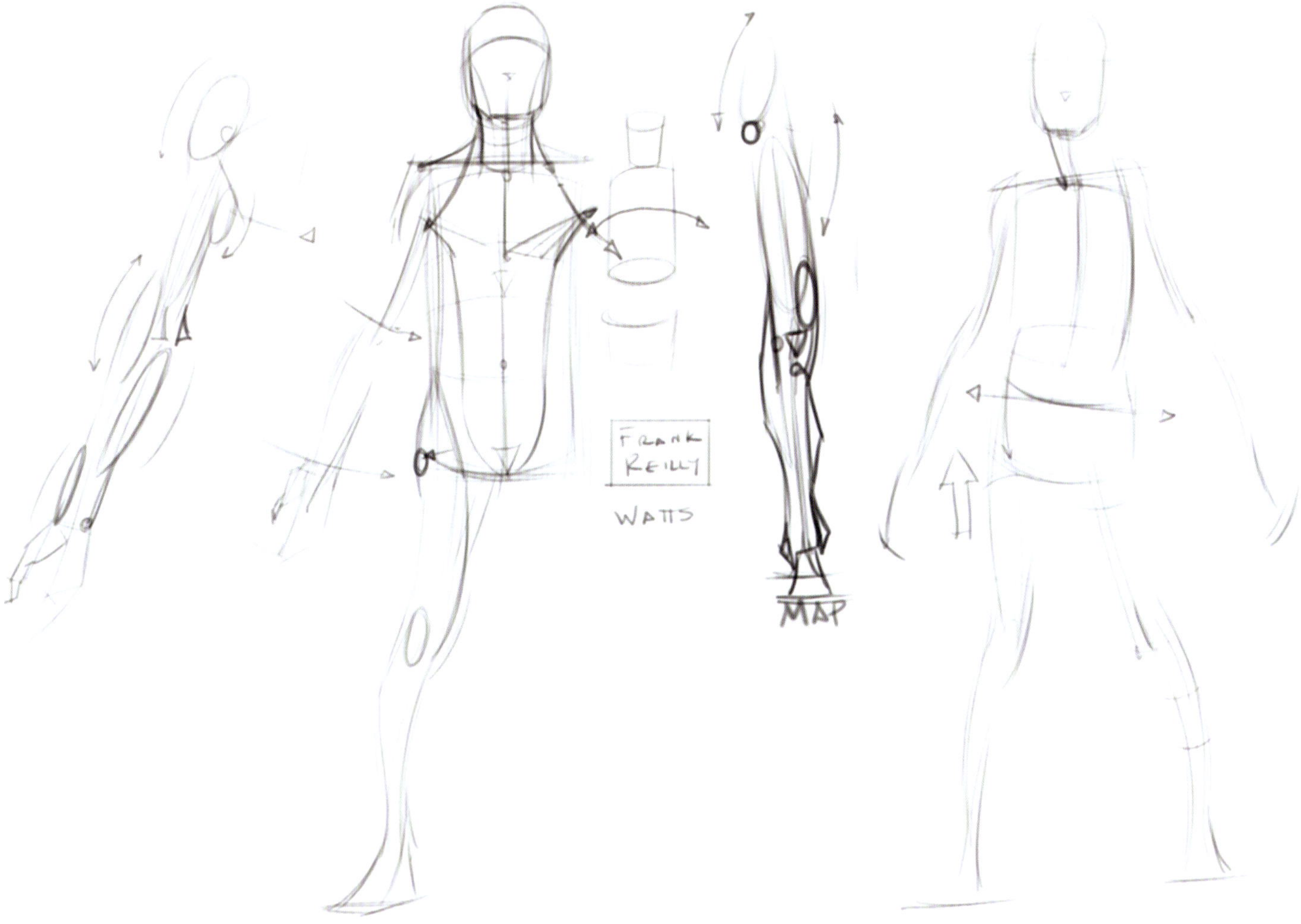

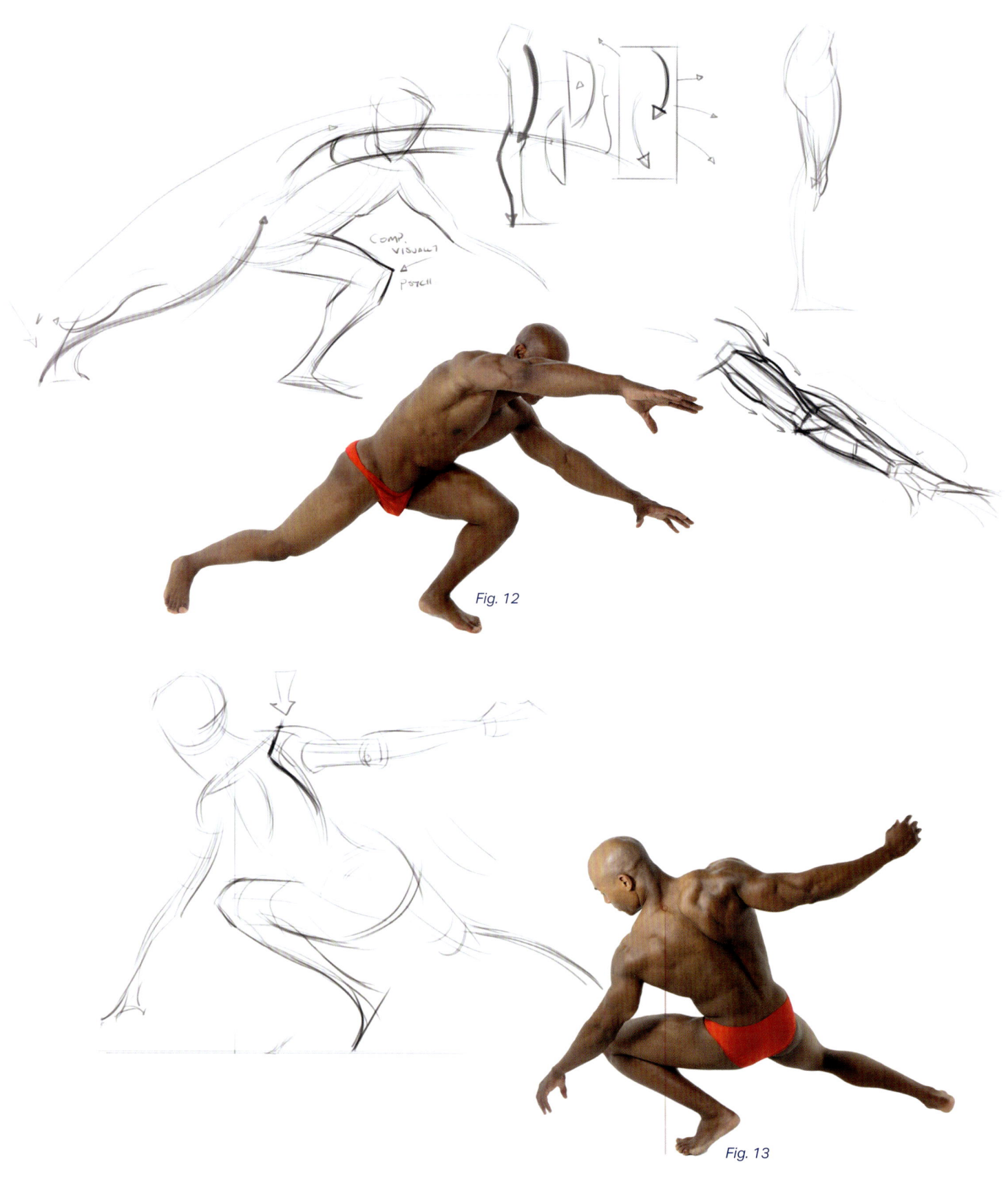

COMP. VISUAL ∆ PSYCH

Fig. 12

Fig. 13

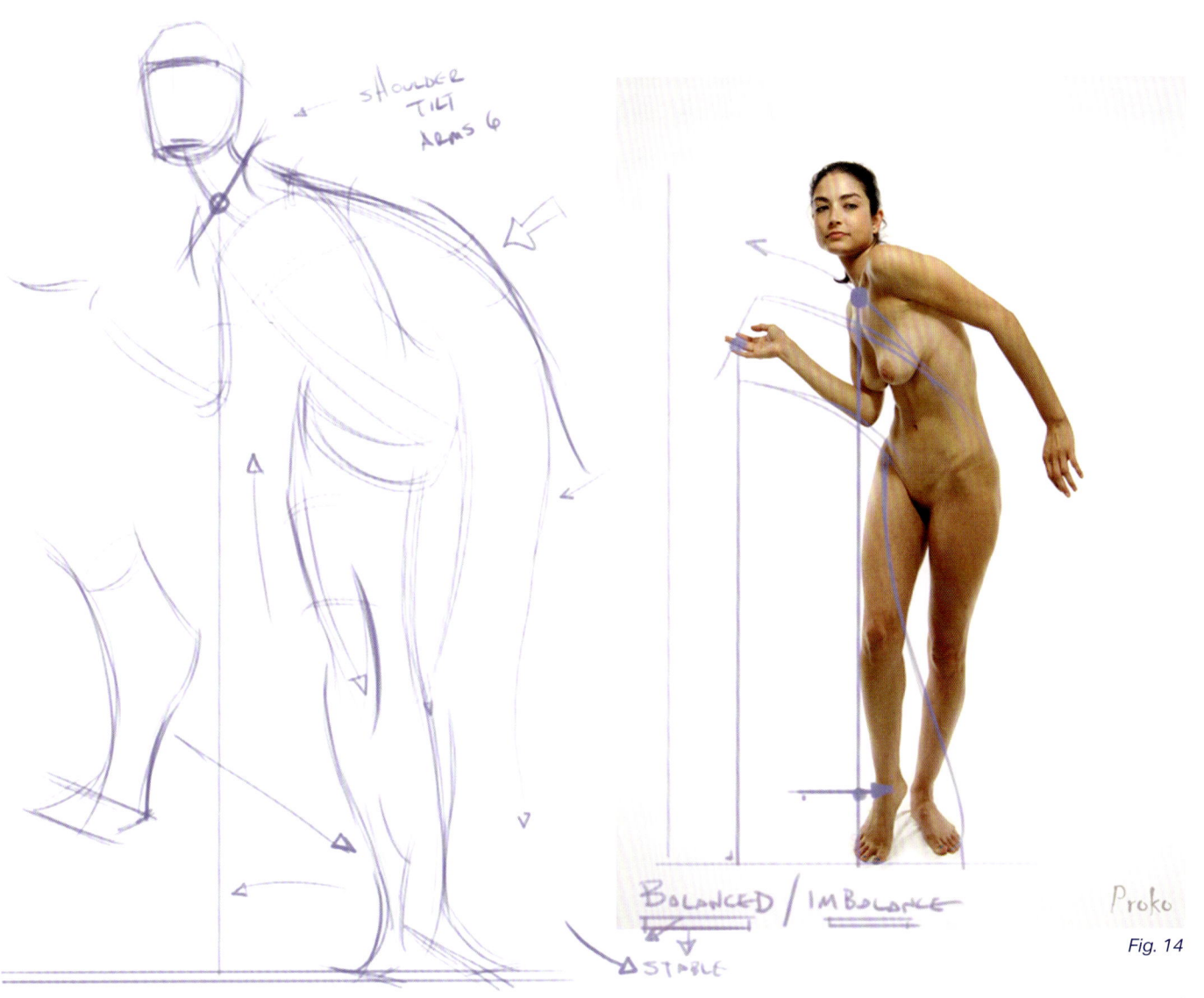

SHOULDER
TILT
ARMS 6

BALANCED / IMBALANCE

STABLE

Proko

Fig. 14

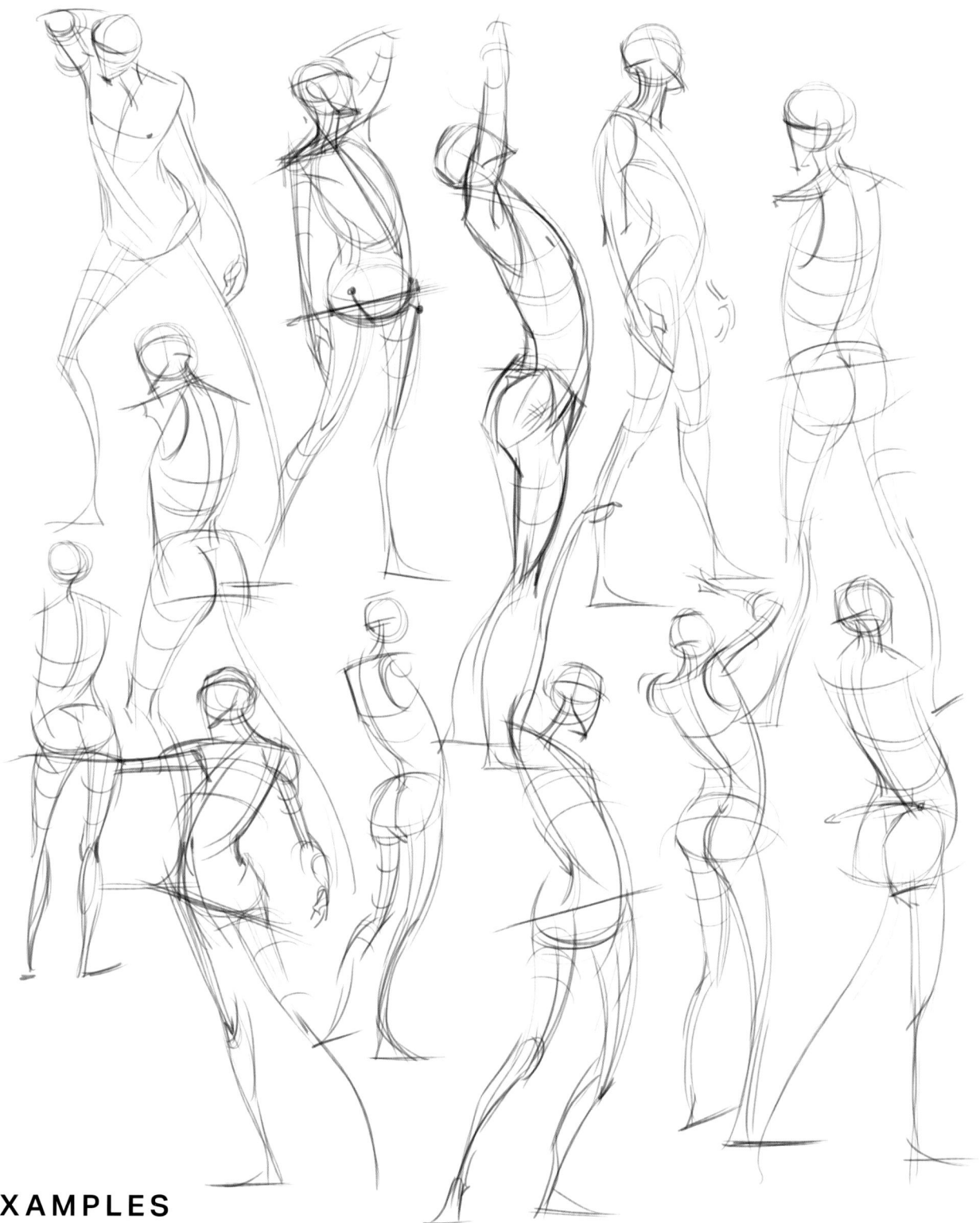

# EXAMPLES

Review the following pages for the ideas and workflow described thus far. See if you can track my use of rhythm using asymmetry. Look for wrapping lines and how they describe the perspective directions. Notice how each gesture curve is oriented at a diagonal tilt.

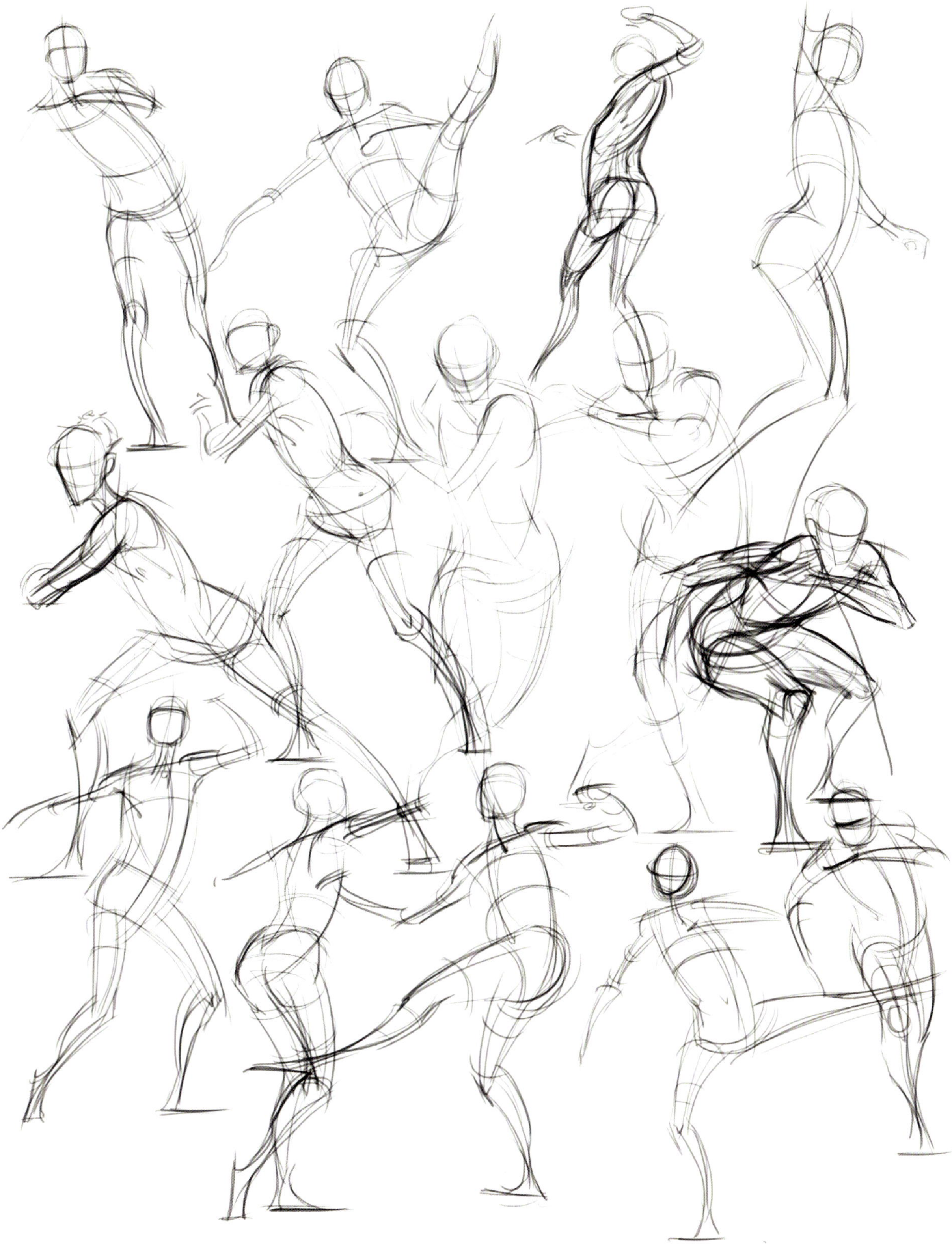

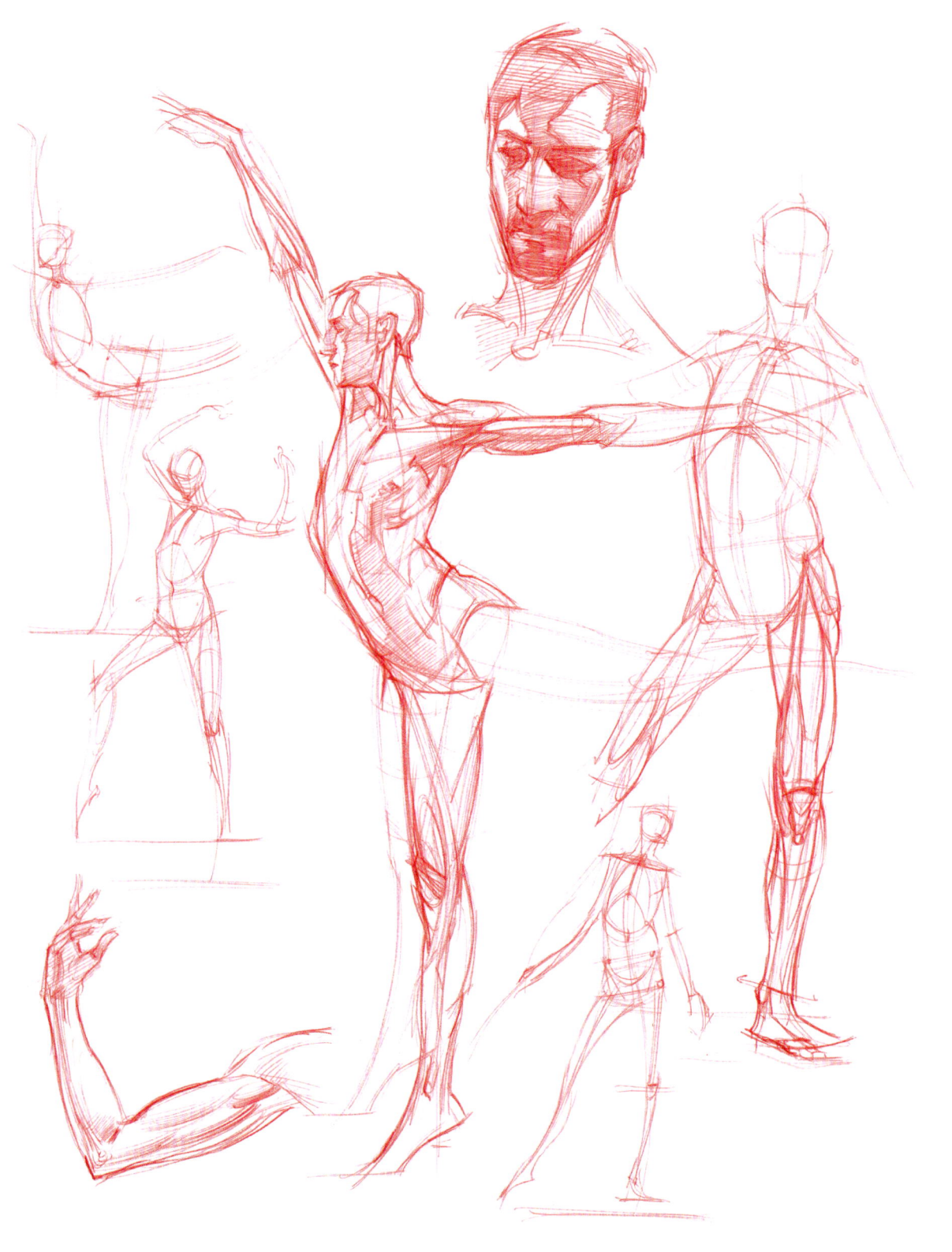

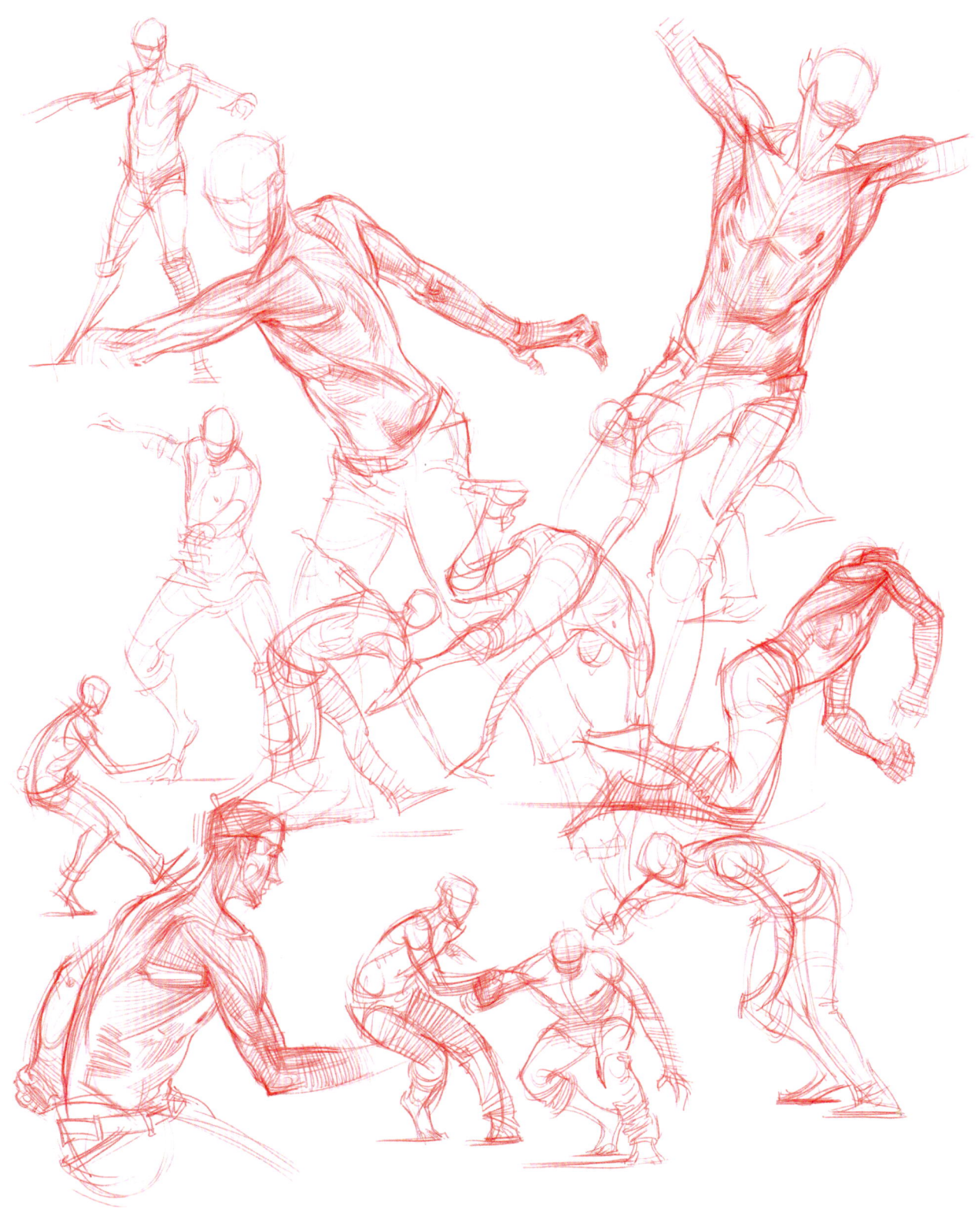

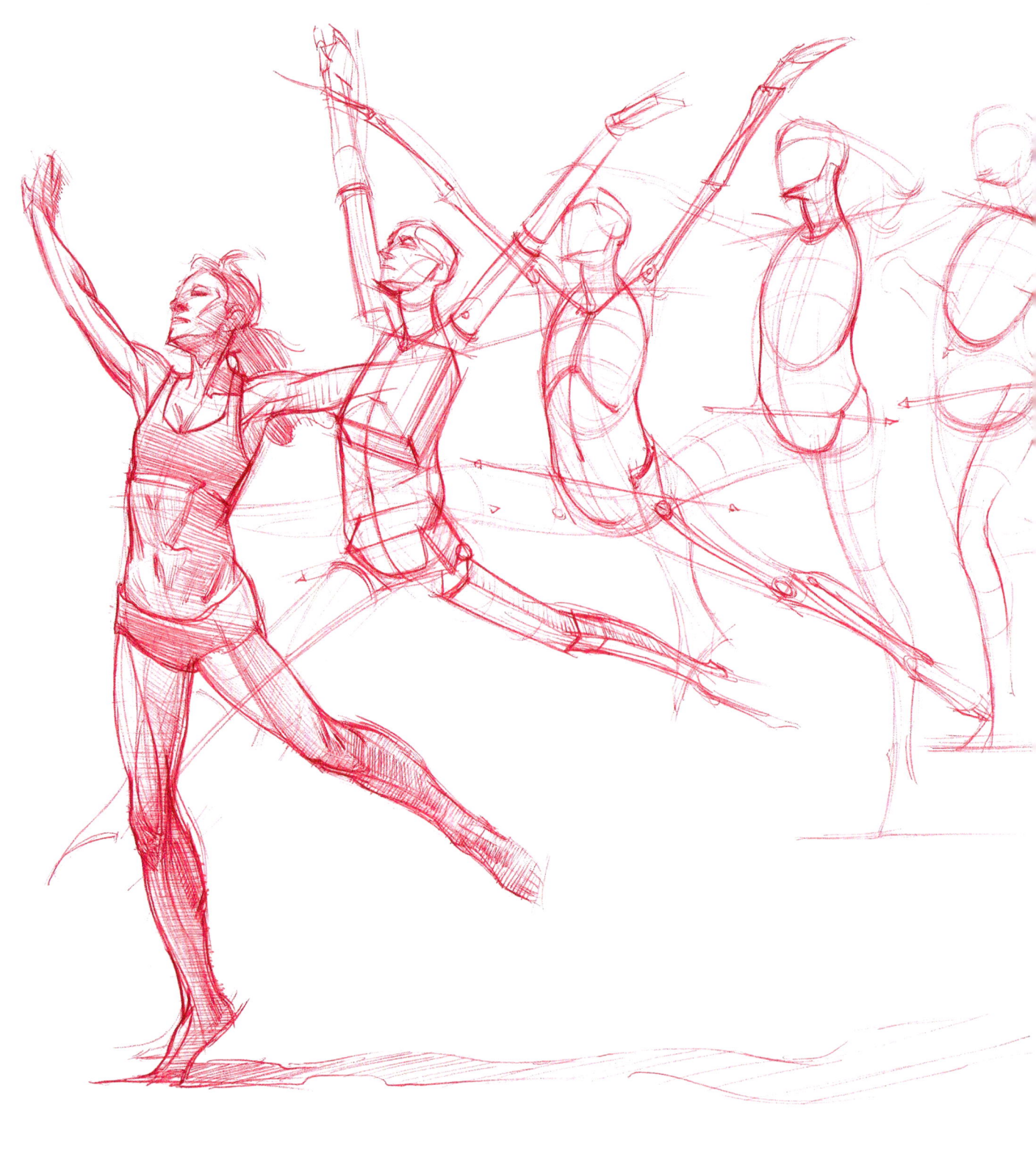

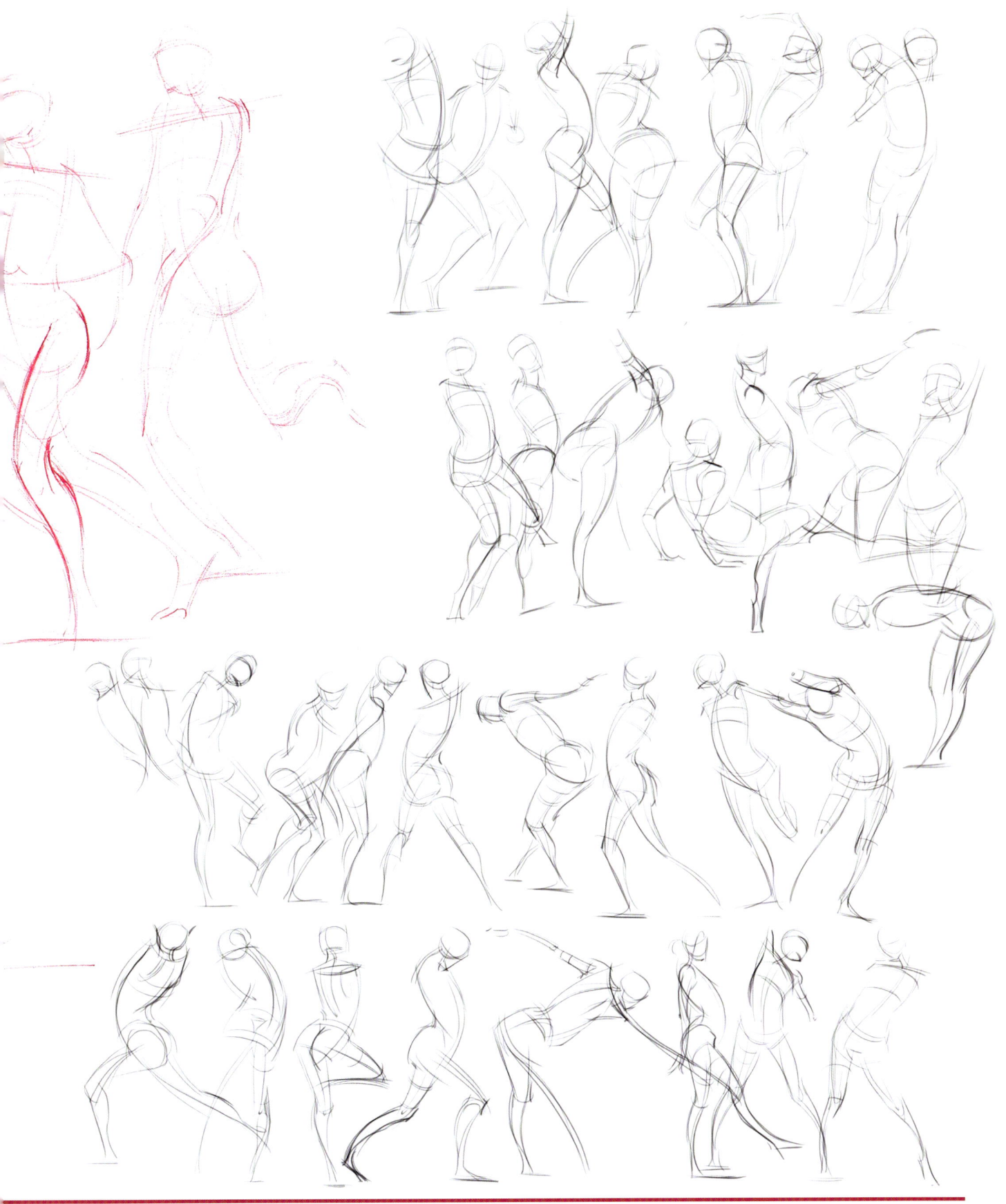

# GESTURE OF THE HEAD, HANDS, AND FEET

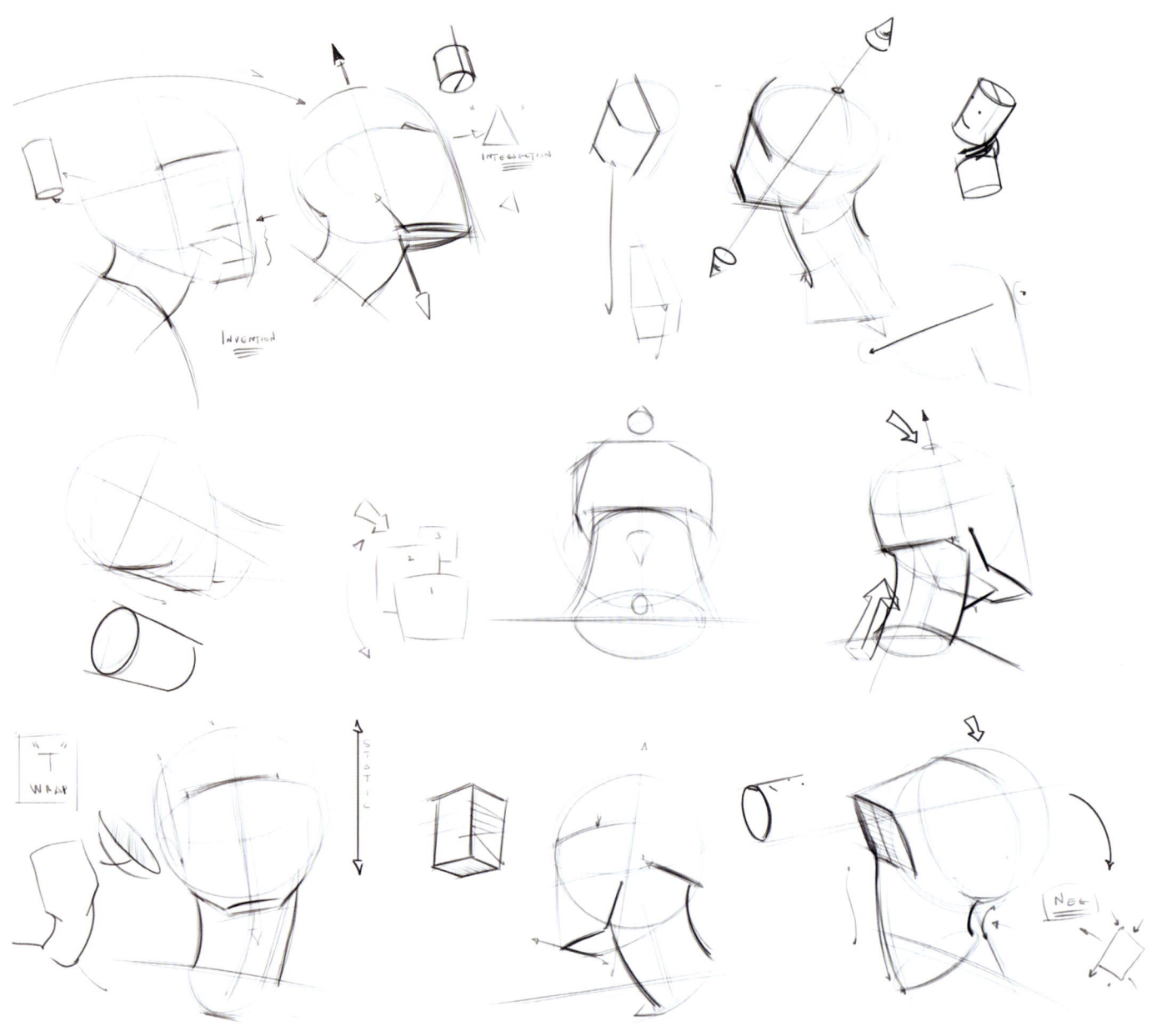

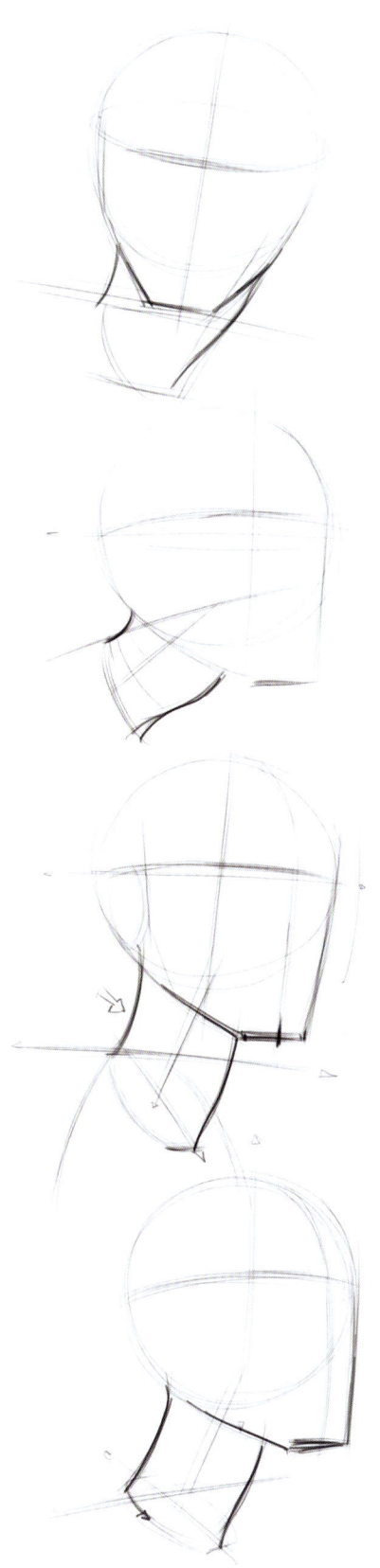

# THE HEAD

When beginning my gestures I start the head as a simple circle or ellipse. However, at times I bring a little more information to specify its position. Here are a few things to think about in the order that I include them:

**HEAD SHAPE**

**TILTS OF HEAD, NECK, AND SHOULDER LINE**

**ADDITION OF THE JAW, CENTER LINE, "T"**

**PERSPECTIVE LINES OF THE HEAD (BROW THROUGH TOP OF EAR)**

As we have already discussed, the lay-in of the head is a simple sphere. That sphere is my simplification of the cranial mass of the skull (feel free to substitute a more complicated form if you like).

My next step attempts to address a consistent problem I see in gestures and head drawing. Mainly that the head, neck, and shoulder are always stiff, too rigid, or otherwise left unconsidered. To address this, on top of my sphere, I indicate the varying leans or tilts of these three areas.

I define the "tilt" of a form as its side-to-side or 2D lean. I always consider the position of the head in relation to the neck and shoulder tilt as there is a considerable amount of nonverbal expression in these simple movements. I can convey annoyance, excitement, arrogance, and so on in the depiction of these three parts. For example, consider a "selfie." Ever notice how common it is for people to offset the angle of their head, neck, and shoulder—usually from an elevated angle? What is the emotion this conveys? Why has it become conventional to do so?

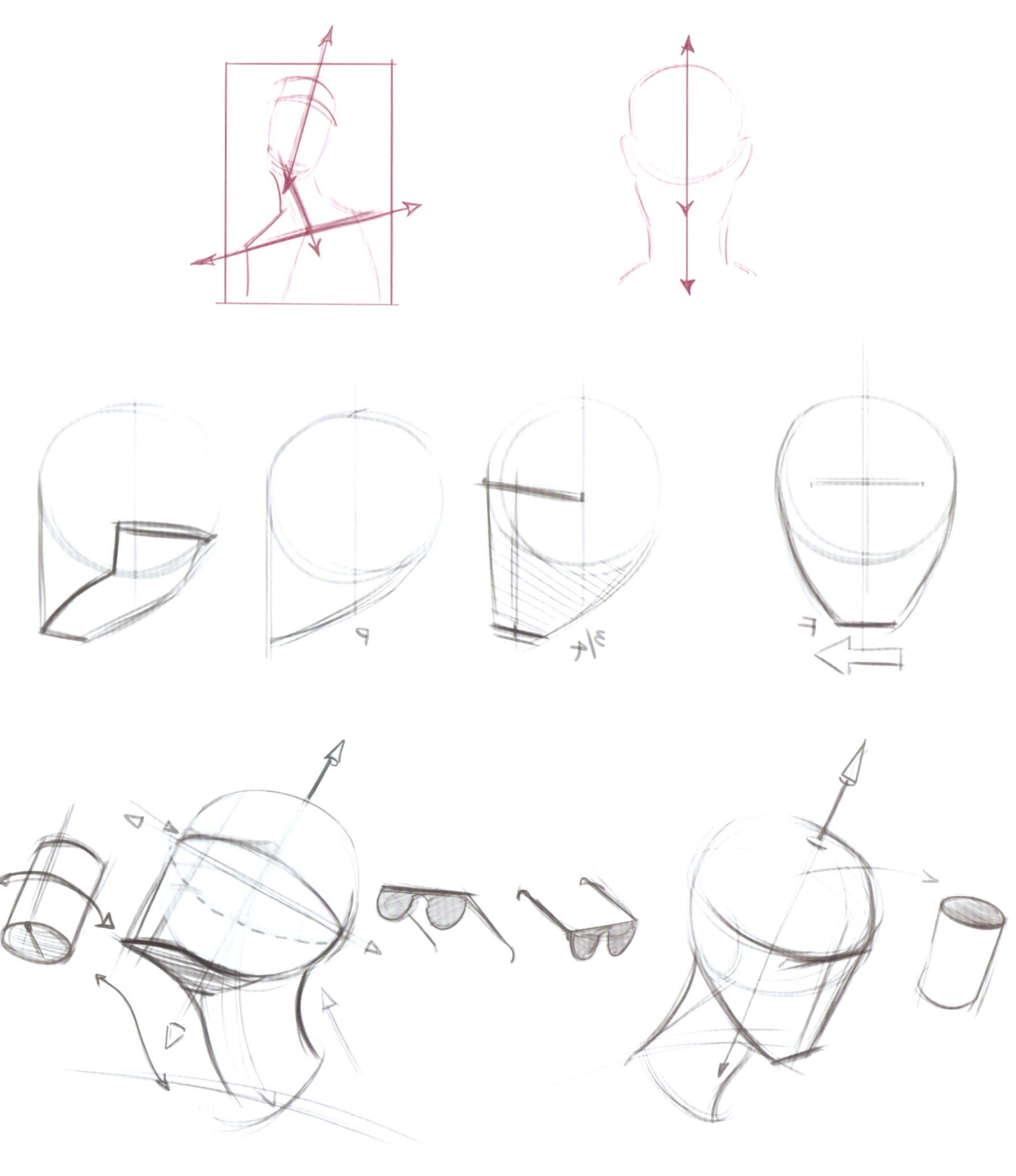

*Tip: I generally don't begin gestures by adding all these elements, instead, as described previously, I begin with a more general egg or oval. However, these might be useful notations to make on a second pass through the gesture stage.*

Next, by adding the shape of the jaw, center line or symmetry line of the face, and "t" with a line between the brow and ear, I can rotate the head to any angle. The trick at this stage is to notice the position of the chin. Notice in the diagram at right that the chin, when facing front, is symmetrical to the center line of the face and that it shifts and shortens as the face rotates toward the profile.

Lastly, by observing that same brow line and its relationship to the ear, I can give a wrapping line (or ellipse) through those points to describe the head seen from below or above.

I consider these four steps the gesture of the head as they explain all possible positions. In that sense, anything beyond these steps would be refining the shape of the head or adding secondary details to it.

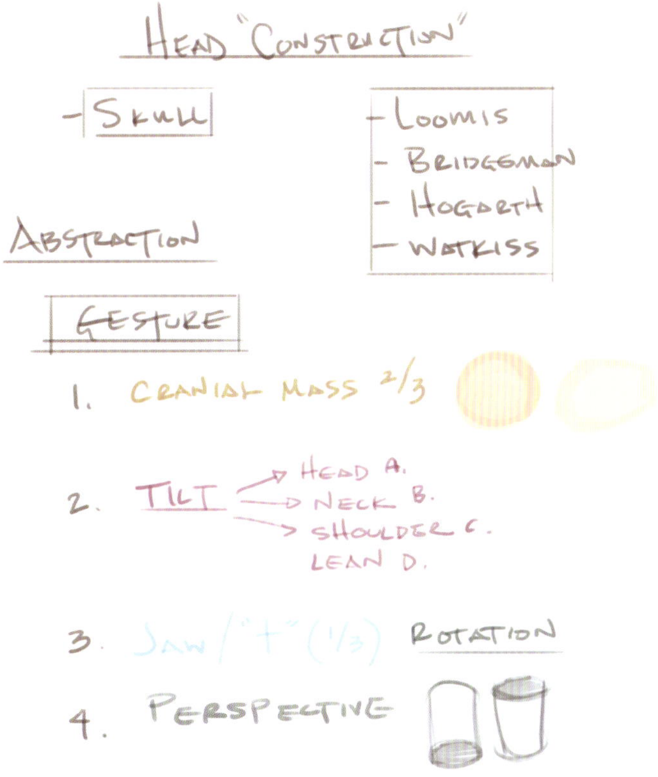

HEAD "CONSTRUCTION"

- SKULL

ABSTRACTION

- LOOMIS
- BRIDGEMAN
- HOGARTH
- WATKISS

GESTURE

1. CRANIAL MASS 2/3

2. TILT → HEAD A.
   → NECK B.
   → SHOULDER C.
   LEAN D.

3. JAW / "t" (1/3)  ROTATION

4. PERSPECTIVE

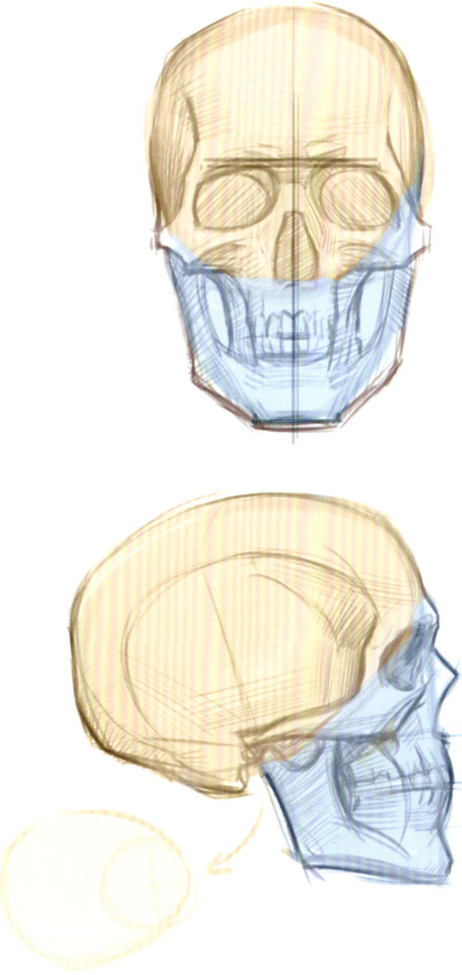

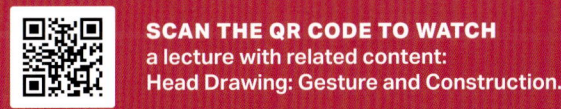

# THE HANDS

As a secondary focal point or area of emphasis, I return to the hands in a secondary pass through my gesture drawing. My first step is the simple "C" or "S" curve summarizing the direction of the forearm and hand into one unified curve. However, like the head, a second pass to describe additional rhythms or shapes can have a massive impact on the way your figures communicate to an audience.

Hands translate and express feelings though gesture, and touch, articulating thoughts and emotions in complex ways. Some studies have shown that the gesture of hands increase the value of a message by 60 percent. In terms of the visual importance of hands, imagine having a conversation with someone with no hand movement at all. This person would likely come across as cold or distant. All because an essential element of conversation is missing. In contrast we tend to think of people who talk with their hands to be warm, agreeable, or energetic.

We gather information from others' body language through the movement and positioning of the hands. Even if this information is processed subconsciously, the value in understanding these behavioral cues is profound when creating believable emotions in your drawings.

For example, if our hands repeatedly touch our face or hair while we're on a date, it can be a sign that we're subconsciously attracted. If that person mirrors our gestures, it reflects and reinforces our own. In this sense, gesture, and the gestures of hands specifically, act as a "second language" revealing what may be absent from our speech.

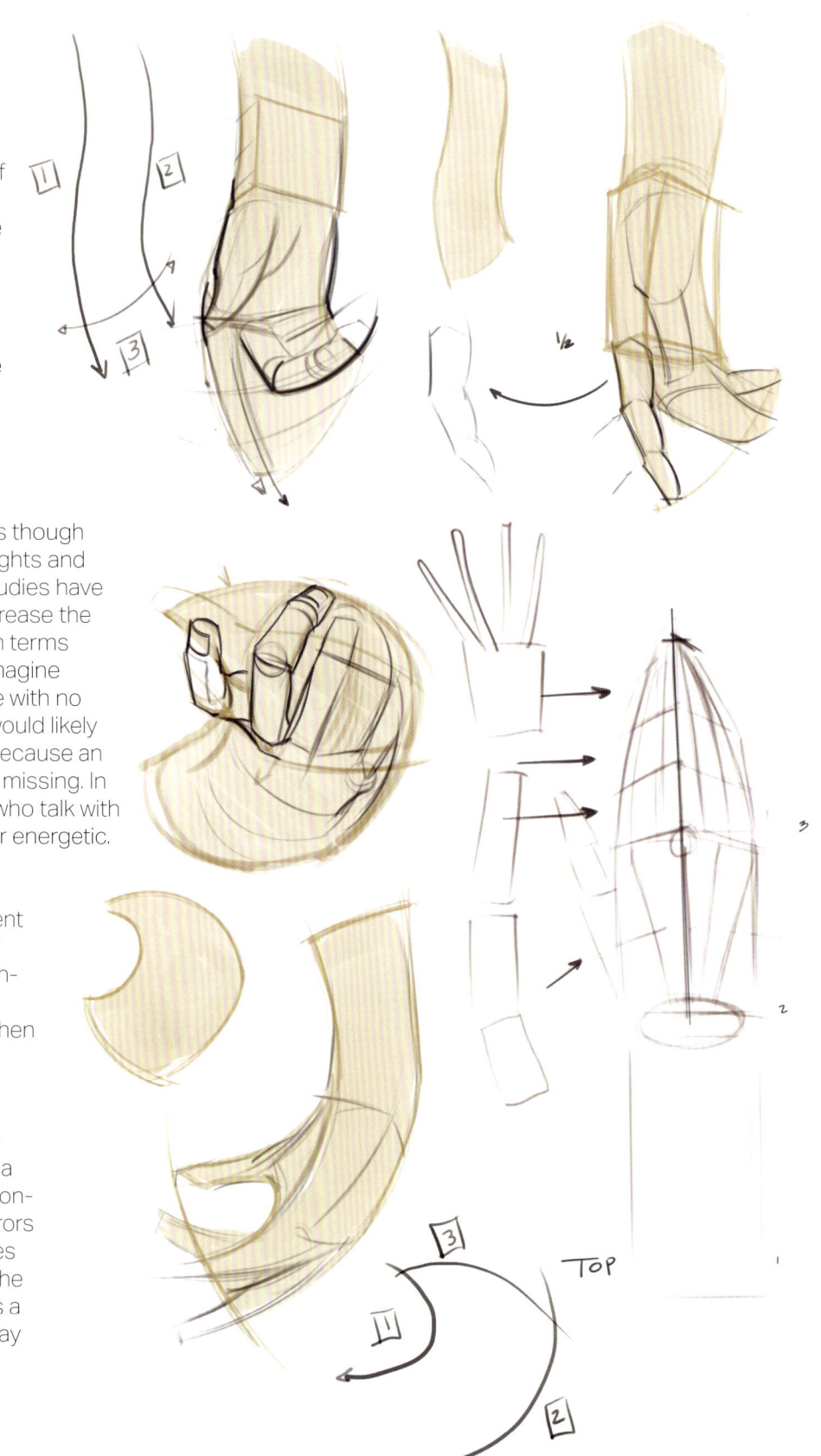

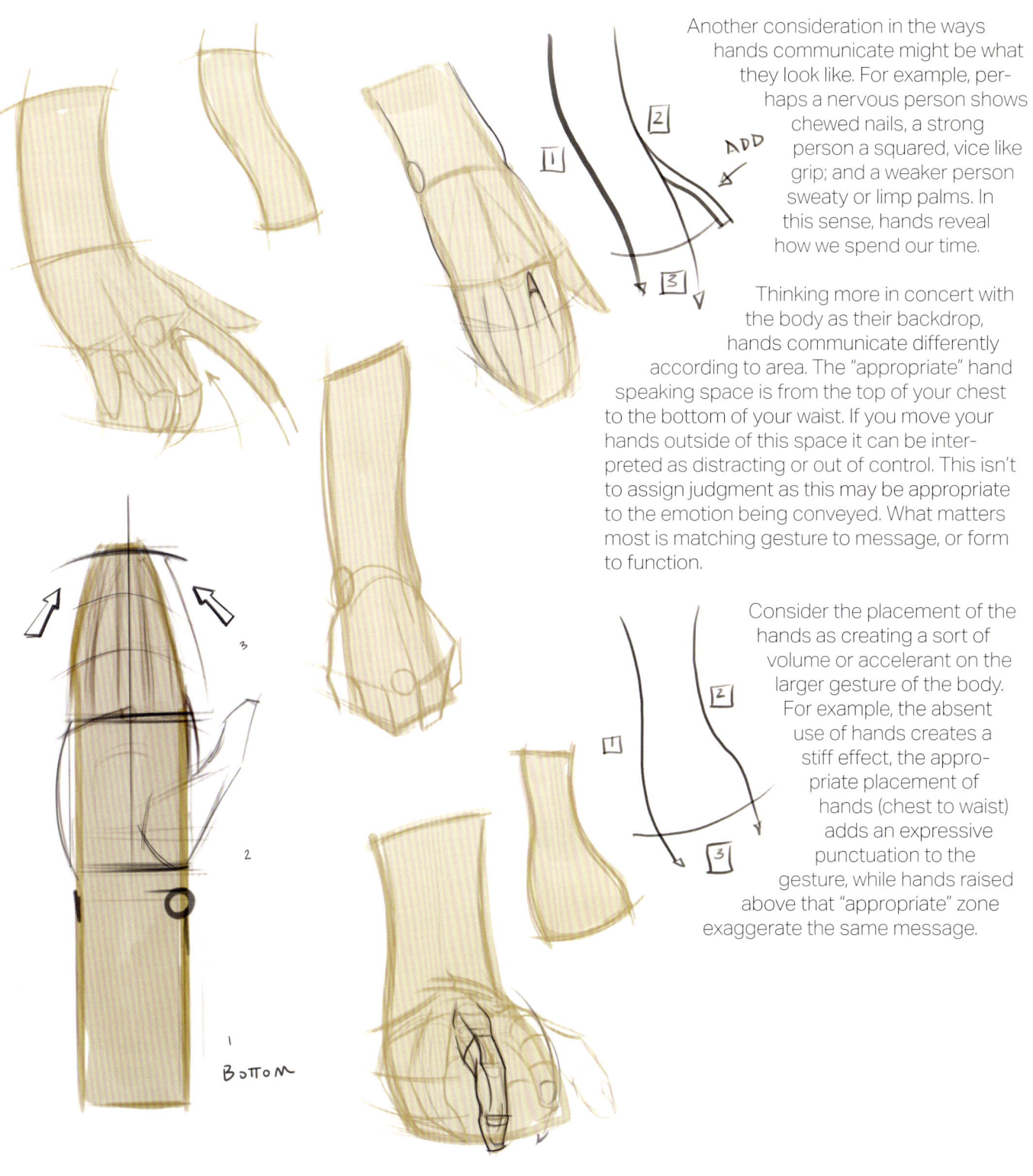

Another consideration in the ways hands communicate might be what they look like. For example, perhaps a nervous person shows chewed nails, a strong person a squared, vice like grip; and a weaker person sweaty or limp palms. In this sense, hands reveal how we spend our time.

Thinking more in concert with the body as their backdrop, hands communicate differently according to area. The "appropriate" hand speaking space is from the top of your chest to the bottom of your waist. If you move your hands outside of this space it can be interpreted as distracting or out of control. This isn't to assign judgment as this may be appropriate to the emotion being conveyed. What matters most is matching gesture to message, or form to function.

Consider the placement of the hands as creating a sort of volume or accelerant on the larger gesture of the body. For example, the absent use of hands creates a stiff effect, the appropriate placement of hands (chest to waist) adds an expressive punctuation to the gesture, while hands raised above that "appropriate" zone exaggerate the same message.

ADD

BOTTOM

Beyond the placement of the hands relative to the body, it may be useful to consider how exactly we use our hands. Whether it be for indicating a number, demonstrating an increase or decrease in emotional intensity (i.e., gesturing toward one's heart), or hand gestures which underly our speech, it's helpful to think of categories or patterns through which story is embellished. For example, consider that we generally read a solid fist as determination, steepling the hands as a confident or wise gesture, hand wringing as a sign of insecurity, a thumbs-up as an indication of confidence, pointing with our hands as aggressive, and so on.

It goes without saying that there is just as much that we can communicate with our hands as with our bodies/heads. To capture this, I choose an edited lay-in to allow a focus on what the hands are saying prior to addressing exactly what they look like. Having briefly identified ways in which you can anticipate the meaning conveyed by the hands, let's next turn to an abbreviated way in which you can draw them to capture that communication prior to focusing on details.

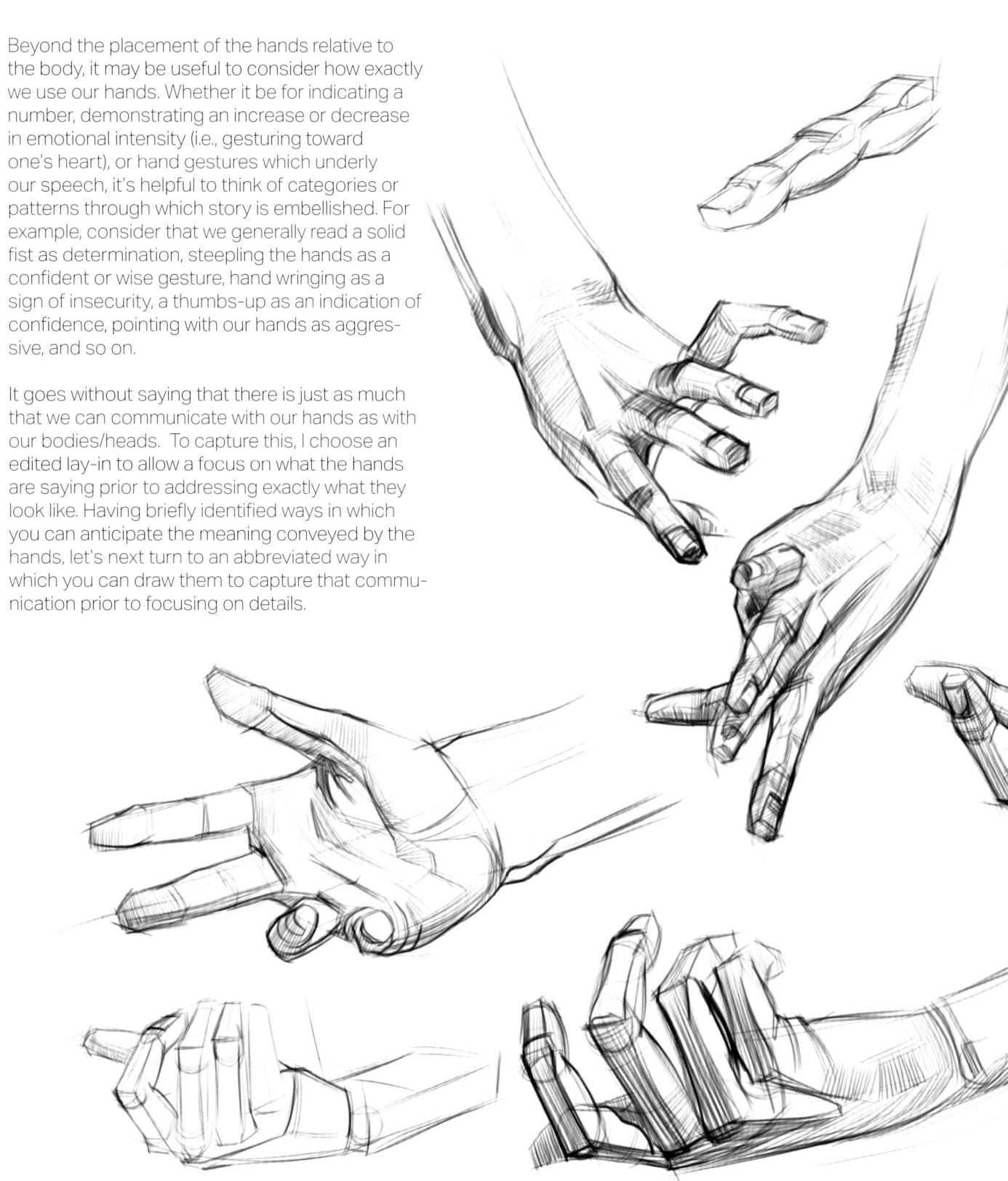

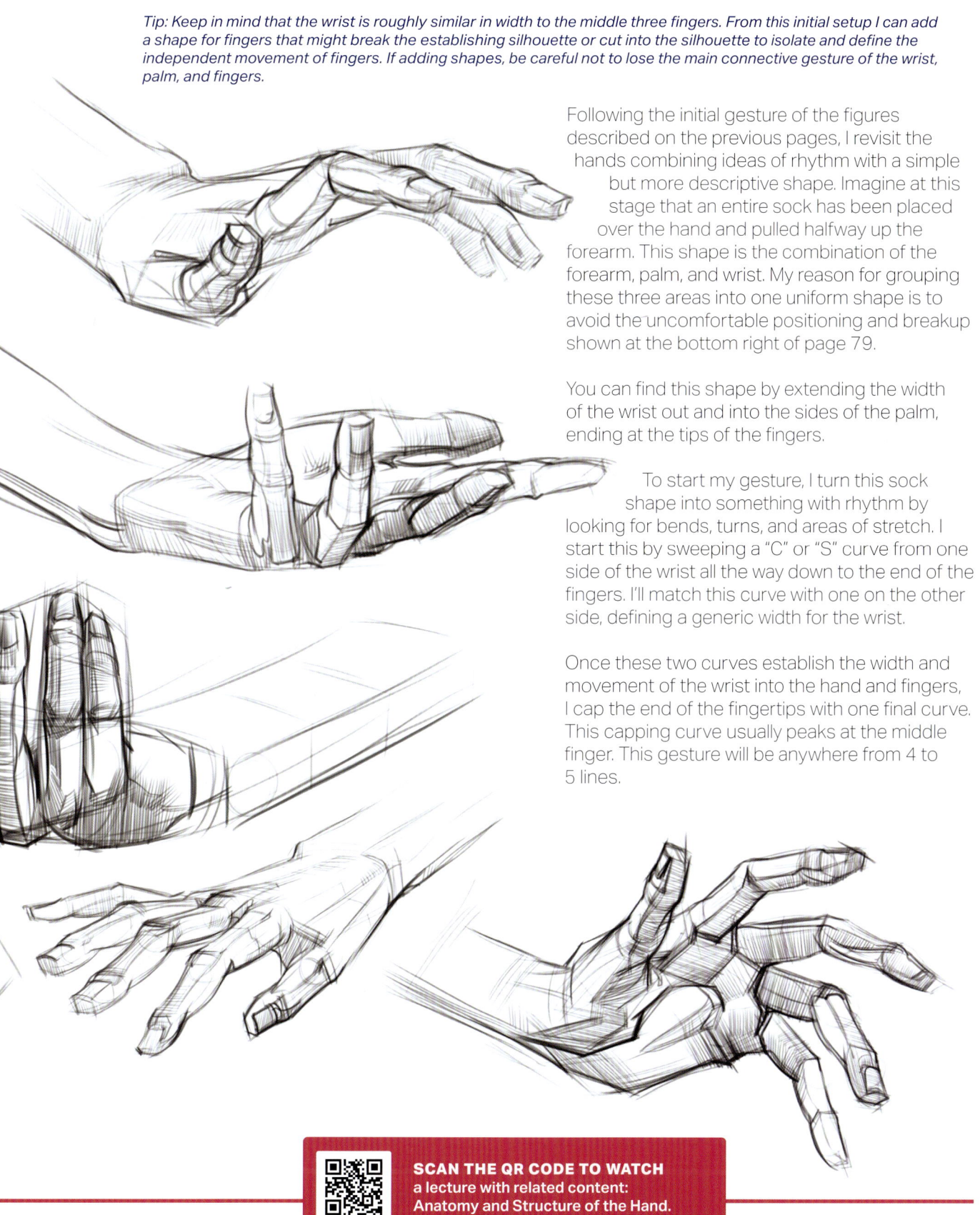

*Tip: Keep in mind that the wrist is roughly similar in width to the middle three fingers. From this initial setup I can add a shape for fingers that might break the establishing silhouette or cut into the silhouette to isolate and define the independent movement of fingers. If adding shapes, be careful not to lose the main connective gesture of the wrist, palm, and fingers.*

Following the initial gesture of the figures described on the previous pages, I revisit the hands combining ideas of rhythm with a simple but more descriptive shape. Imagine at this stage that an entire sock has been placed over the hand and pulled halfway up the forearm. This shape is the combination of the forearm, palm, and wrist. My reason for grouping these three areas into one uniform shape is to avoid the uncomfortable positioning and breakup shown at the bottom right of page 79.

You can find this shape by extending the width of the wrist out and into the sides of the palm, ending at the tips of the fingers.

To start my gesture, I turn this sock shape into something with rhythm by looking for bends, turns, and areas of stretch. I start this by sweeping a "C" or "S" curve from one side of the wrist all the way down to the end of the fingers. I'll match this curve with one on the other side, defining a generic width for the wrist.

Once these two curves establish the width and movement of the wrist into the hand and fingers, I cap the end of the fingertips with one final curve. This capping curve usually peaks at the middle finger. This gesture will be anywhere from 4 to 5 lines.

# THE FEET

The gesture of the foot is easily represented using a simple triangle. Viewing the foot as a triangle allows me to customize its position by making subtle but deliberate alterations to this shape. To this point, review my early steps for placing the head, specifically the position of the chin in showing the head's rotation. I'm using the exact same thinking here with the foot.

I establish the initial triangle of the foot from the front view by creating a straight line across the toes. This will represent the front plane of the foot (consistent with how the line of the chin tracked the front plane of the face). As the foot rotates into three-quarter or profile views, I will alter the length of this line and introduce a side/ length to the shape of the foot. This sets up an understanding of how the foot, when placed on the ground, is visualized from a three-quarter view. To create a profile gesture, I remove the front and extend the length, for the back I'll use the straight of the heel to represent the plane change from back to side.

My steps when visualizing the foot as a gestural envelope are very similar to that of the hand. If the envelope of the hand was compared to a glove, imagine the foot as a simple sock form. With these four basic positions in mind, I can go one step further through consideration of how each may move. Look at the three-quarter diagram at the top right. It still has all the basic components of three-quarter except I've exaggerated the bounding lines. On the bottom of the foot, as it raises to the heel, I've created an "S" curve to communicate that stretch. On the front, a "C" curve to show a greater compression.

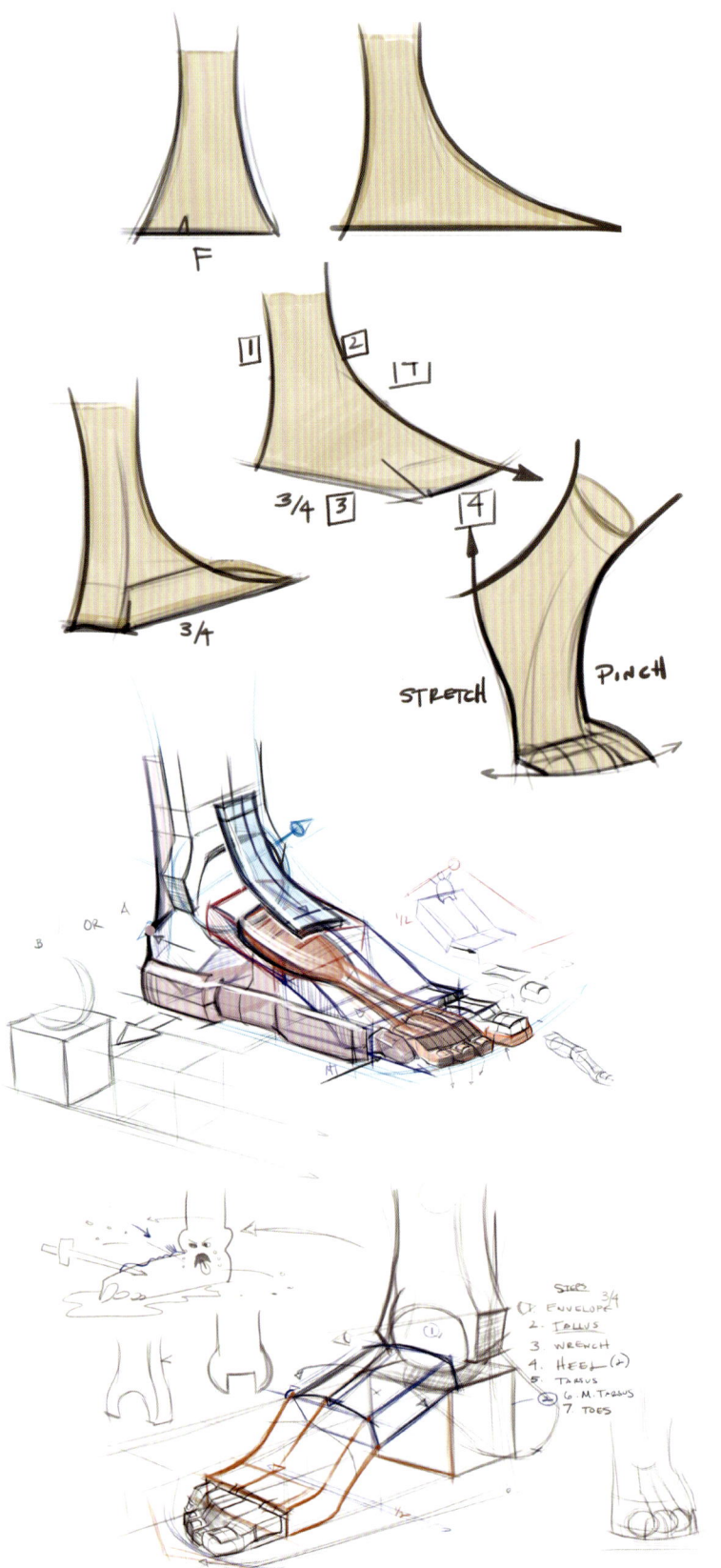

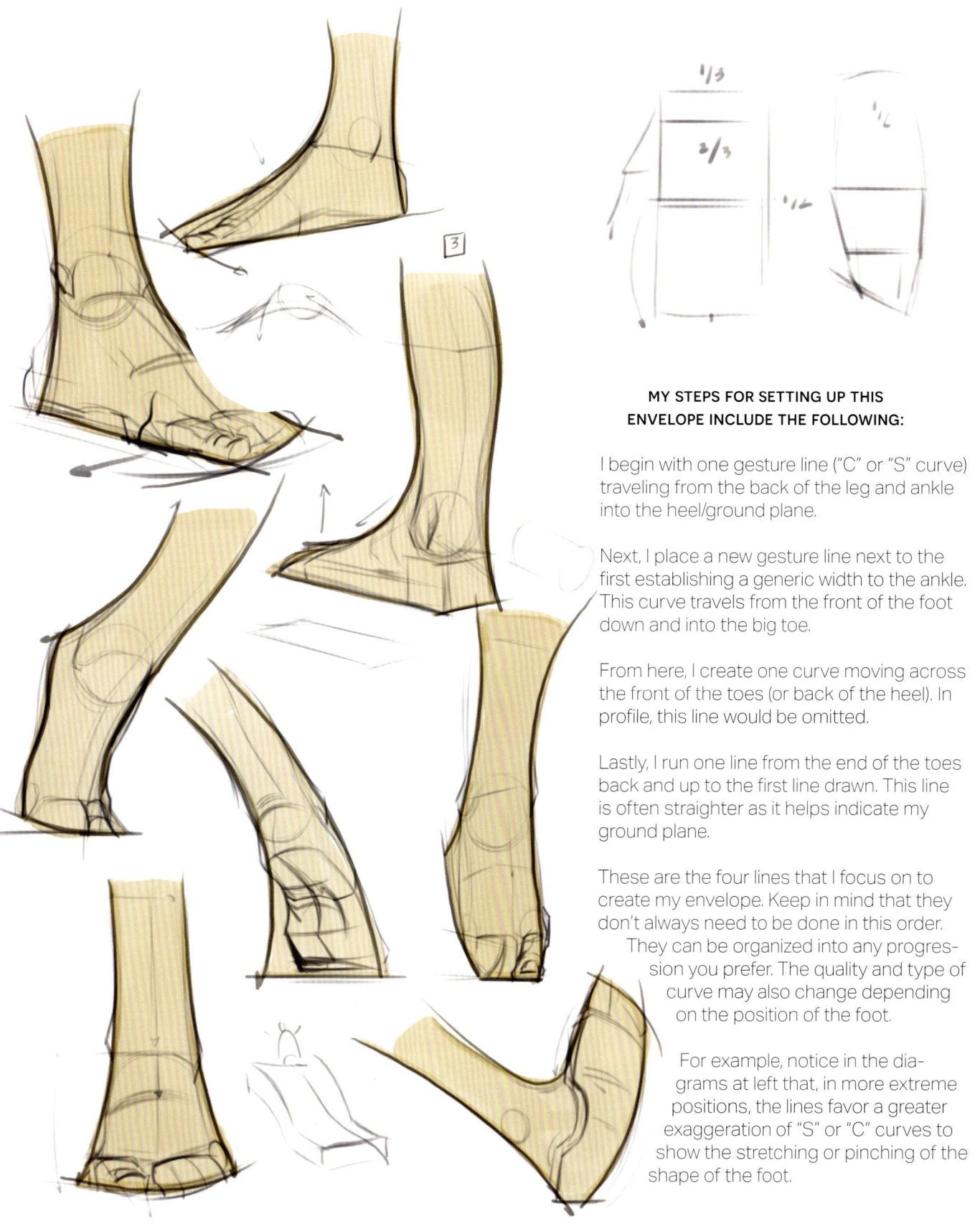

## MY STEPS FOR SETTING UP THIS ENVELOPE INCLUDE THE FOLLOWING:

I begin with one gesture line ("C" or "S" curve) traveling from the back of the leg and ankle into the heel/ground plane.

Next, I place a new gesture line next to the first establishing a generic width to the ankle. This curve travels from the front of the foot down and into the big toe.

From here, I create one curve moving across the front of the toes (or back of the heel). In profile, this line would be omitted.

Lastly, I run one line from the end of the toes back and up to the first line drawn. This line is often straighter as it helps indicate my ground plane.

These are the four lines that I focus on to create my envelope. Keep in mind that they don't always need to be done in this order. They can be organized into any progression you prefer. The quality and type of curve may also change depending on the position of the foot.

For example, notice in the diagrams at left that, in more extreme positions, the lines favor a greater exaggeration of "S" or "C" curves to show the stretching or pinching of the shape of the foot.

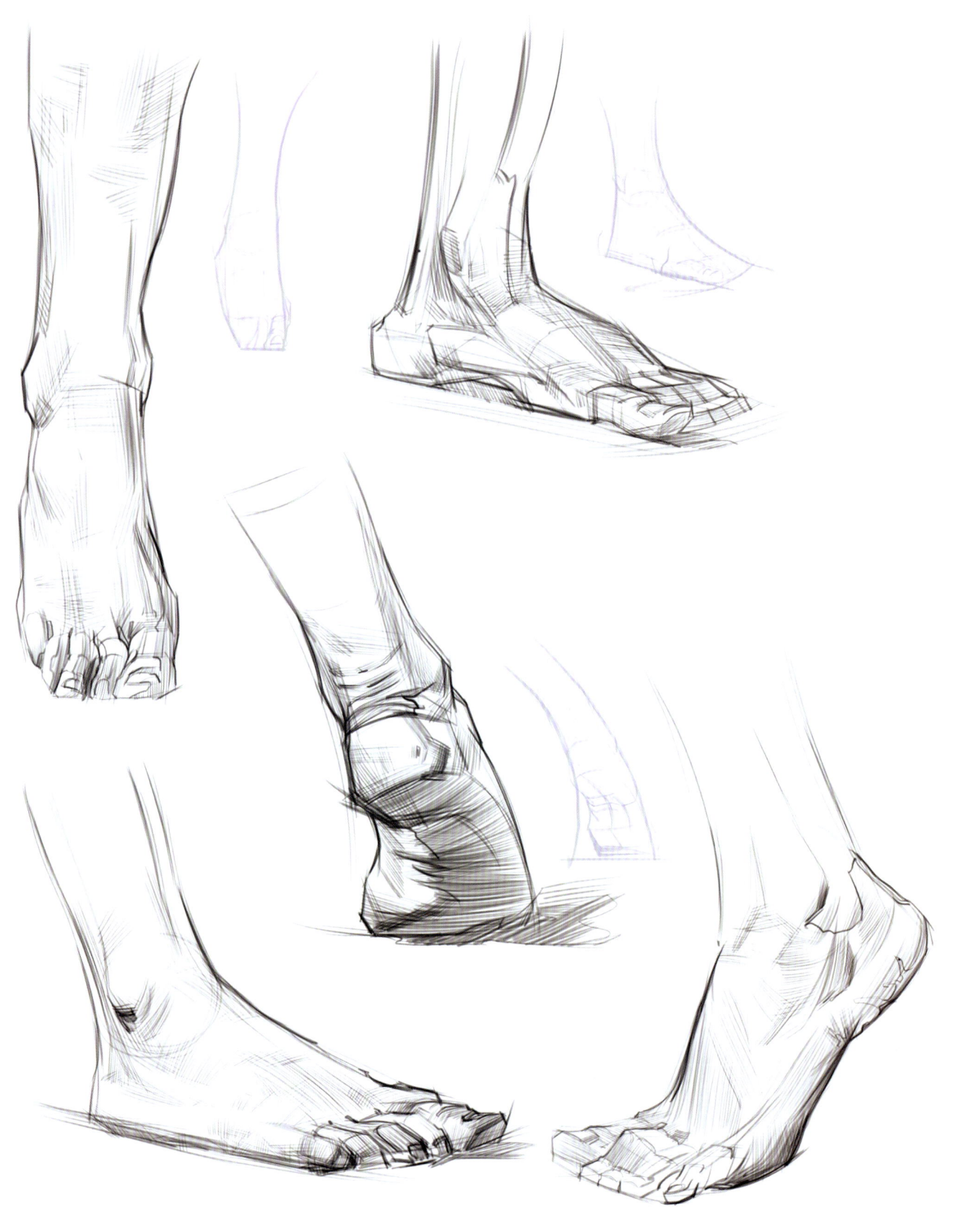

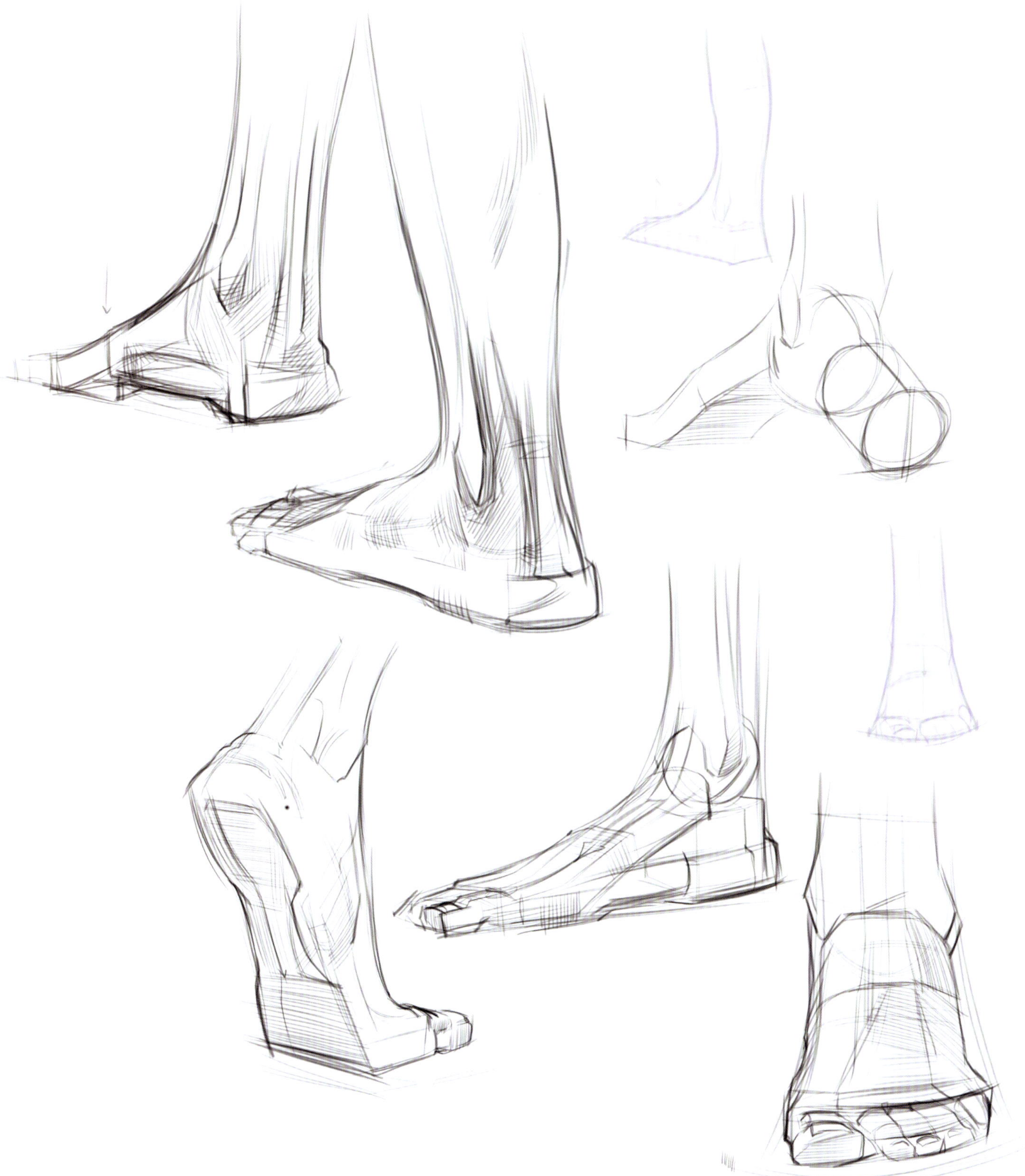

SCAN THE QR CODE TO WATCH
a lecture with related content:
How to Draw the Foot.

# THE CENTER OF GRAVITY AND "ABOUT TO" POSE

Now that I've gone through a more detailed explanation of the "how" of my gesture, what I'm thinking, and how I tackle smaller parts (head, hands, and feet), let's try to loop back to the beginning.

A common question many ask is, "When do you know to push a pose?" To the great disappointment of most my answer is always, "Whenever you want." As you might expect, this is related to the subjective "why" of the pose that I began this book attempting to describe.

There are an endless number of different ways you might push a pose. You might distort proportions, change positions, exaggerate shapes, and so on.

All of these are viable and will undoubtedly result in some expressive exaggeration. Again, the only thing that matters is that you communicate with intention to your audience.

I realize this isn't easy to just do. So, in this last section, and with all our pieces and process described, I'd like to share the way I think about pushing poses that you might want to try in your own gestures. Keep in mind, this is just one way.

To begin pushing an existing pose I start by analyzing the quality and type of balance that the pose has. My view toward "pushing" a pose is through the creation of tension, as such I attempt to create or exaggerate an imbalance. My hope is that this takes a pose from feeling stationary to feeling as if there is a motion in progress. I call this exercise creating an "about to..." pose. An "about to..." pose positions

a figure in a way that imbalance dominates leaving no conclusive or stationary quality.

The open-ended "about to..." leaves the pose indeterminate with the hopes of engaging the audience in anticipation.

There are a few ways we can look for this. One way to begin is by looking for a plumb line representing the center of gravity. This can be found by looking for the pit of the neck (look for the purple circle near the

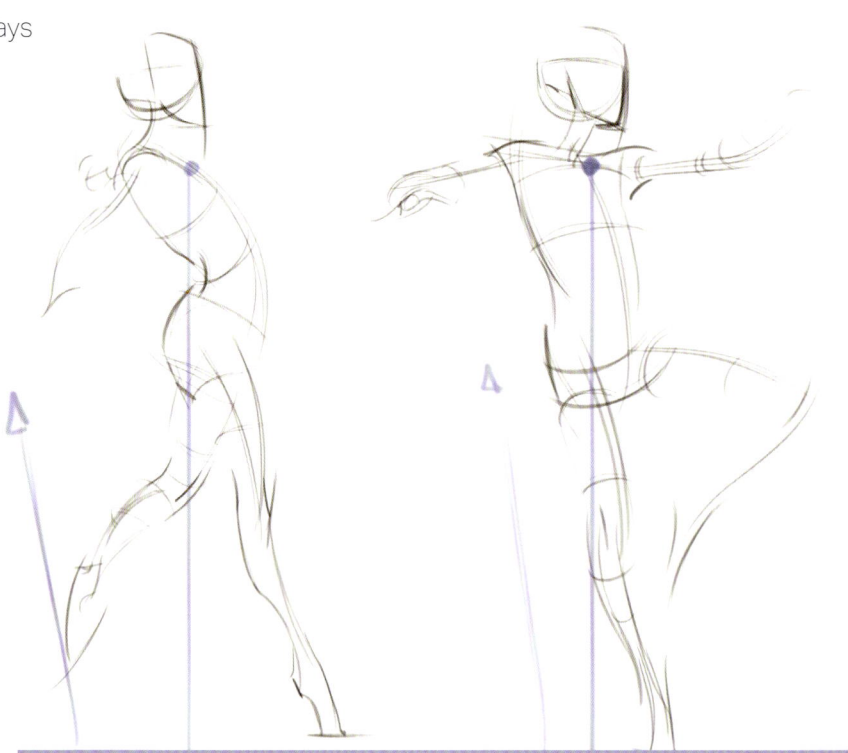

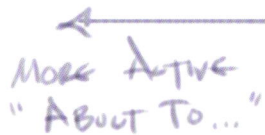

MORE ACTIVE
" ABOUT TO..."

bottom of the throat in the diagrams on this and the prior pages. From there, I plumb a straight line down toward the ground.

Depending on where this line hits relative to the placement of the weight-bearing ankle/foot you can determine the degree to which your figure is balanced.

Go back through the earlier gesture examples and see if you can find this line. Try and notice where the feet land relative to it and the quality or effect of balance resulting.

If this plumb line/center of gravity hits near the ankle on the weight-bearing leg, you likely have a balanced position.

A secondary way you can look for this is to notice the placement of both feet/legs and the negative shape they create. In a more balanced position, you will find a static or equilateral triangle in the negative space of the legs.

With this idea in mind, if I decide to push a pose to have a greater sense of exaggeration, movement, anticipation, and so on, I might choose to create instability by shifting that area of balance.

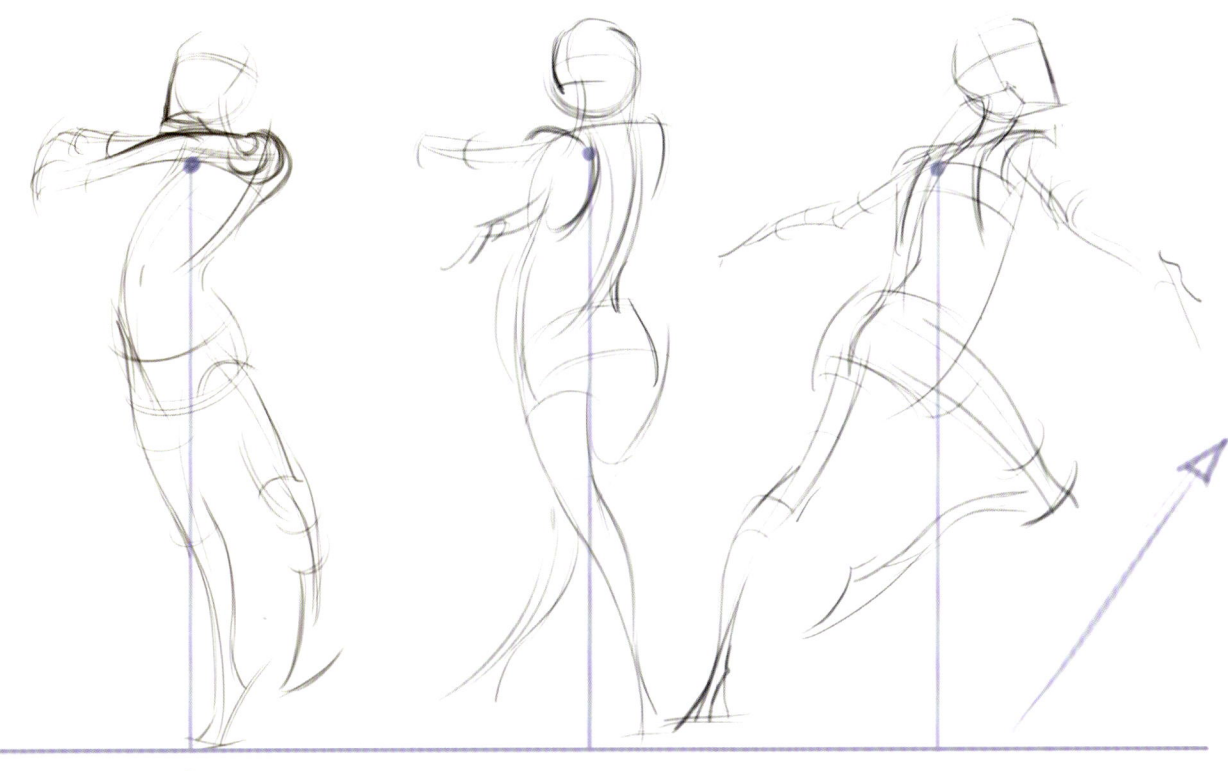

MORE BALANCED
CENTER OF GRAVITY

MORE ACTIVE

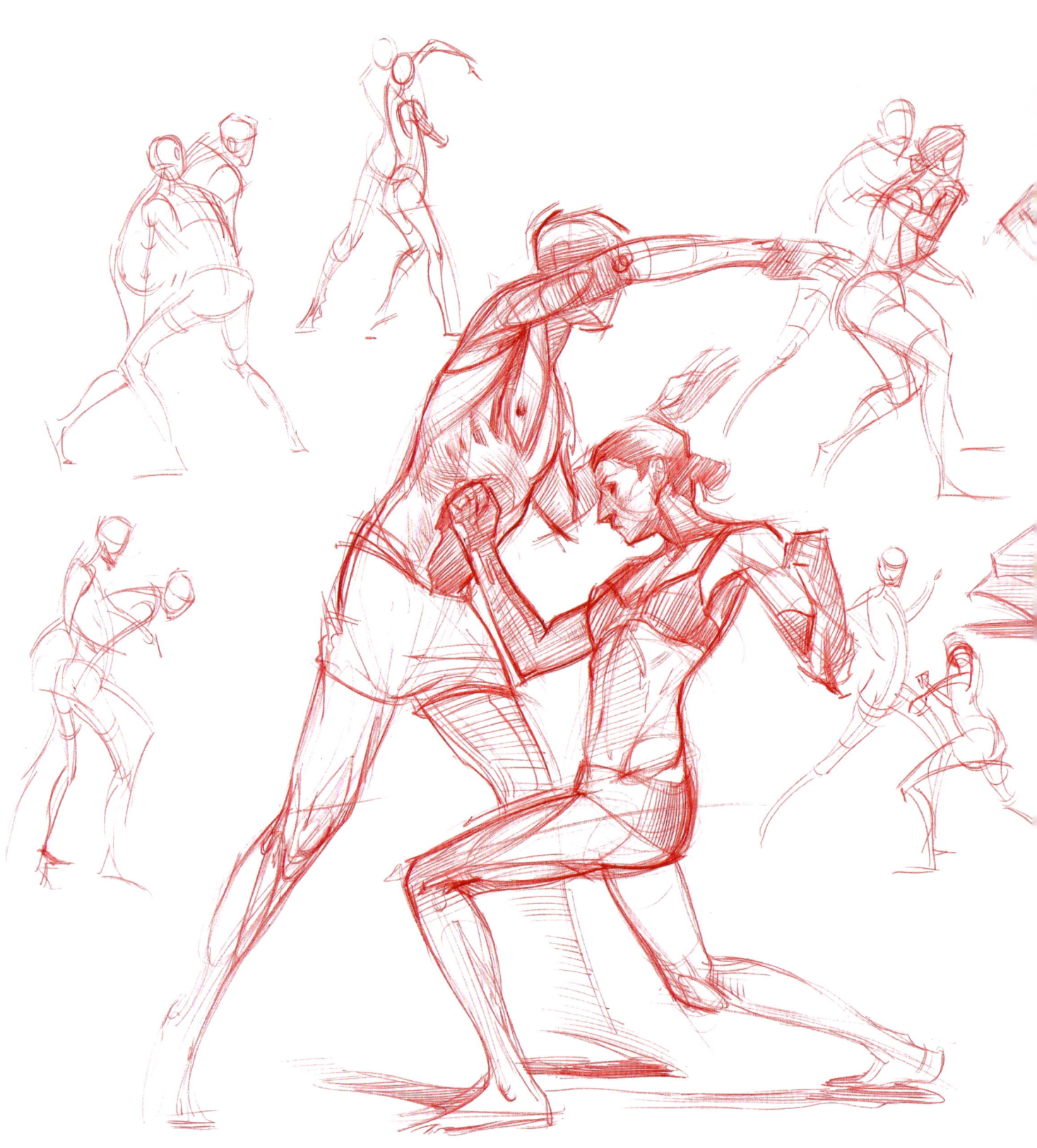

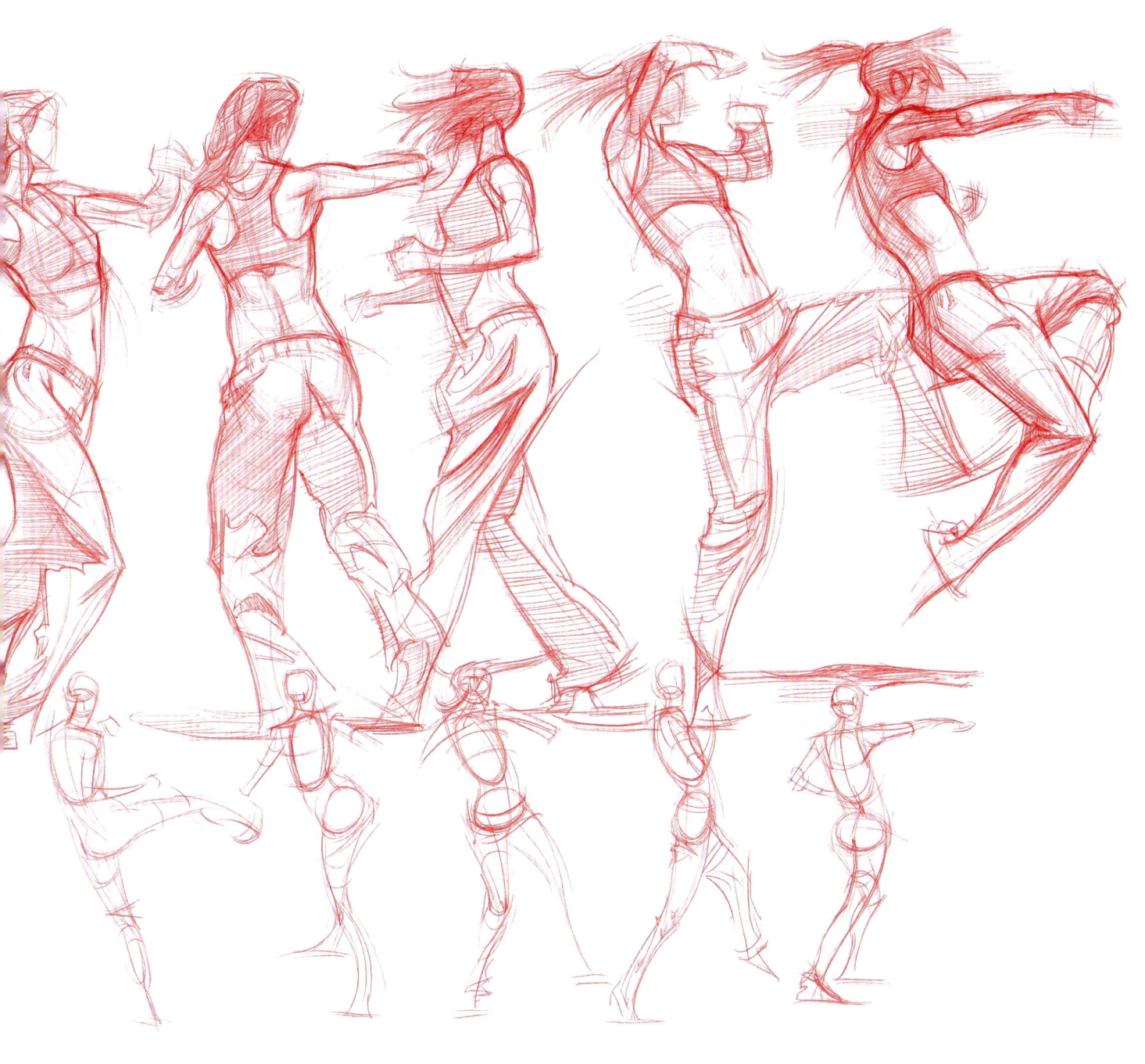

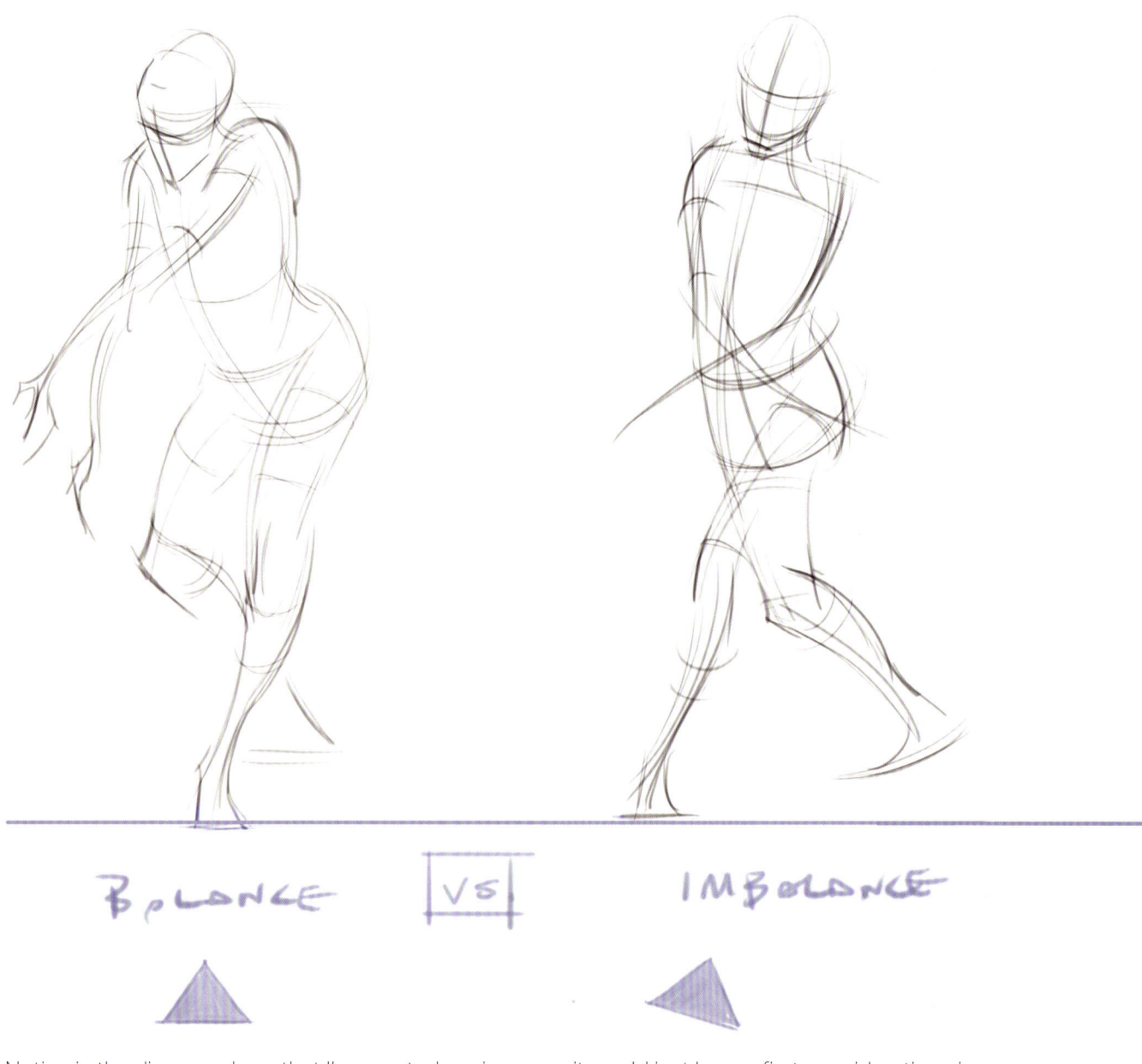

BALANCE  VS  IMBALANCE

Notice in the diagrams here that I've created positions which shift the weight-bearing leg farther away from the area of balance. This is a way that I can think of each pose with gradations of stability or instability. This can result in figures that accent an impression of motion in action.

Using this idea for the center of gravity is the most common way I push poses in this style of gesture as the emphasis here is on the global treatment of the figure, its design, and overall positioning. This doesn't mean that it's the only way to play with exaggeration,

it would just be my first consideration since my workflow is geared toward addressing the largest, most general issues first and then moving more and more toward smaller, more detailed areas.

In conclusion, Part 2 describes the "how" of my approach to gesture. Beginning from the use of asymmetry and rhythm to the 16-line figure, to adjustments that depict sitting, foreshortened, or pushed and exaggerated positions. This is a great process for quick indications, invention, and pushing a feeling of motion. However, not every approach

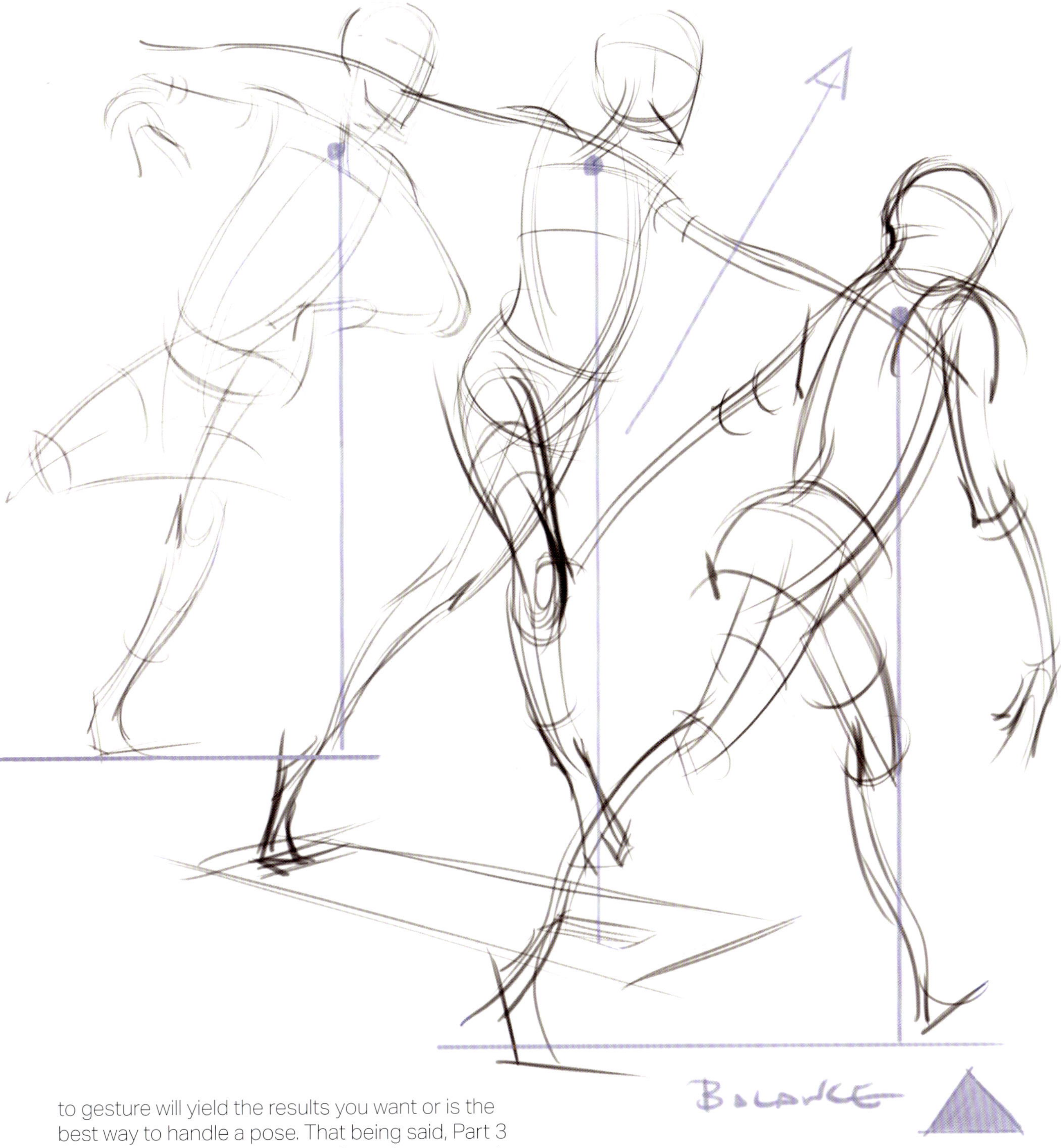

BALANCE

to gesture will yield the results you want or is the best way to handle a pose. That being said, Part 3 will cover a way of drawing the figure in gesture that prioritizes shape as a complement to our linear approach discussed previously.

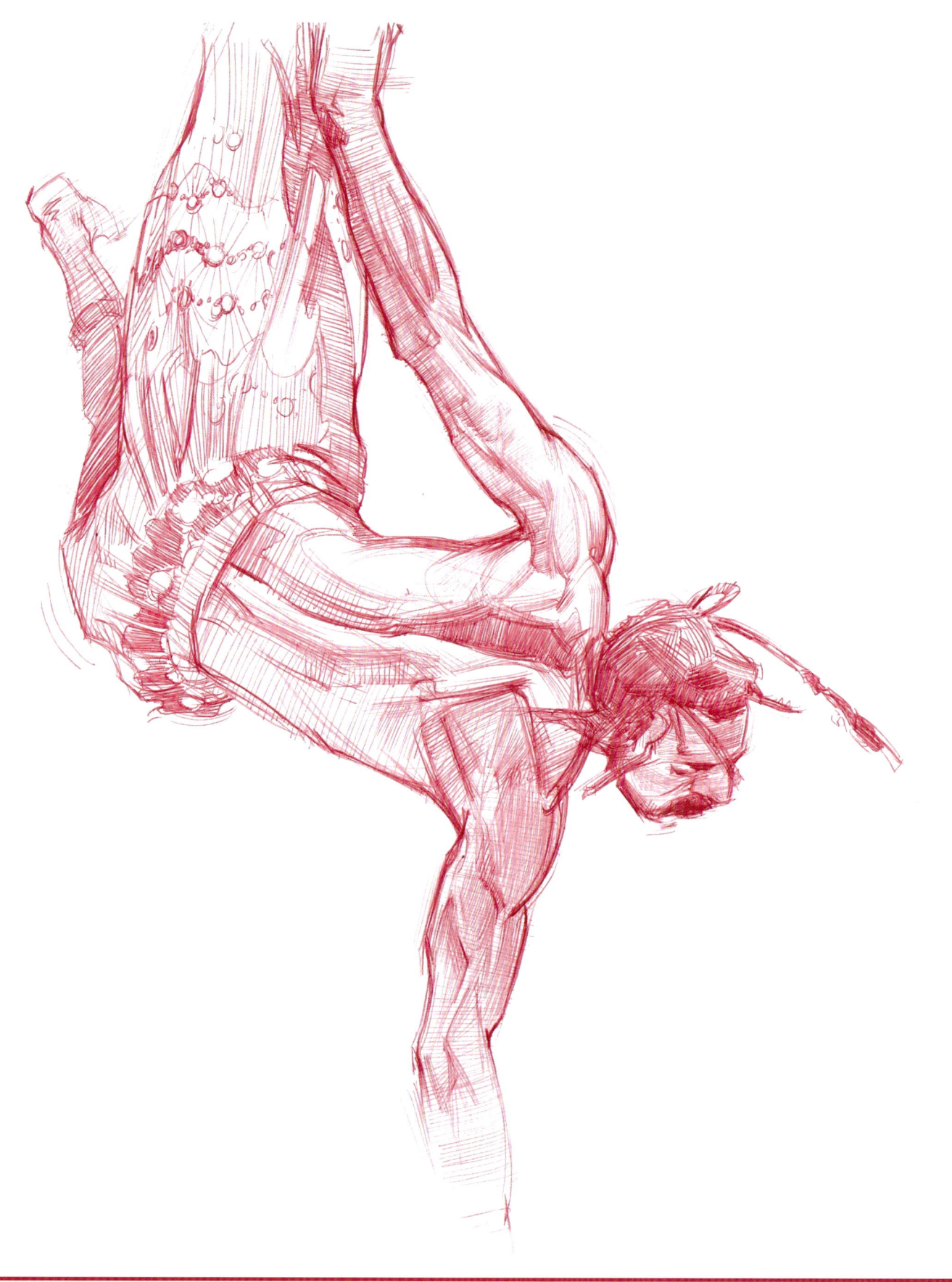

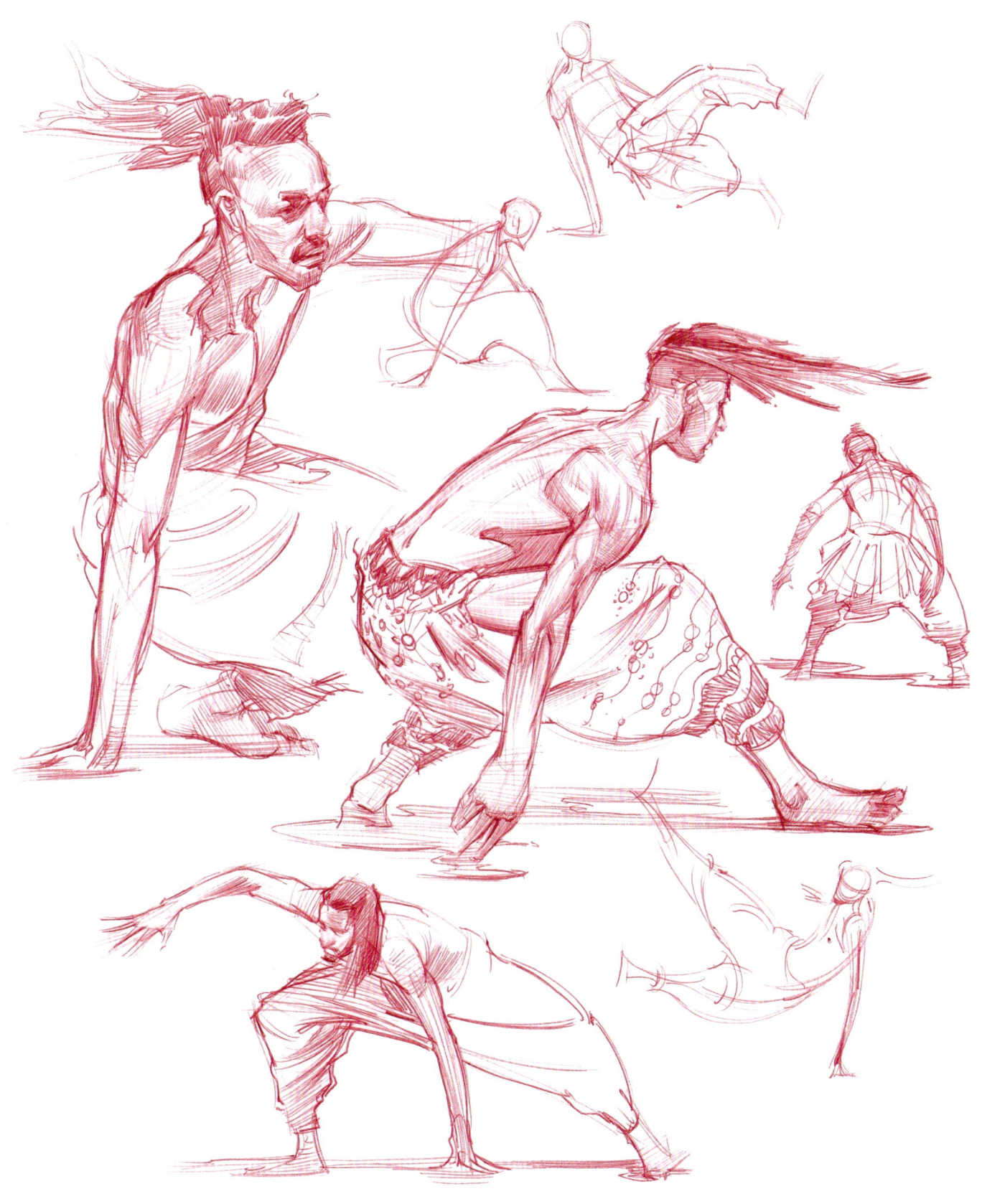

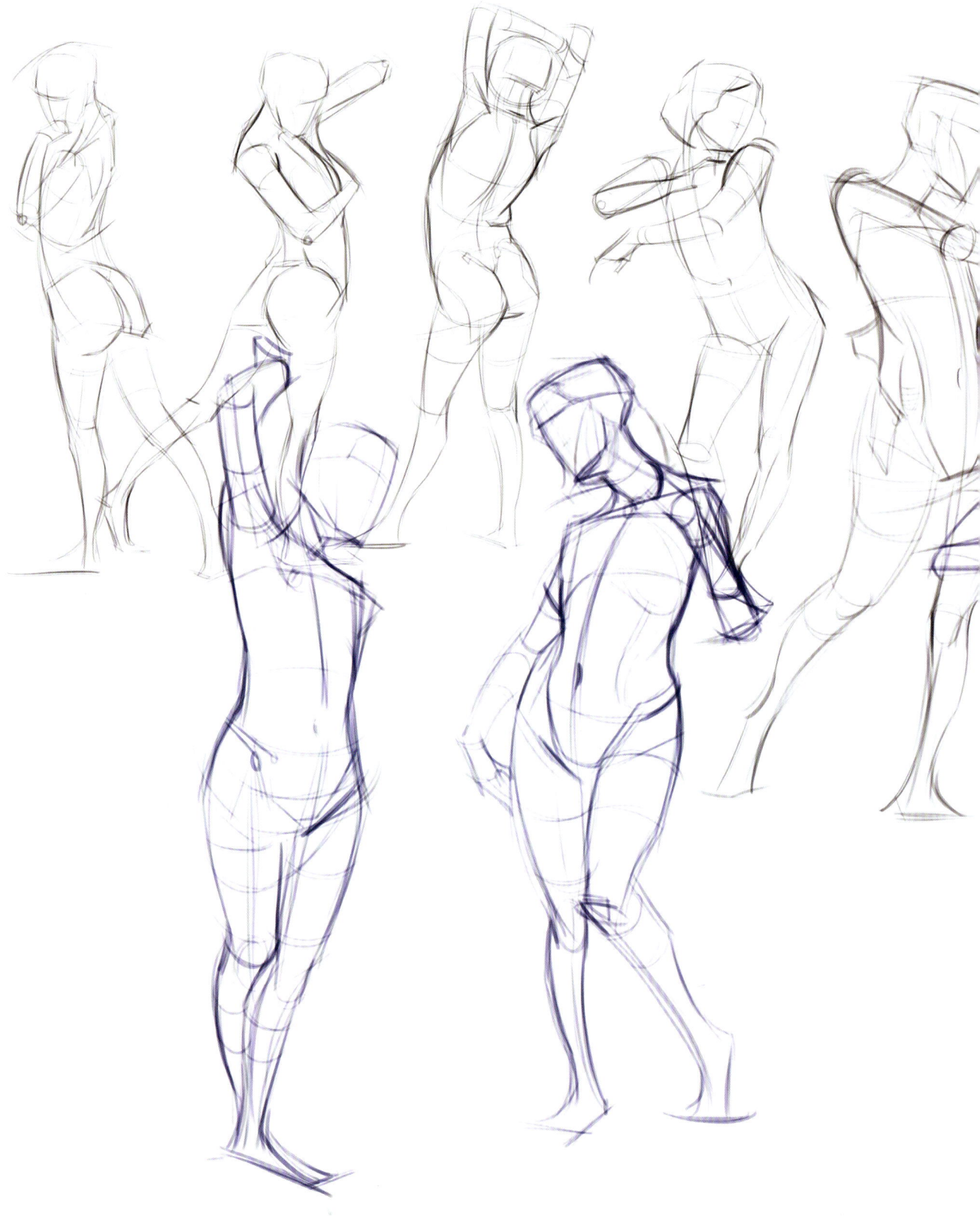

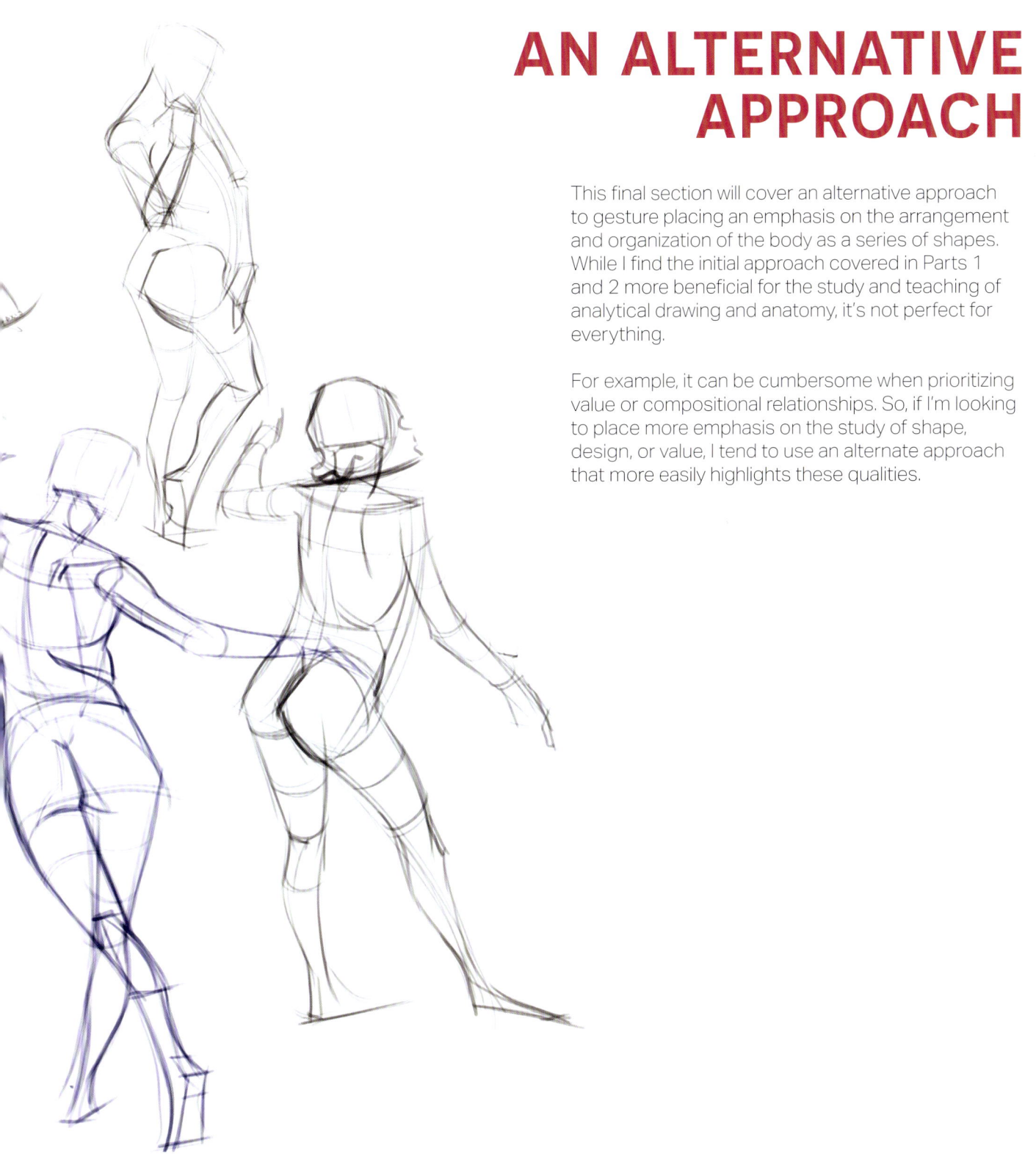

# AN ALTERNATIVE APPROACH

This final section will cover an alternative approach to gesture placing an emphasis on the arrangement and organization of the body as a series of shapes. While I find the initial approach covered in Parts 1 and 2 more beneficial for the study and teaching of analytical drawing and anatomy, it's not perfect for everything.

For example, it can be cumbersome when prioritizing value or compositional relationships. So, if I'm looking to place more emphasis on the study of shape, design, or value, I tend to use an alternate approach that more easily highlights these qualities.

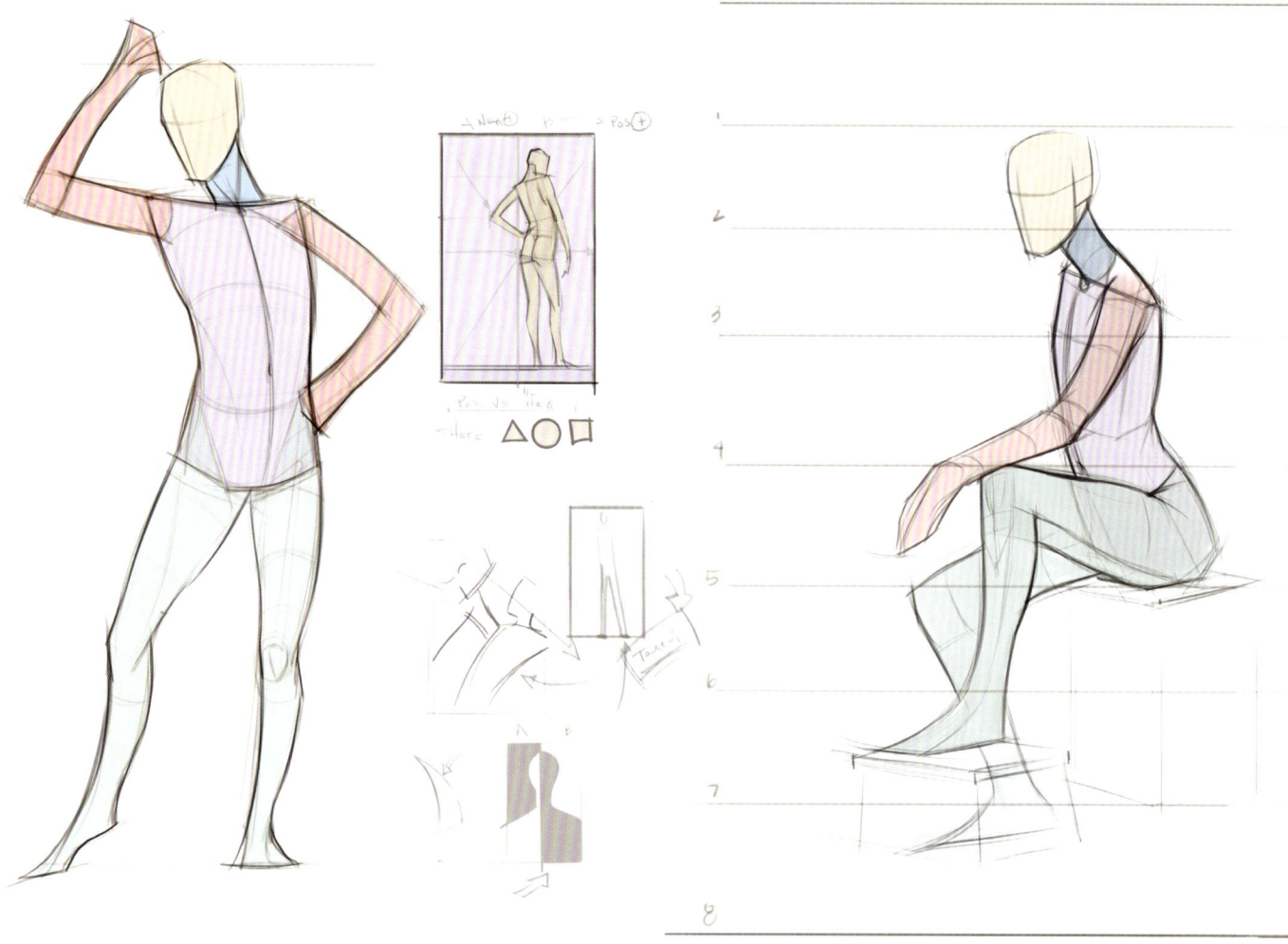

This approach varies from the first in a few important ways. First, instead of dissolving the figure into asymmetrical relationships for the creation of a rhythm, I focus on the design of each of the parts separately and then assemble them with a more cautious series of steps.

The importance of proportion, posing, weight, and the nonverbal communication of the figure (covered in the initial approach) all remain the same. However, working more directly with shape allows me to add layers of information previously not included, specifically, a more direct study of body type, value, and composition.

As mentioned, for this shape-based approach, I break the figure into distinct parts. These include the head, neck, torso (combination shape of the rib cage, waist, and pelvis), and arms/legs. I've highlighted the distinct shapes using color throughout. For the head I use a combination shape of the skull and jaw; the neck becomes a column or pillar; the torso a basic tube

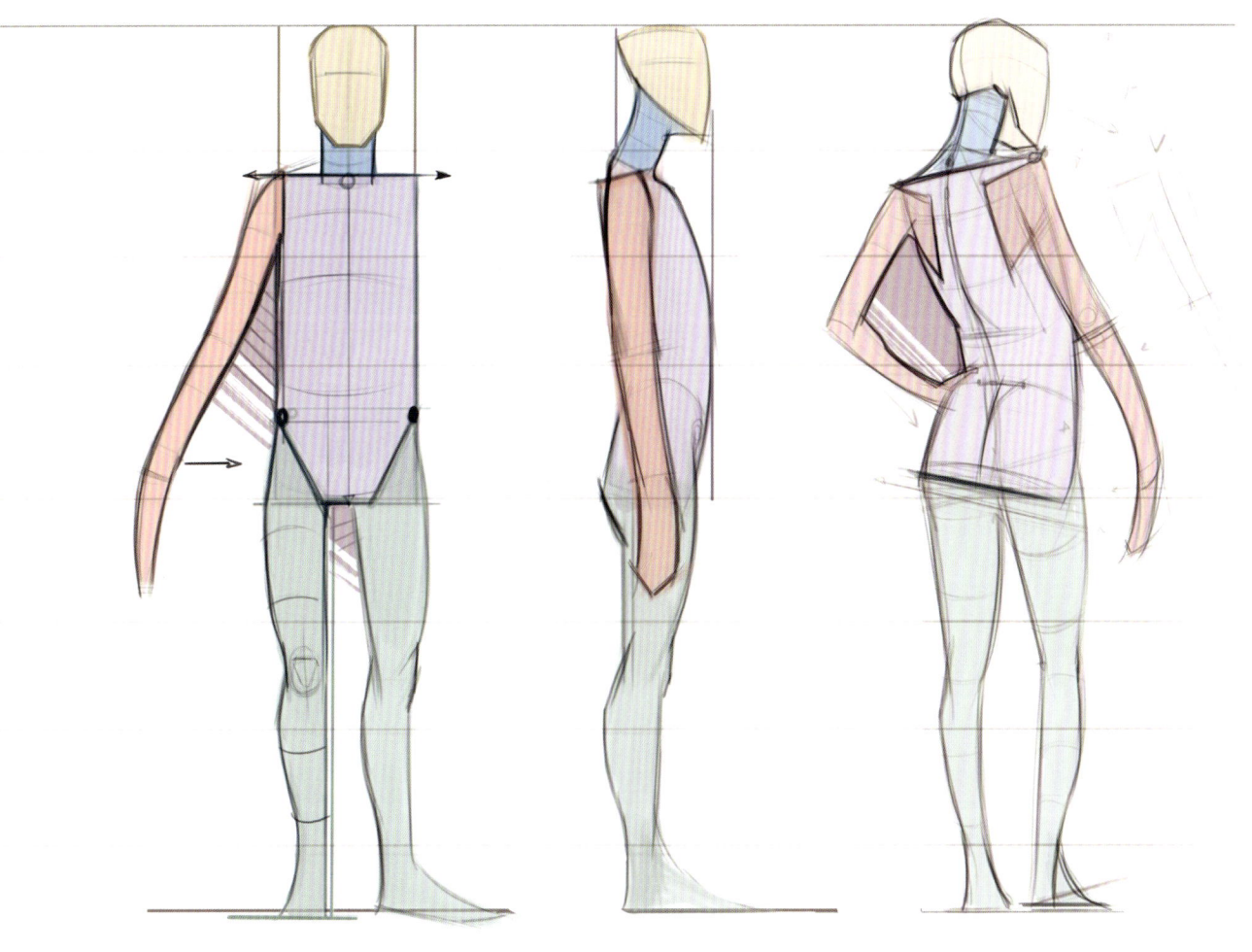

or elongated rectangle: the legs a "B" if front or back, an "S" curve if three-quarter or profile, and a triangle if bent. Lastly, the arms become an "S" if extended or triangle/"C" shape if bent.

These generic shapes edit the figure into simple masses and their proportional relationships; however, I run each individual shape through the process to avoid a static or boring interpretation.

## SHAPE:
A 2D DESIGN SUMMARIZING THE PART(S).

## GESTURE:
A TILT, TURN, SQUASH, STRETCH, OR MODIFICATION OF THE INITIAL SHAPE.

## PERSEPCTIVE:
INDICATION, USING WRAPPING LINES, OF THE SHAPE LEANING FORWARD OR BACK IN 3D.

## CONNECTION:
POSITION IN RELATION TO THE PRIOR SHAPE. A CONNECTION CAN BE ESTABLISHED USING LONGER CONNECTIVE RHYTHMS, OVERLAPS, OR INTERLOCKING SHAPES (TO NAME A FEW).

Notice in the diagrams on page 99 how each part of the body has gone through a consideration of the previously discussed Shape, Gesture, and Perspective steps to customize its position and appearance. Let's discuss a few parts to clarify the workflow I'm proposing.

Take the head to start. Notice on my initial diagram of the figure at right that the head has a distinct shape. I initially visualized this shape as a generic combination of the skull and jaw. What interests me, however, from an iconic- or simple-shaped beginning, is the potential for variation. In the diagram to the right (or the body type lineup on page 100), notice that by altering the head shape to be more squared and box-like or smooth and more curved that I can create sympathy with different character/likeness effects. These effects come by way of building visual continuity with a square, circle, or triangle (for extreme versions of this, refer to the brief discussion on character archetypes introduced in Part 1).

Second, notice that the shape of the head has been titled (leaned to the left or right) or rotated. The rotation of the head is a little trickier but can be easily accomplished by shifting the symmetrical line and chin to favor one side or the other. Remember, rotation is the result of moving your center line closer to one side or the other.

Lastly, notice the wrapping line, usually around the area of brow to ear, indicating a three-dimensional view (under or over). I won't develop the perspectives any further in this approach as I'll use light and shadow effects to create plane changes and a more organic feeling of dimensionality when ready.

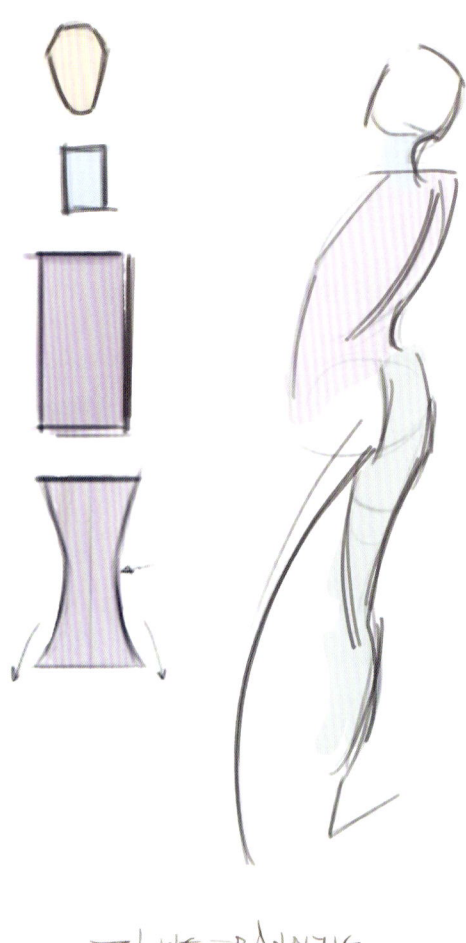

LINE → ANALYTIC
TONAL → OBSERVATION

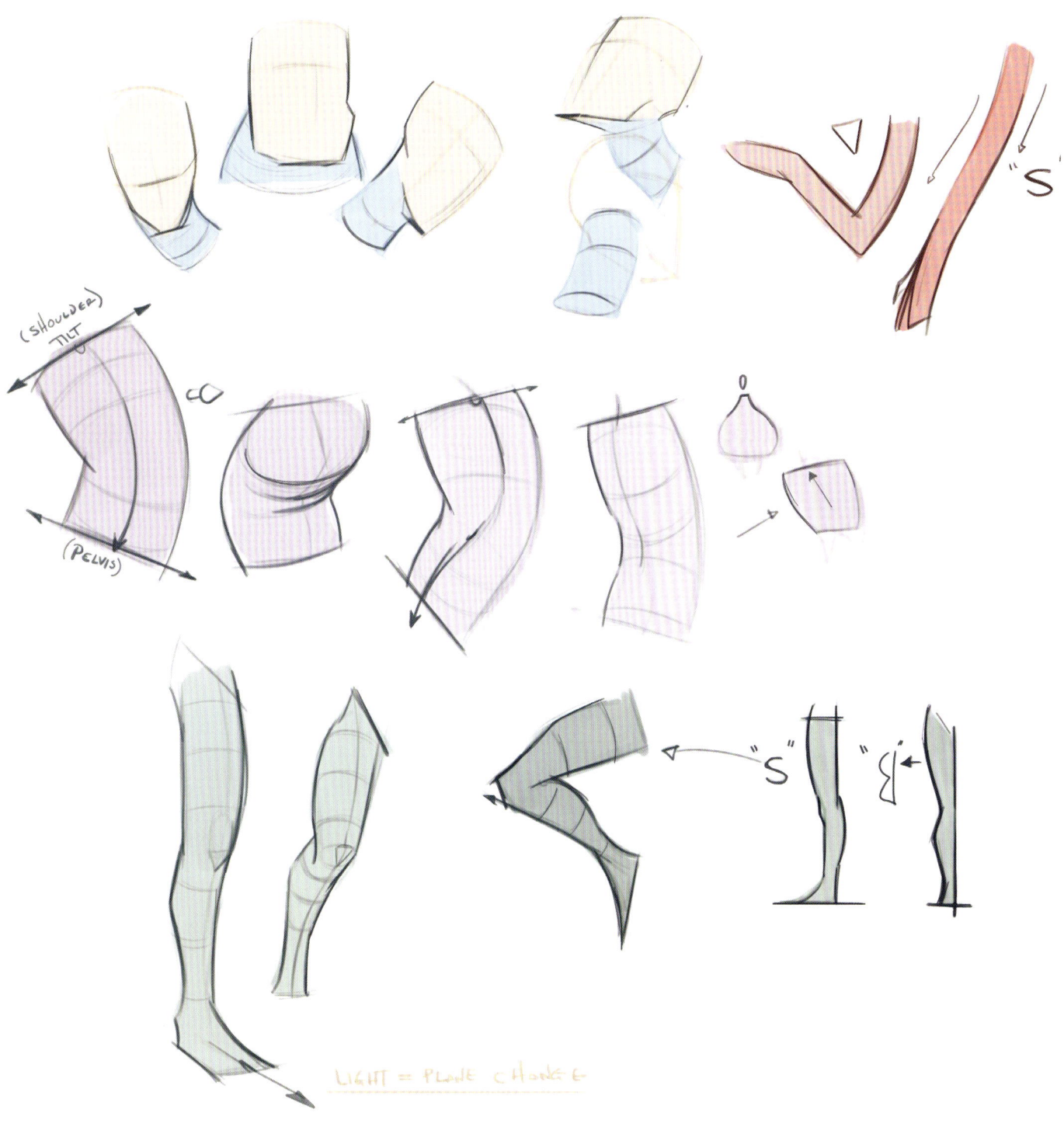

*Tip: Try to keep your basic design(s) of parts as simple as possible to begin. Four to five lines would be a good max.*

*Tip: What I'm doing with this approach is attempting to create an extremely simplified version of the Reilly figure abstraction. I'd recommend looking at the original version of this for ideas on additional rhythms and ways to connect areas and parts.*

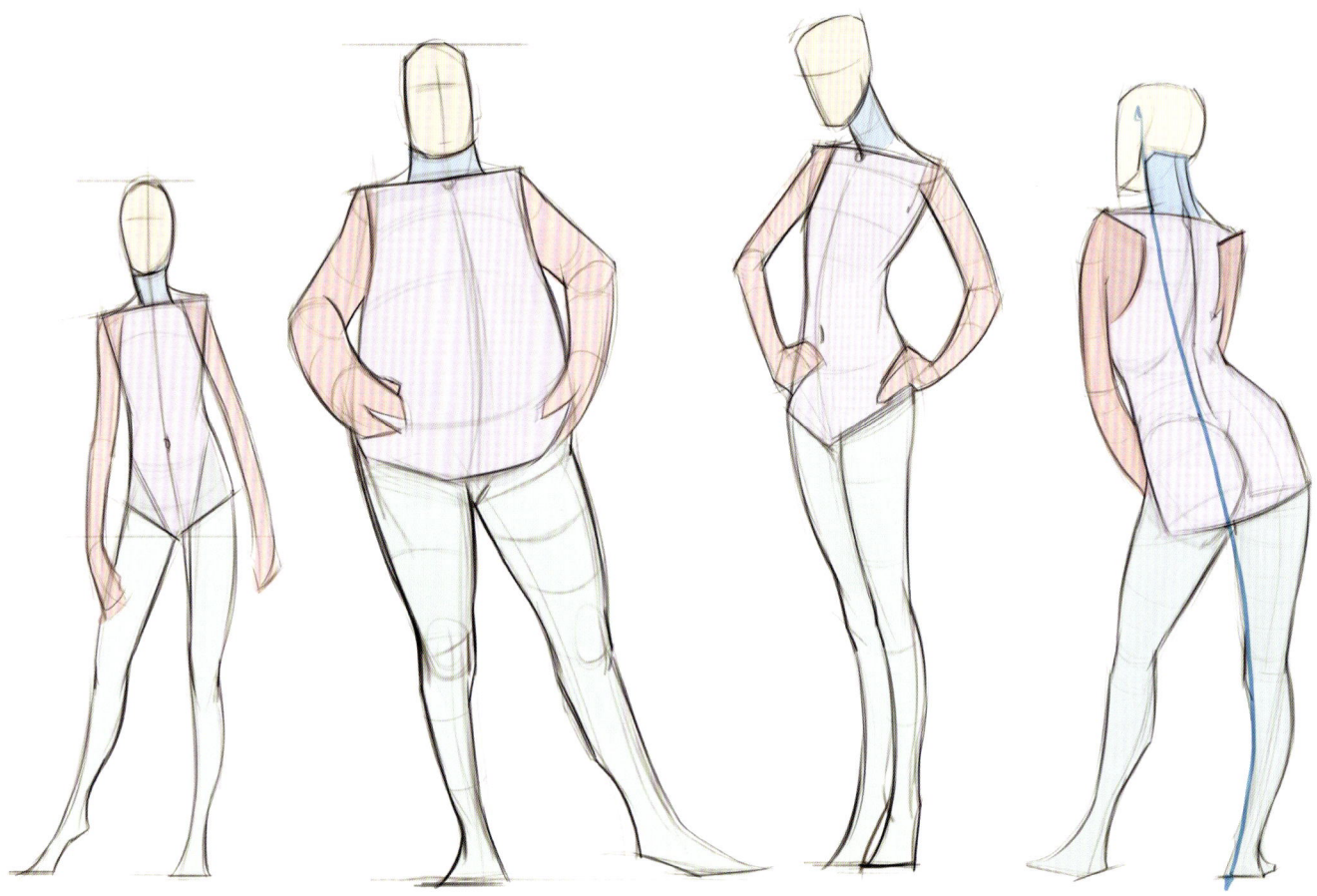

Refer to the diagrams (on this page and the next) for the ways in which I am designing each part, addressing their gesture, and bringing a perspective to each. Notice that for the soft areas (i.e., neck, torso, or transitional areas of anatomy) that I am pushing a much greater stretch vs pinch design than I would for any of the hard surface area and shapes.

Once I have two parts established, I spend time addressing the relationship between forms, or their connection.

To begin, when adding a part to an existing one, I begin by sighting the width and placement relative to the last. This means I aim to tie the new part by judging its shape and placement to fit the visual relationship I see. From there I connect the two with "T" overlaps (placing a line behind or in front).

See if you can identify this usage of "T" overlaps at the junction of every two parts.

*Tip: As a strategy for connecting forms, in the diagrams on this and the previous page, notice the long blue "S" curve running down the front and back views of the figures connecting the center lines of the head, neck, and torso into the weight-bearing leg.*

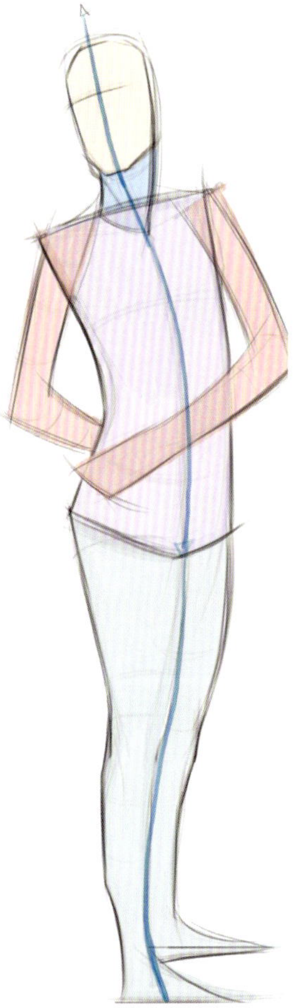

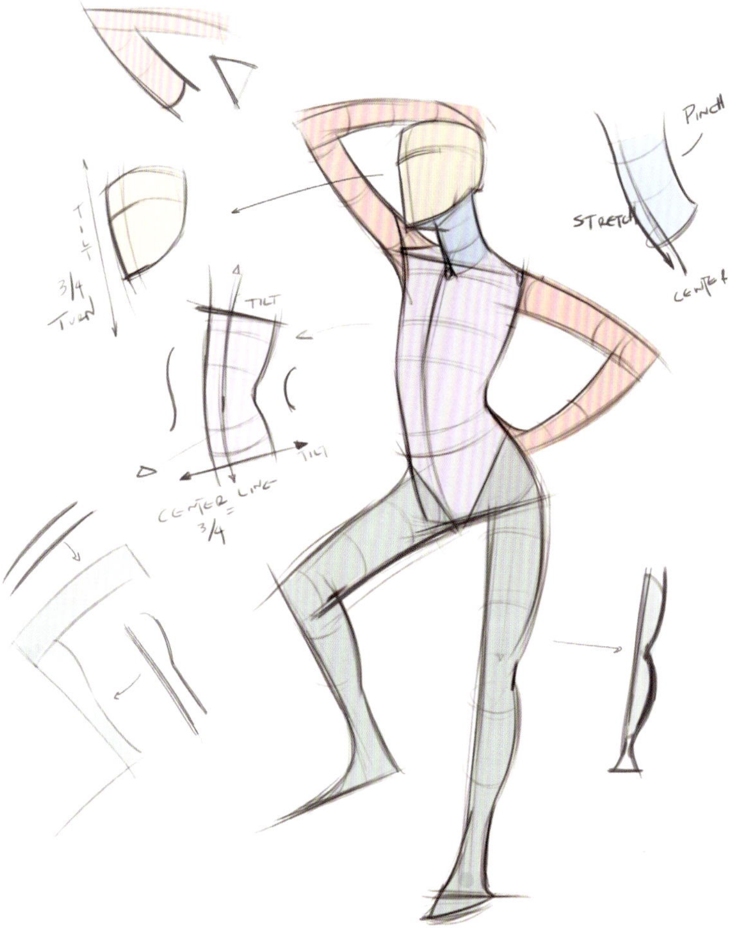

Another strategy for creating a fluid relationship between parts is by bridging the center lines of forms through longer "S" or "C" curves. In the diagrams (on this and the previous page) track the long "C" or "S" curves which begin with the center line of the face (or sometimes from the point of the ear if the head is turned), through the center of the neck, and torso, and into the weight-bearing leg. This especially works well in standing poses. In nonstanding poses you can still find rhythm-based relationships between the forms and their center lines, it may just not tie together as many parts.

Arms present a different challenge when attempting a connection. A potential solution here might be bringing the sides of the neck into each arm, relating the rhythm of the arms across the torso shape into the arm on the opposing side.

In the examples that follow, see if you can understand the original shape, gesture, perspective, and connecting strategy for each part.

**SCAN THE QR CODE TO WATCH**
a lecture with related content:
A Shape-Based Approach.

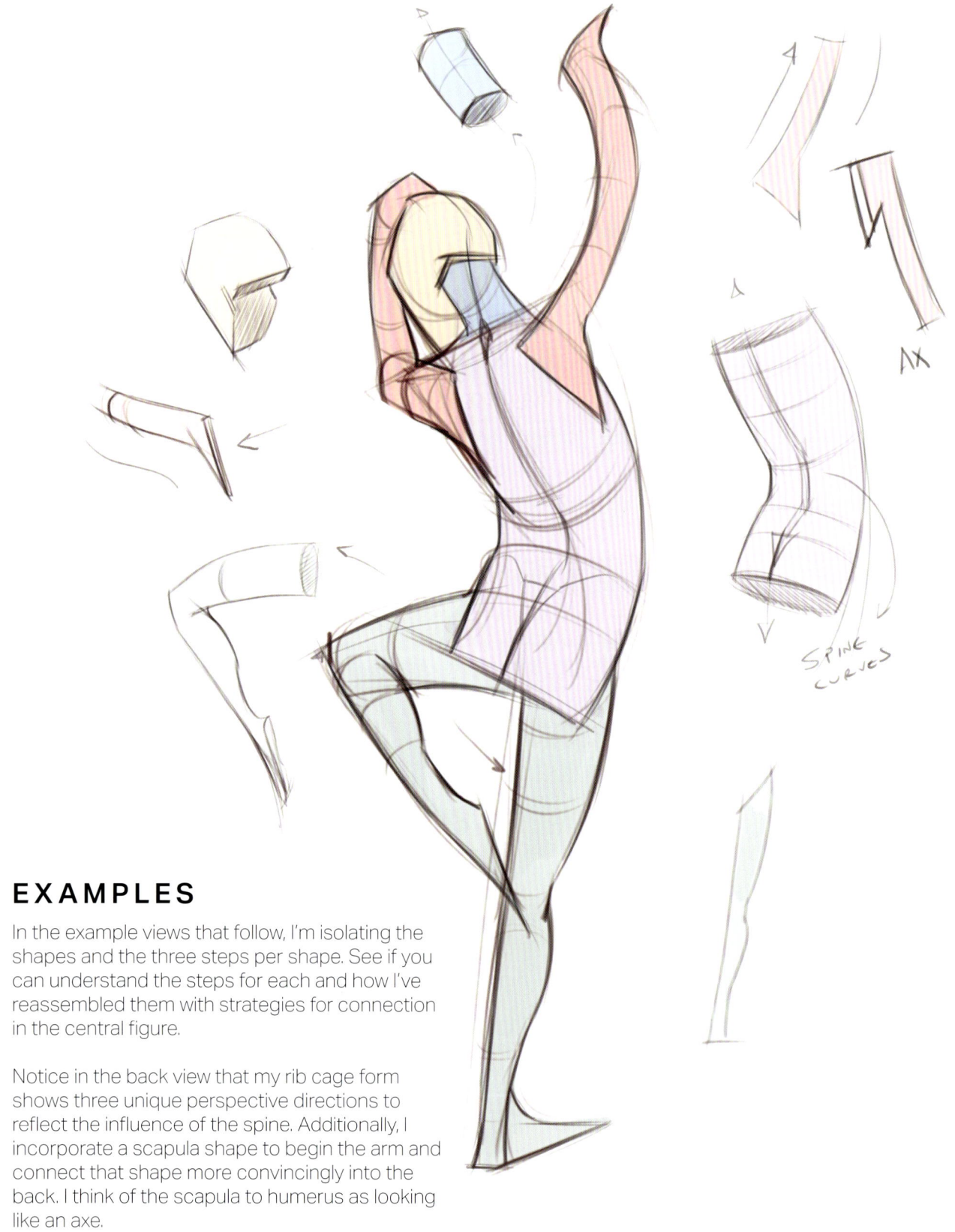

SPINE
CURVES

# EXAMPLES

In the example views that follow, I'm isolating the shapes and the three steps per shape. See if you can understand the steps for each and how I've reassembled them with strategies for connection in the central figure.

Notice in the back view that my rib cage form shows three unique perspective directions to reflect the influence of the spine. Additionally, I incorporate a scapula shape to begin the arm and connect that shape more convincingly into the back. I think of the scapula to humerus as looking like an axe.

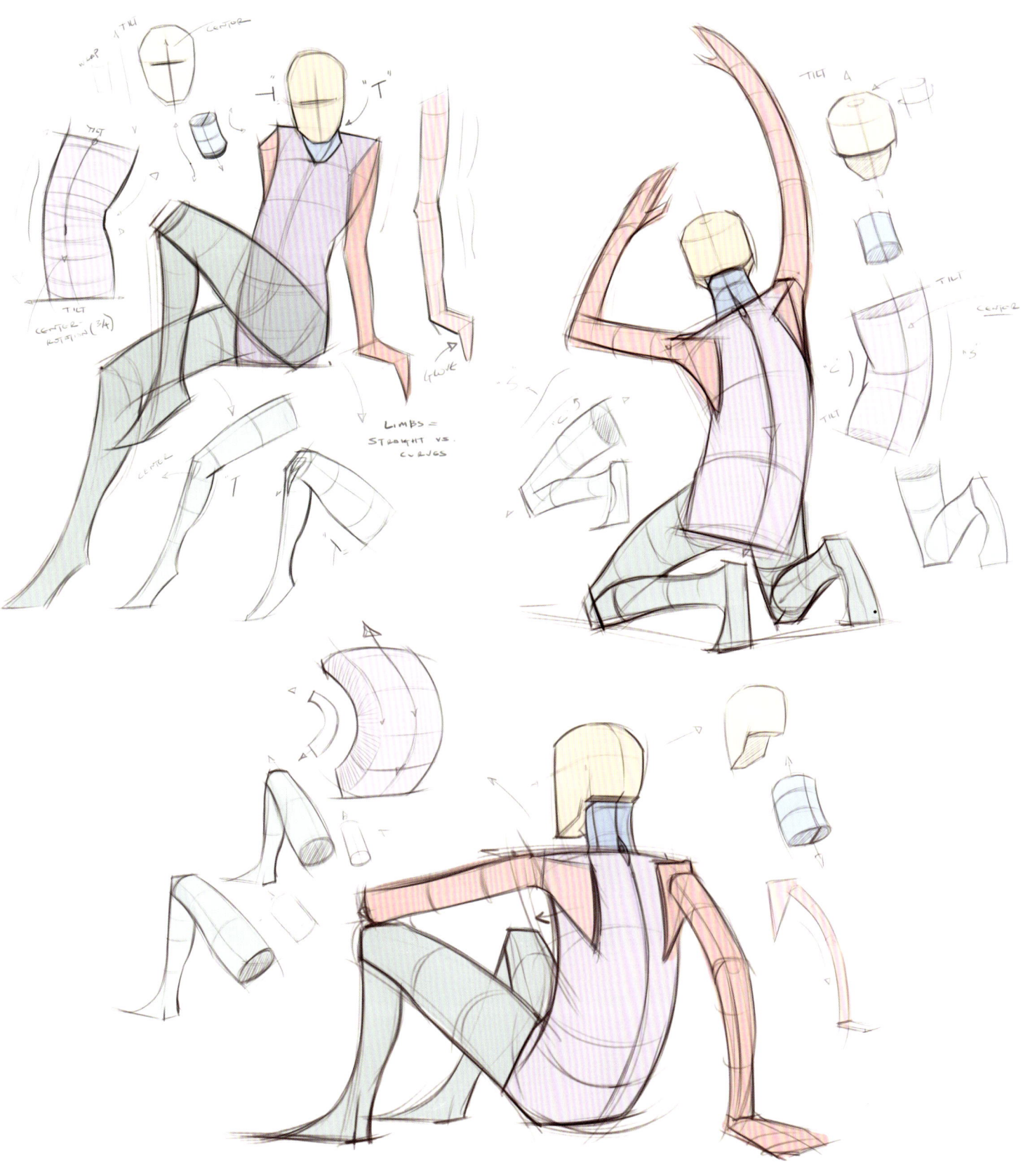

LIMBS = STRAIGHT VS. CURVES

# GESTURE AND THE FRAME

One truly beneficial reason for approaching the figure with this technique is that it allows for an easier study of composition. One level of composition already discussed is the purposeful distortion of your individual parts. This might be the way we create, exaggerate, or push these pieces to reflect body type.

However, using this method of gesture allows me to explore a larger compositional study—the effect created through the figure's position in a frame. This adds a level of artistic difficulty and storytelling that is beyond the more random creation of "studies" which we all make. However, instead of indiscriminately arranging figures in the space of my sketchbook or drawing page, an emphasis on simple composition studies allows me to explore the gesture of the frame and how the figure can interact with it in a variety of ways.

First, take a moment to consider how ubiquitous the frame is (even if we pay little attention). While it's certainly normal to overlook its importance, it conditions everything we see. Every painting, ad, comic, or visual is in some sense responsive and designed according to a frame, boundary, or surrounding context. An exercise like I'm suggesting focuses on setting a figure within a frame to develop greater sensitivity to an endless array of messages a figure might convey.

Take the example on the opposite page to start. This is everything that we've been looking to develop in this approach so far. There is a part to part lay-in of the figure with each part having gone through its three steps (shape, gesture, and perspective). There is an adequate connection between the parts using overlaps and a longer rhythmic tie developed between the centers of the head, neck, torso, and into the weight-bearing leg.

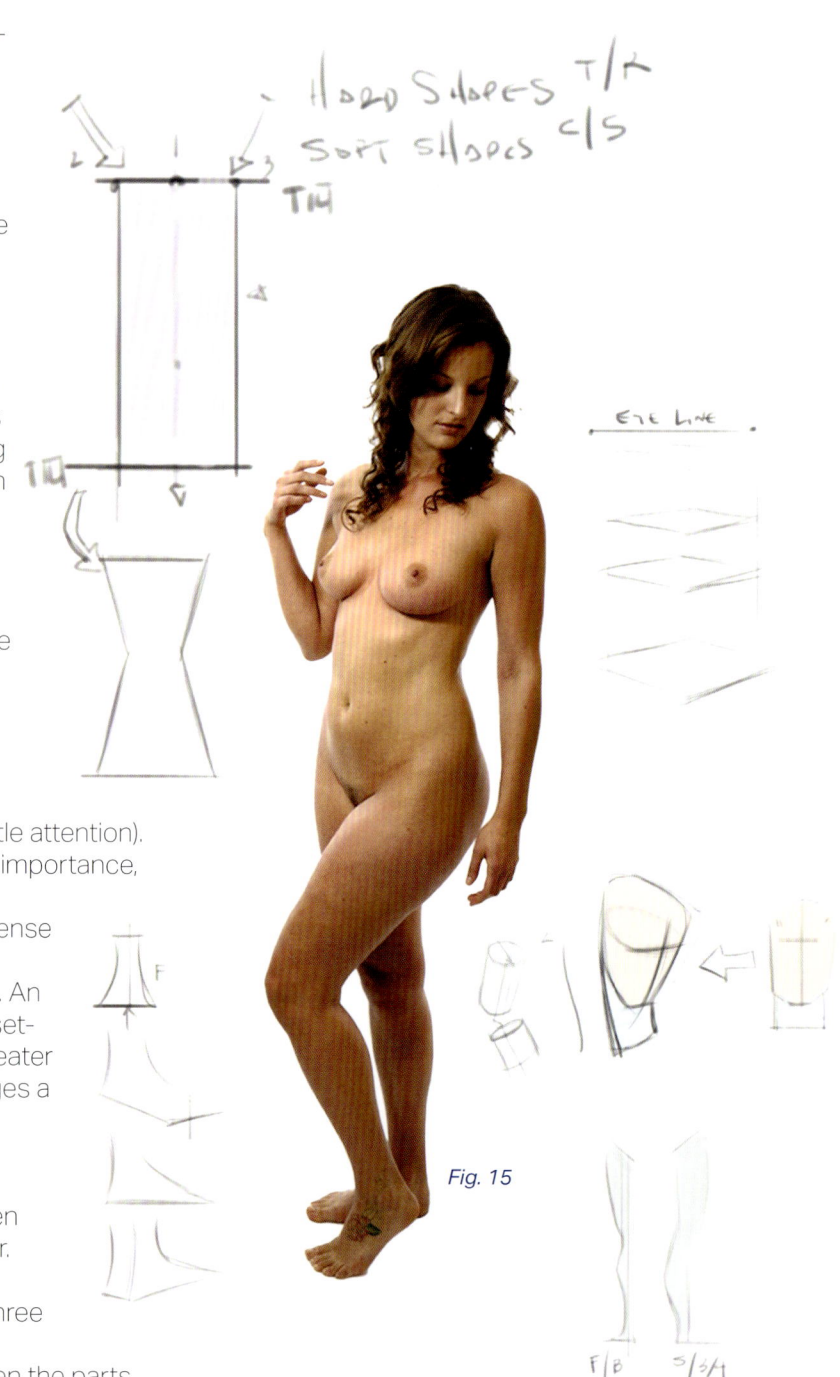

Fig. 15

However, the figure still exists in a blank void. While the study is sufficient, and a story exists for the pose itself, there is still a degree of ambiguity present. So, to push my thinking of gesture further I incorporate a frame. You can choose any format of frame you like. I'm fond of using a simple portrait format to start.

Within a portrait-formatted rectangle I subdivide the frame with diagonals (upper left to lower right, upper right to lower left), a vertical division, and a horizontal. These divisions intersect at a center and divide the frame into what I think of as a skeleton of sorts. The reason for this more anthropomorphic description

is that the lines themselves offer "feelings" based on if/how they are amplified by the figure interacting with them.

For example, if I am to place a figure on or accentuate a diagonal division, I will create a greater sense of movement. If my figure remains vertical or is placed directly on the central vertical division, a feeling of stability will result. And lastly, anything used on the horizontal will offer greater passivity. Notice that these are external qualities in excess of the figures own gesture that can be added to the initial idea/story of a pose.

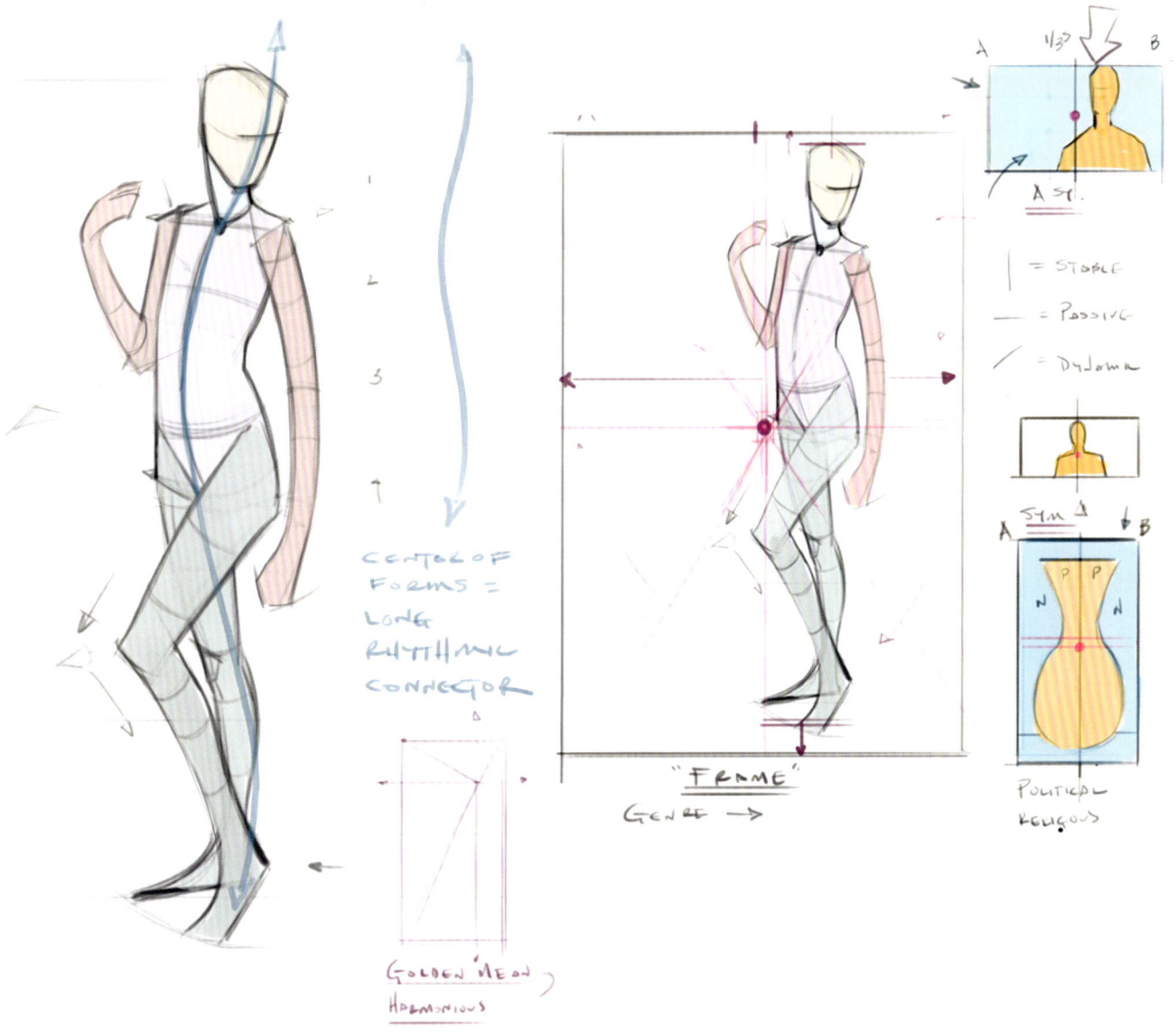

*Fig. 15 – Courtesy of Proko™*

105

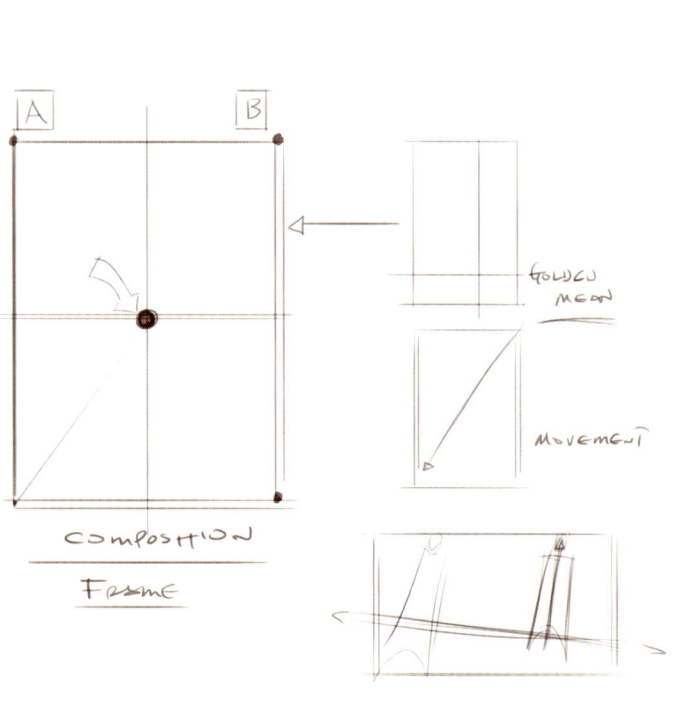

COMPOSITION
FRAME

GOLDEN MEAN

MOVEMENT

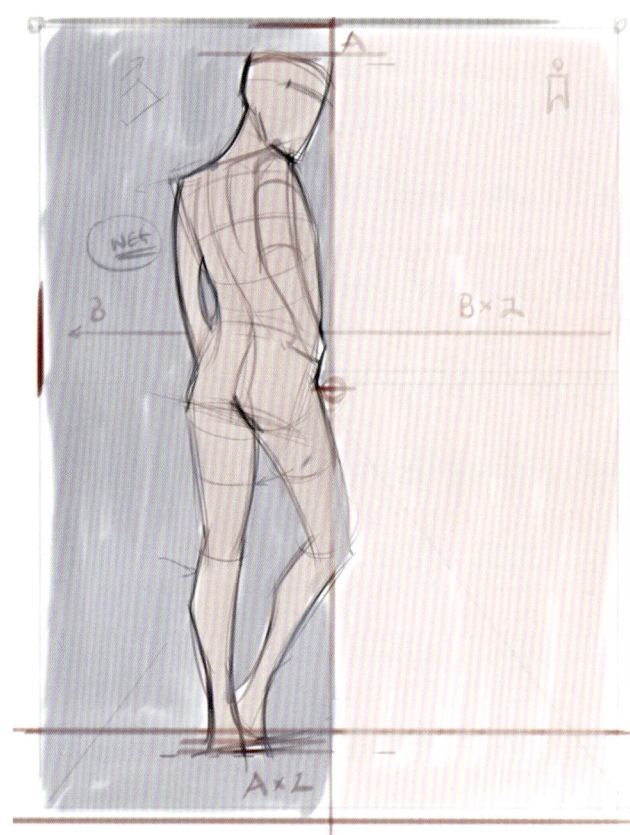

Look at the example on the opposite page for how this exercise was executed using the preceding description.

Notice in the diagram on the opposite page that there is a diagonal, horizontal, and vertical division in red within. In a generic study of composition, I use these divisions to understand and think through the placement of my figure and resulting effects. As it seems common for most of us to want to center our compositions, I make a concerted effort to do the opposite here.

My assigned goal in an early compositional exercise is to bring the figure as close to the center of the composition as possible without putting it directly on top. This is to create a composition with asymmetry and visual tension.

Another challenge in terms of placement and the frame is asymmetry when spacing the figure to the

boundaries of the frame. In the illustrations on this page and the next, note that the distance from the head to the top of the frame is doubled from the foot to the bottom of the frame. The right side of the figure to the frame is then doubled from the left side to the left of the frame.

As far as shape is concerned, pay special attention to how the two sides of the frame are used. Notice that I have labeled the left side as "A" and the right as "B." A further goal in these compositions is to create an asymmetry of positive vs negative shapes and their proportion from side A to side B.

In the smaller diagrams on the previous page, notice how the interplay of positive and negative shape is different in an asymmetrical composition compared to a to symmetrical one. This isn't to assign value of any kind but to help you become sensitized to the myriad of compositional possibilities to choose the one best suited to your story, figure, or concept.

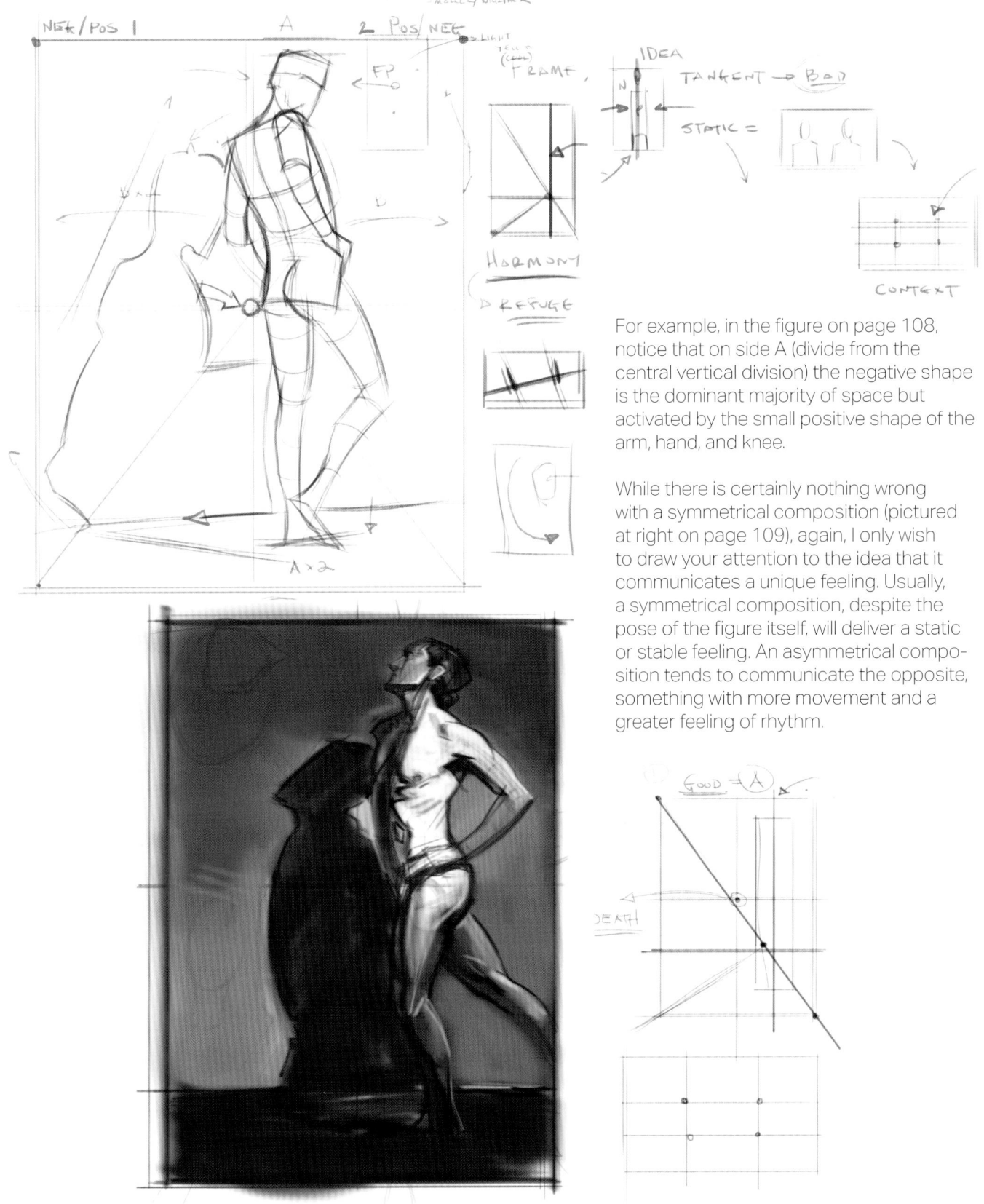

For example, in the figure on page 108, notice that on side A (divide from the central vertical division) the negative shape is the dominant majority of space but activated by the small positive shape of the arm, hand, and knee.

While there is certainly nothing wrong with a symmetrical composition (pictured at right on page 109), again, I only wish to draw your attention to the idea that it communicates a unique feeling. Usually, a symmetrical composition, despite the pose of the figure itself, will deliver a static or stable feeling. An asymmetrical composition tends to communicate the opposite, something with more movement and a greater feeling of rhythm.

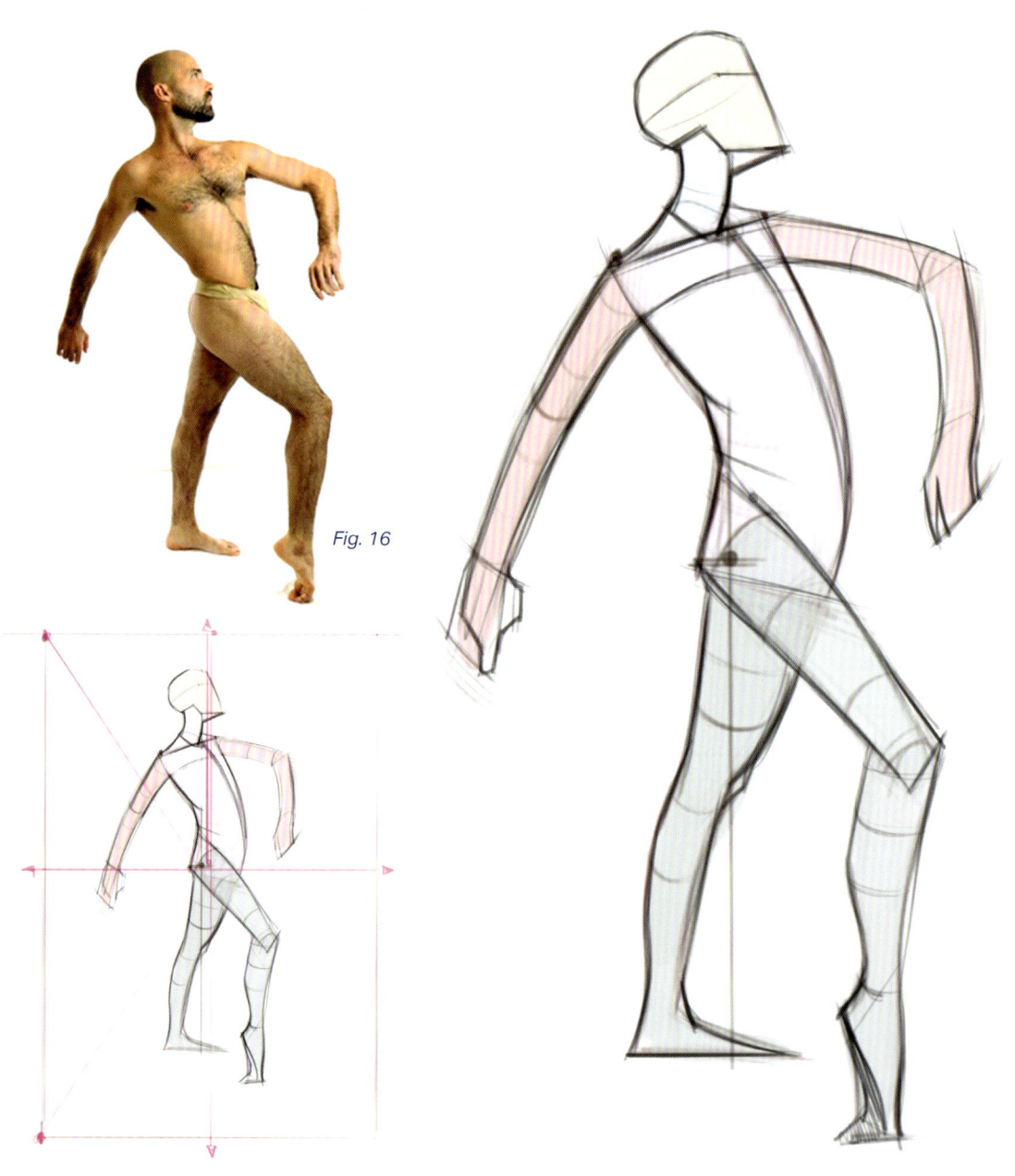

Fig. 16

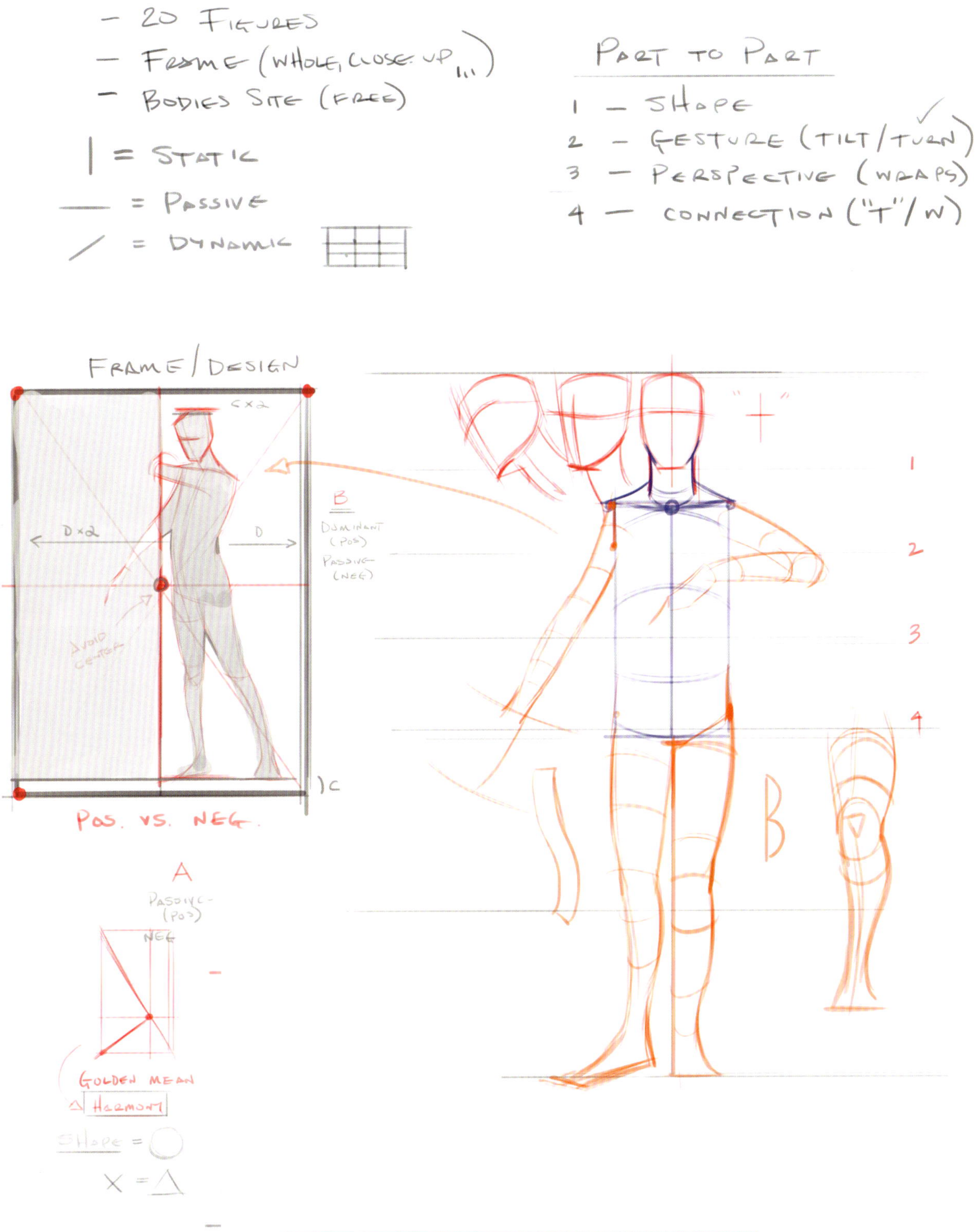

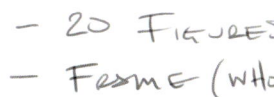

- 20 FIGURES
- FRAME (WHOLE, CLOSE-UP...)
- BODIES SITE (FREE)

| = STATIC

— = PASSIVE

/ = DYNAMIC

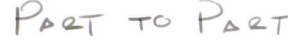

PART TO PART

1 — SHAPE ✓
2 — GESTURE (TILT/TURN)
3 — PERSPECTIVE (WRAPS)
4 — CONNECTION ("T"/W)

FRAME/DESIGN

C×2

D×2

D

B
DOMINANT (POS)
PASSIVE (NEG)

AVOID CENTER

)C

POS. VS. NEG.

A
PASSIVE-(POS)

NEG

GOLDEN MEAN
△ HARMONY
SHAPE = ○
X = △

"+"

1

2

3

4

B

**SCAN THE QR CODE TO WATCH**
a lecture with related content:
Basics of Composition.

*Fig. 16 – Courtesy of Proko™*

109

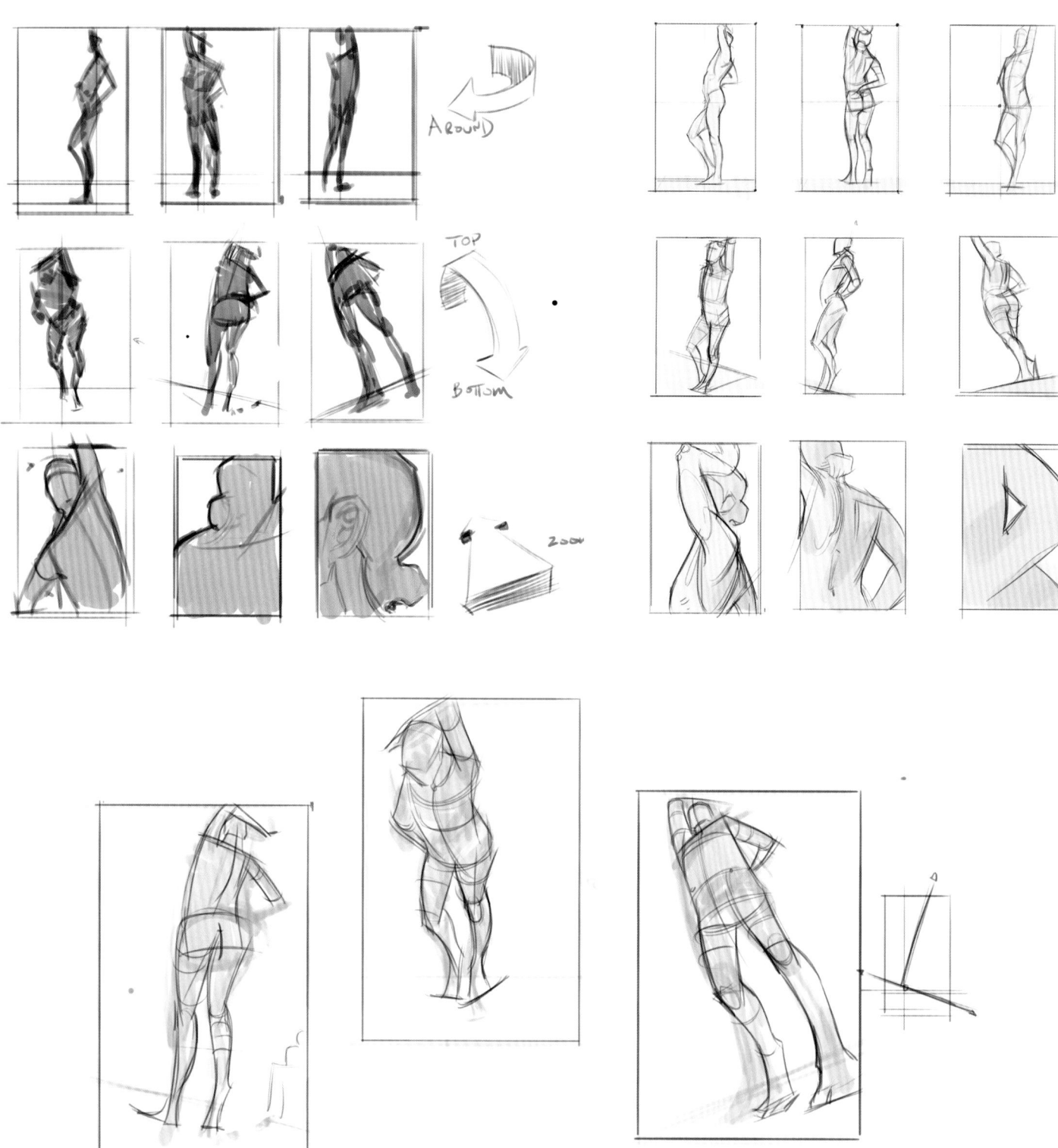

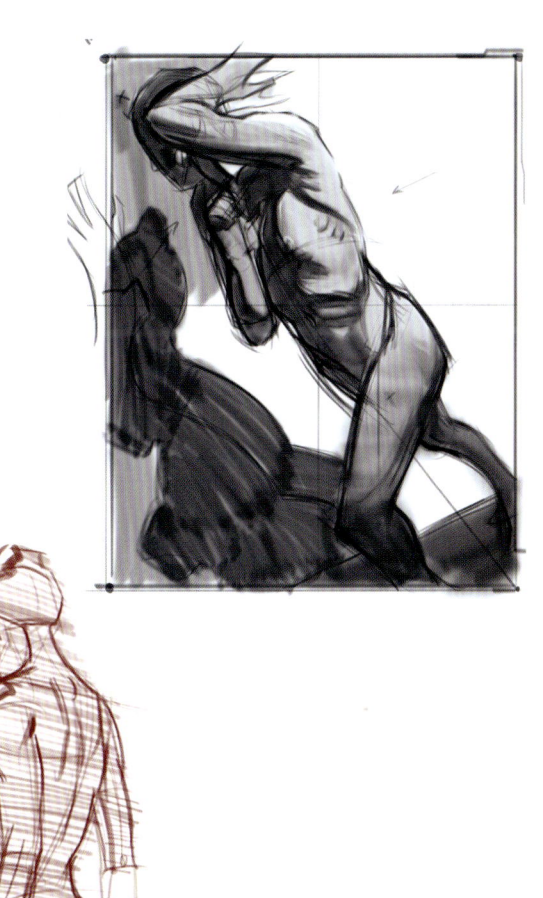

In the loose sketches shown here, notice that this can also be a more exploratory process and doesn't necessarily require careful planning as I've explained previously. Again, the notes discussed are just to give you some rules and ideas to keep as guardrails as you begin this process.

When working more loosely with these ideas it can be nice to use a sharpie or other style of brush pen. This keeps us from getting drawn into details and forces our focus into shape and its organization. Sometimes, as pictured on the opposite page, I stick with one reference image and try to move the camera around, top to bottom, and then zoom it to explore the figure in a more cropped relationship to the frame. This is an exercise I did when in classes with John Watkiss, a master anatomist, artist, and inspiring teacher. The goal is to see that myriad of effects one can create with a single figure just by changing the orientation to the frame and camera angle.

I'm going to stop myself here as this isn't intended to be a book or manual on composition. My intention is only to provide examples for the benefit of thinking about this alternate gestural style. However, if you are interested in pursuing this line of inquiry further, there are additional video tutorials on my YouTube channel that may help you get started.

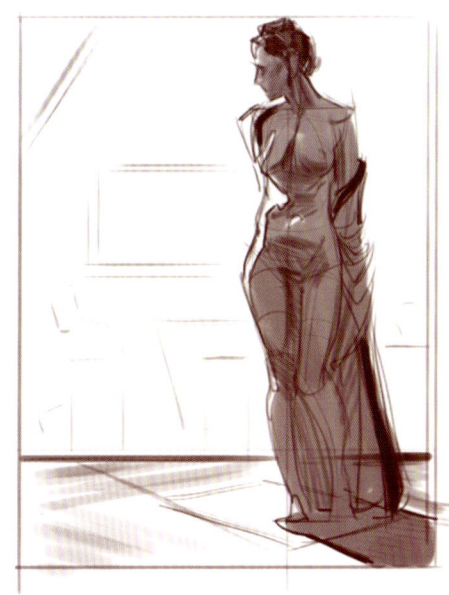

**SCAN THE QR CODE TO WATCH**
a lecture with related content:
Composition Study.

# LIGHT AND SHADOW

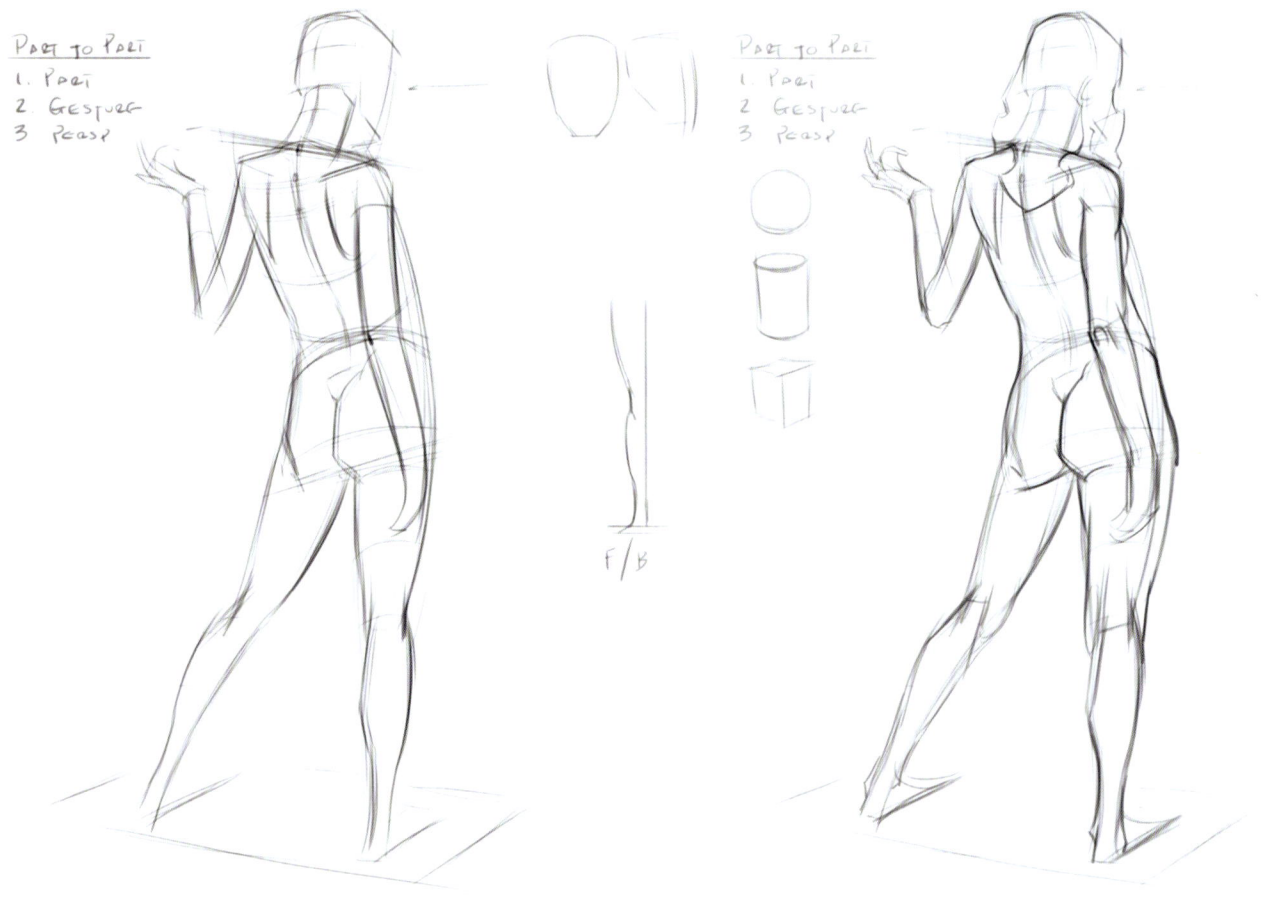

For those of you who rightly observe that we are still dealing with a mannequin of the figure and not something that looks organic/detailed, yes, I totally agree. If possible, try and delay that judgment as, again, we are only focused on gesture here. However, I would like to at least give you an idea of how the process of tonal development is supported by this beginning.

Once we've posed and designed our figures within the confines of a frame, my next step would be to add some exterior details and map light and shadow relationships onto the existing shapes of the figure. Though this remains outside the scope of our overview on gesture it's important to mention as a more modeled or three-dimensional appearance may be created through the addition of light/dark shapes here.

In the images shown here, you can see the importance of the gesture stage. This reflects what we covered so far and is foundational to the structure and position.

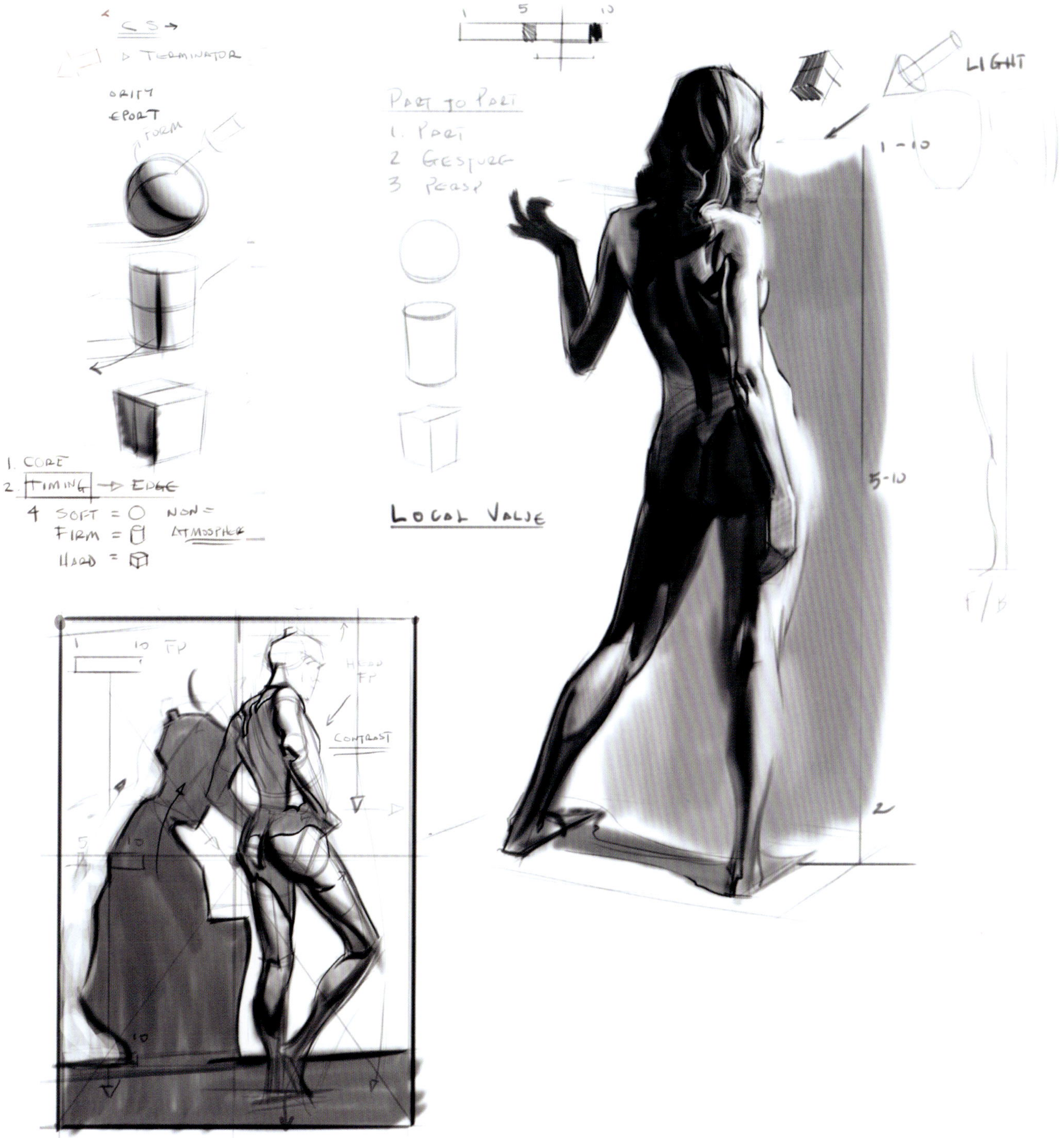

C S →

▷ TERMINATOR

ORITY
EPORT
FORM

1. CORE
2. TIMING → EDGE
4. SOFT = ◯ NON =
   FIRM = ⬭ ATMOSPHER
   HARD = ⬡

PART TO PARI
1. PARI
2. GESTURE
3. PERSP

LOCAL VALUE

1   5   10

CONTRAST

LIGHT

1-10

5-10

In essence, it gives me the forms I light. All my thinking via lighting boils down to the use of three basic volumes (a sphere, cylinder, and box), and four edge types (soft, firm, hard, and lost).

When lighting the figure, I separate the light and dark into graphic shapes in reference to the underlying mannequin form. Once designed, I describe the quality or timing of the surface by using one of the four edges (soft edge is a sphere-like form, firm edge is cylindrical, and hard edge is boxed).

Though these often look as though there are lots of smaller details and surface variations, I am almost always just lighting the largest volumes and manne-quin that we've outlined previously. To say too much more here would be to stray from our emphasis on gesture; however, the QR code on the next page links to a short summary that illustrates lighting the figure in more detail for those interested.

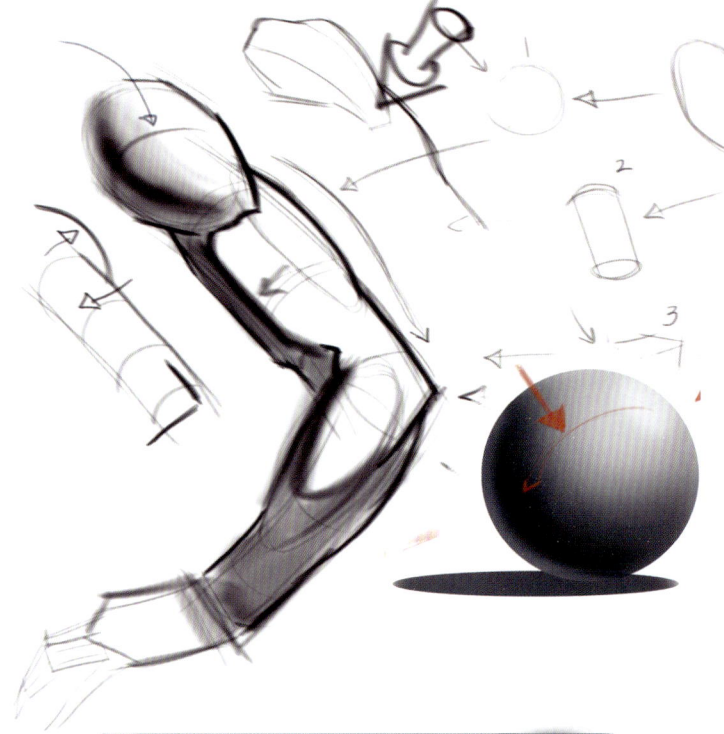

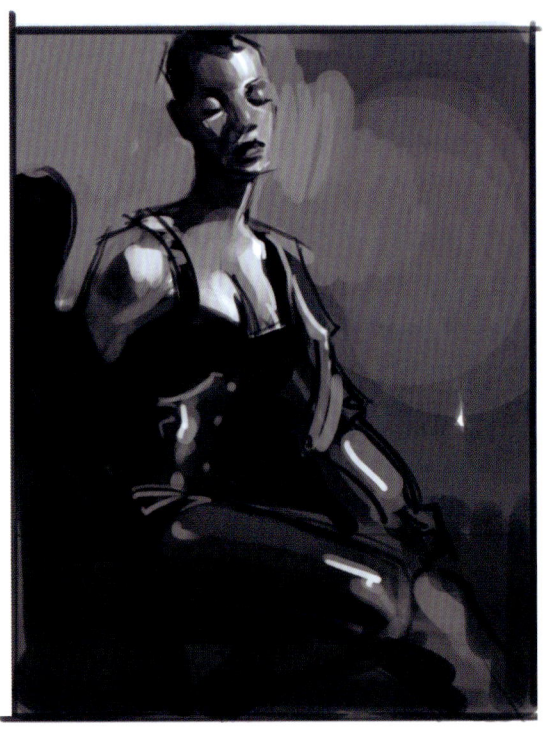

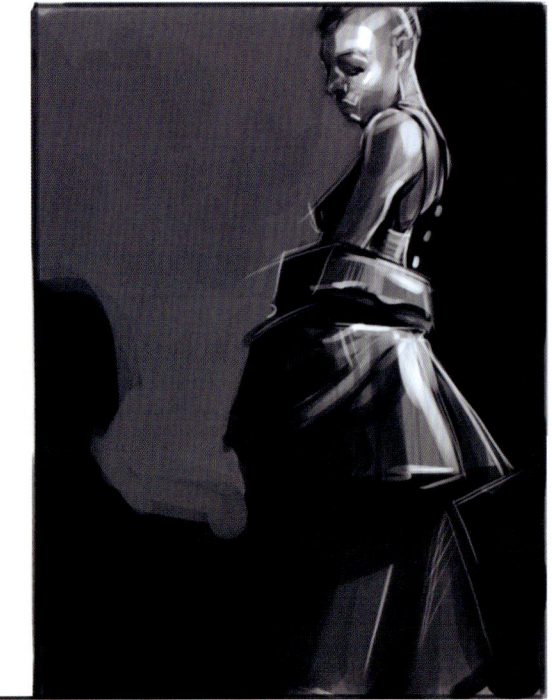

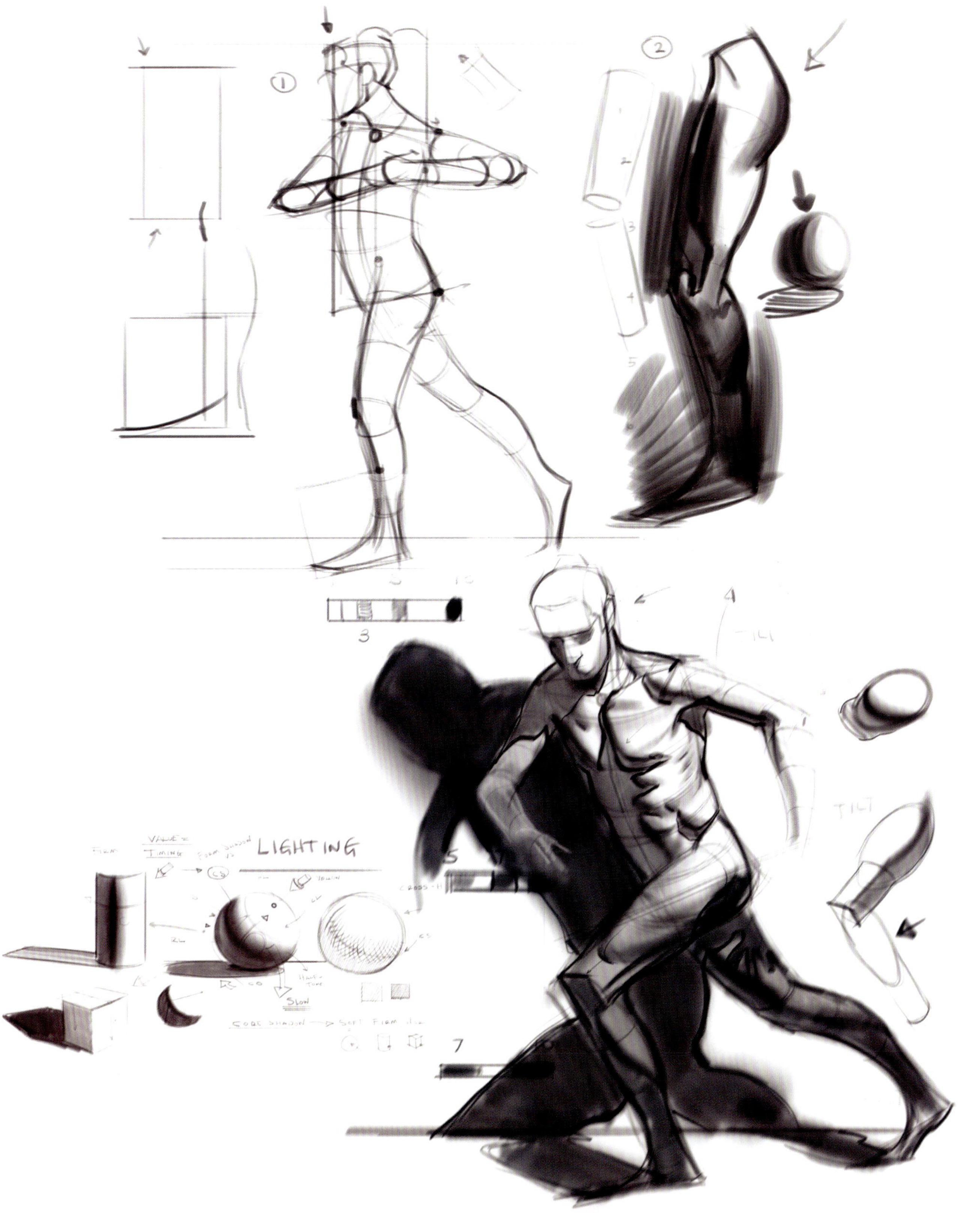

LIGHTING

**SCAN THE QR CODE TO WATCH**
a lecture with related content:
Shading Gesture Easy.

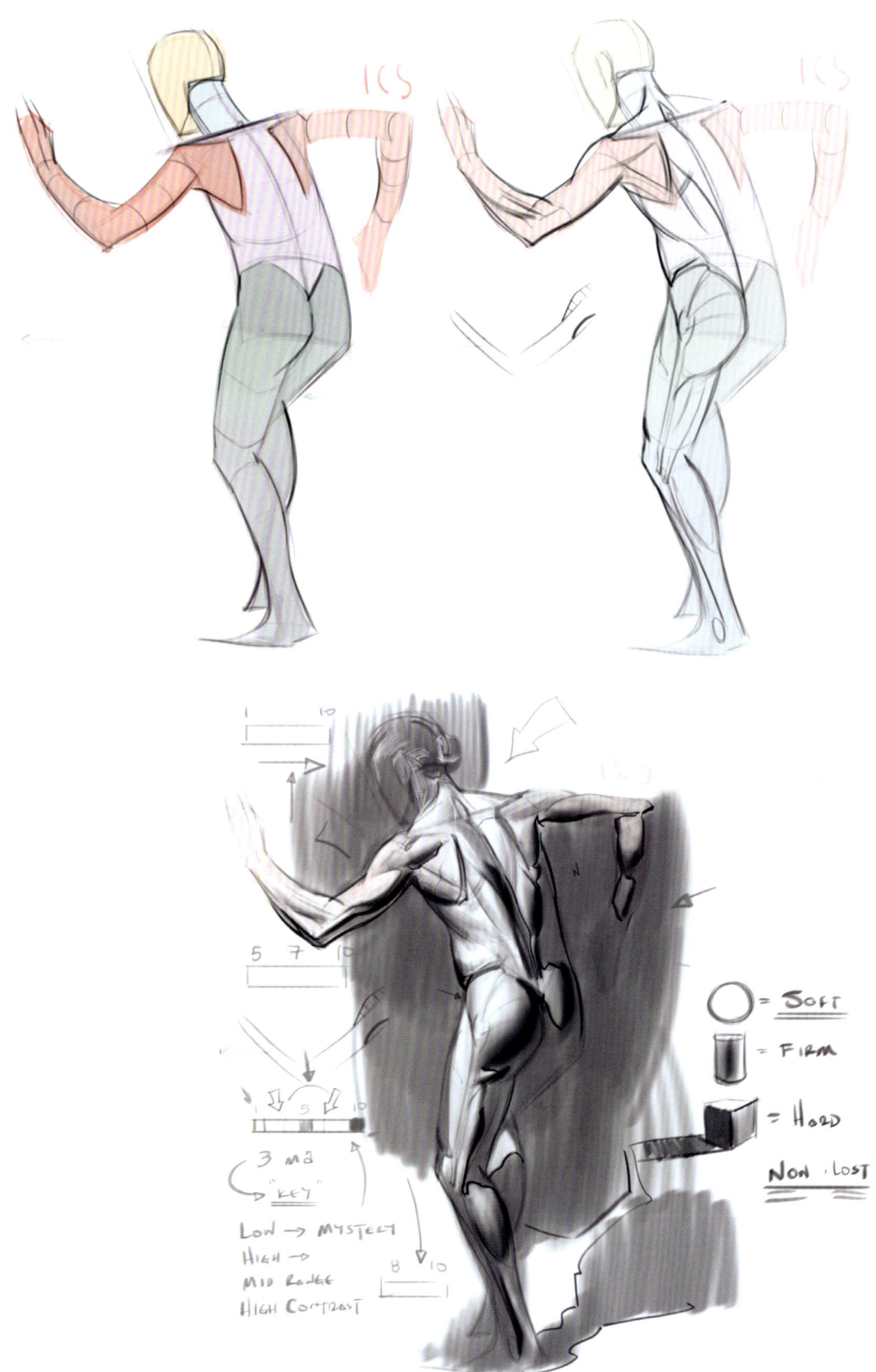

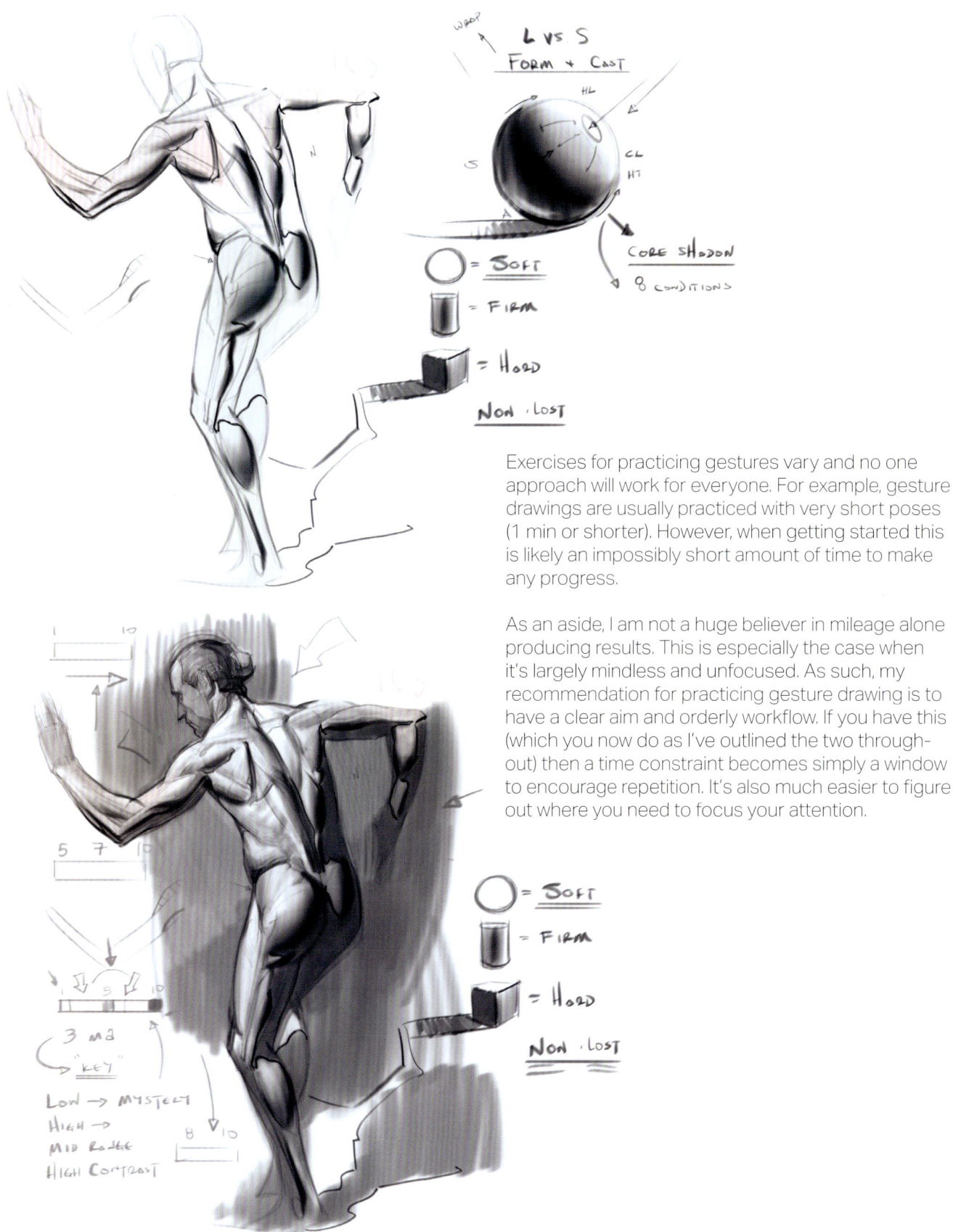

Exercises for practicing gestures vary and no one approach will work for everyone. For example, gesture drawings are usually practiced with very short poses (1 min or shorter). However, when getting started this is likely an impossibly short amount of time to make any progress.

As an aside, I am not a huge believer in mileage alone producing results. This is especially the case when it's largely mindless and unfocused. As such, my recommendation for practicing gesture drawing is to have a clear aim and orderly workflow. If you have this (which you now do as I've outlined the two through-out) then a time constraint becomes simply a window to encourage repetition. It's also much easier to figure out where you need to focus your attention.

For example, take our 16-line approach, described previously, as the workflow. To begin your practice, start with an amount of time that allows you to get through the total rhythmic breakdown of the eight parts.

When working through this, don't allow yourself more time than it takes get from head to foot and then into the arms, as we don't want to fall back into bad habits or old routines. If you keep your approach consistent, you'll eventually develop a familiarity with the 16 lines, their placement, what works, what doesn't, and so on, because of this repetition. Familiarity develops greater economy, which will in turn translate into speed.

A good longer-term goal would be to aim to get down to 1 min poses. This seems to be an ideal window of

time as it's brief enough to capture an initial impression of the figures "idea" or "story" and interpret it in a reactive way.

I'd recommend you start out with standing poses, work from the head through the spine, look for the weight-bearing leg, supporting leg, and the arms. Once comfortable here, move into sitting poses, leaning, leaping, and eventually foreshortening and difficult angles. Once you've become comfortable interpreting poses you observe, next try and design poses from your imagination. This will aid in transitioning into figure invention.

Again, there isn't one right way to study so take these recommendations as general guardrails for things to consider and implement.

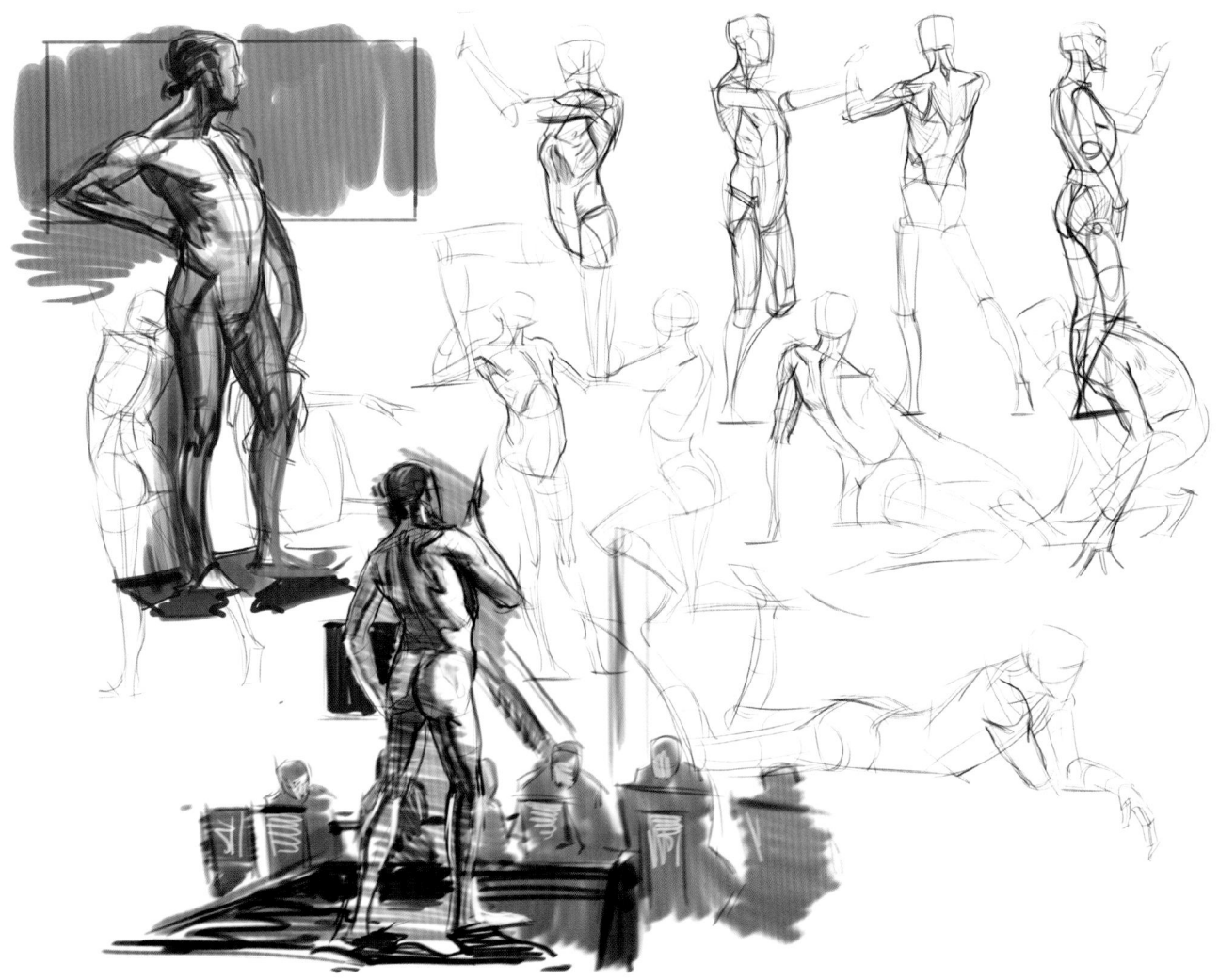

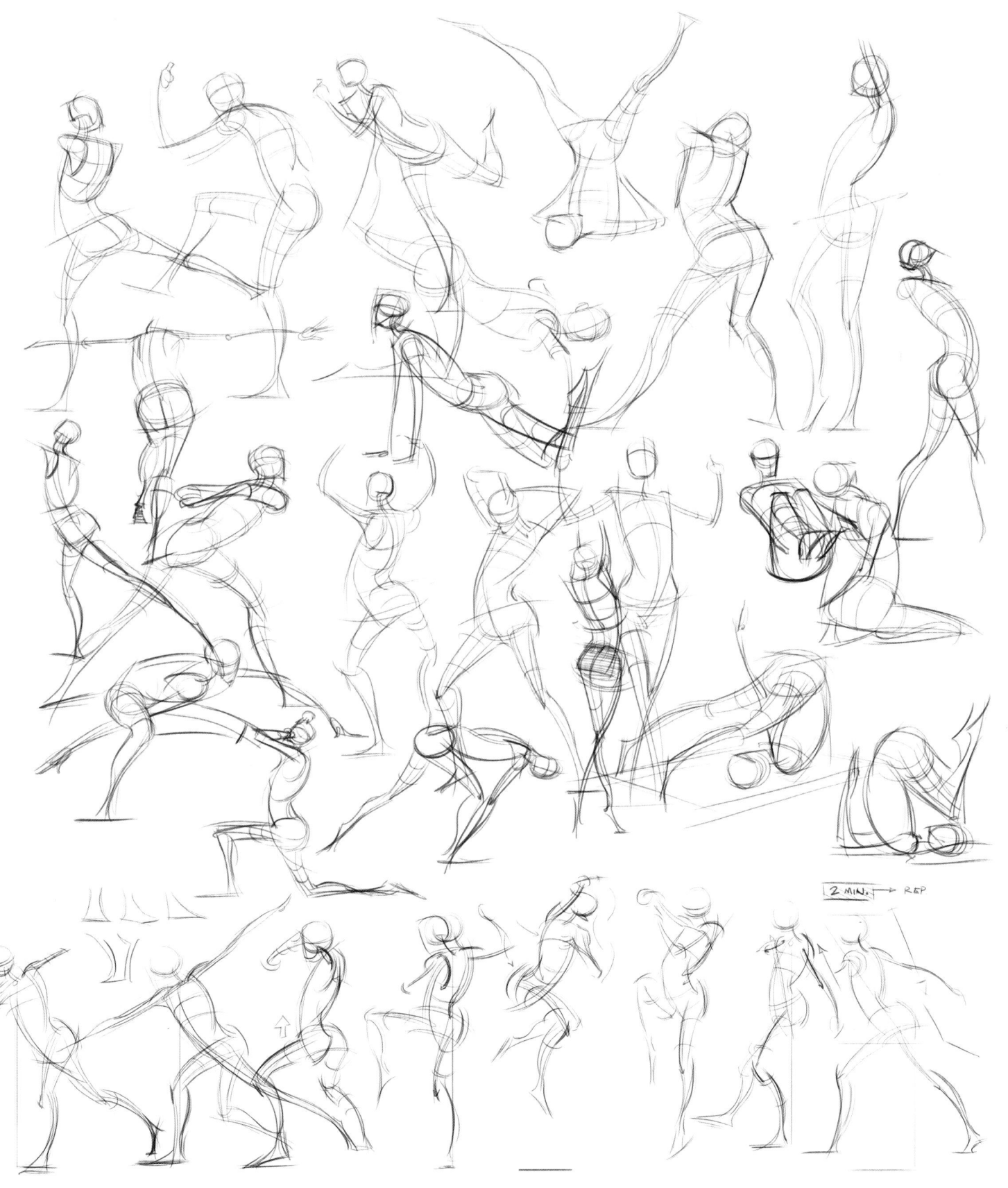

2 MIN. → REP

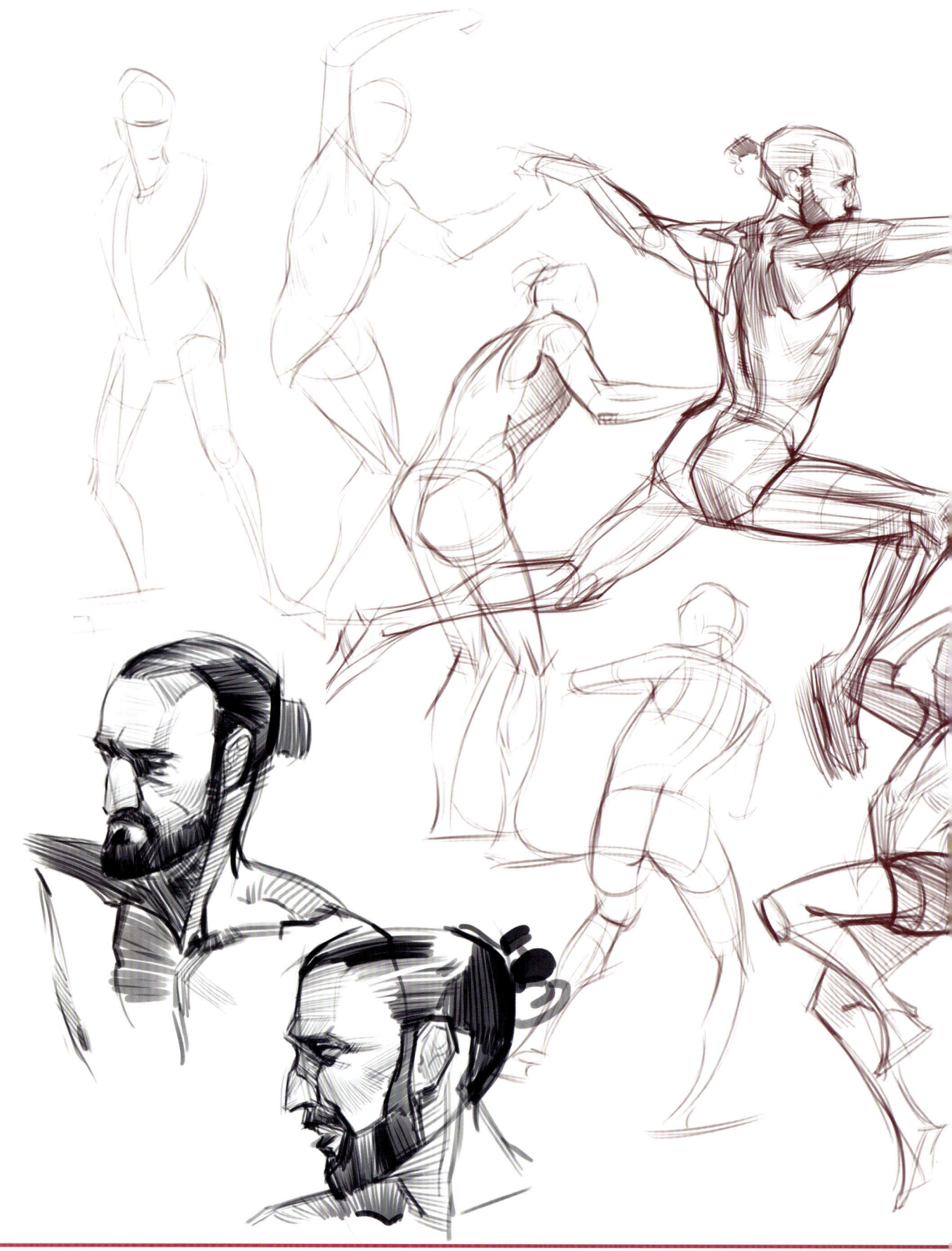

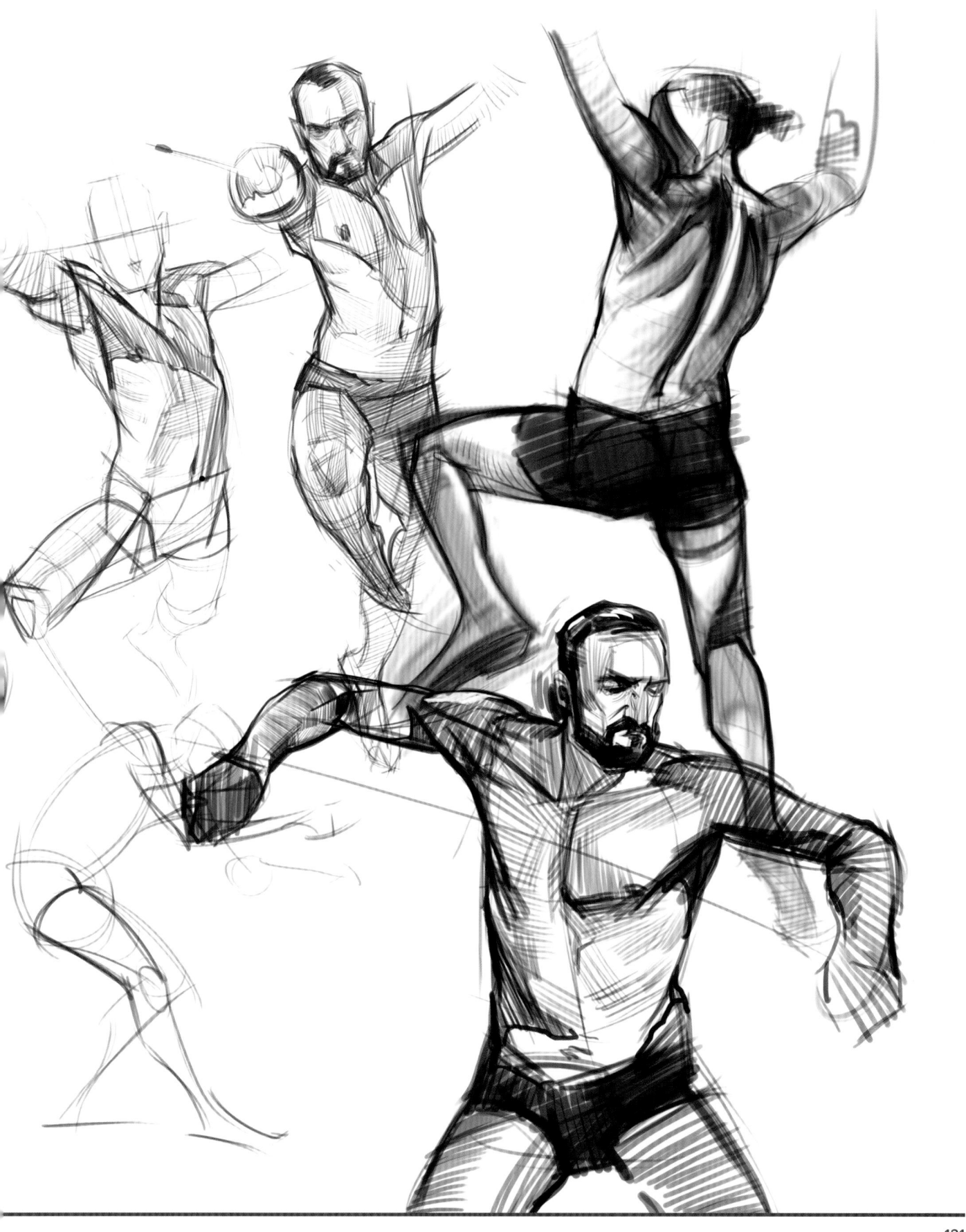

# CONCLUSION

One of the most common questions I hear from students at this point is, "should I master gesture before moving on to other subjects?" While I completely understand the reasoning behind this question my answer is always, "absolutely not."

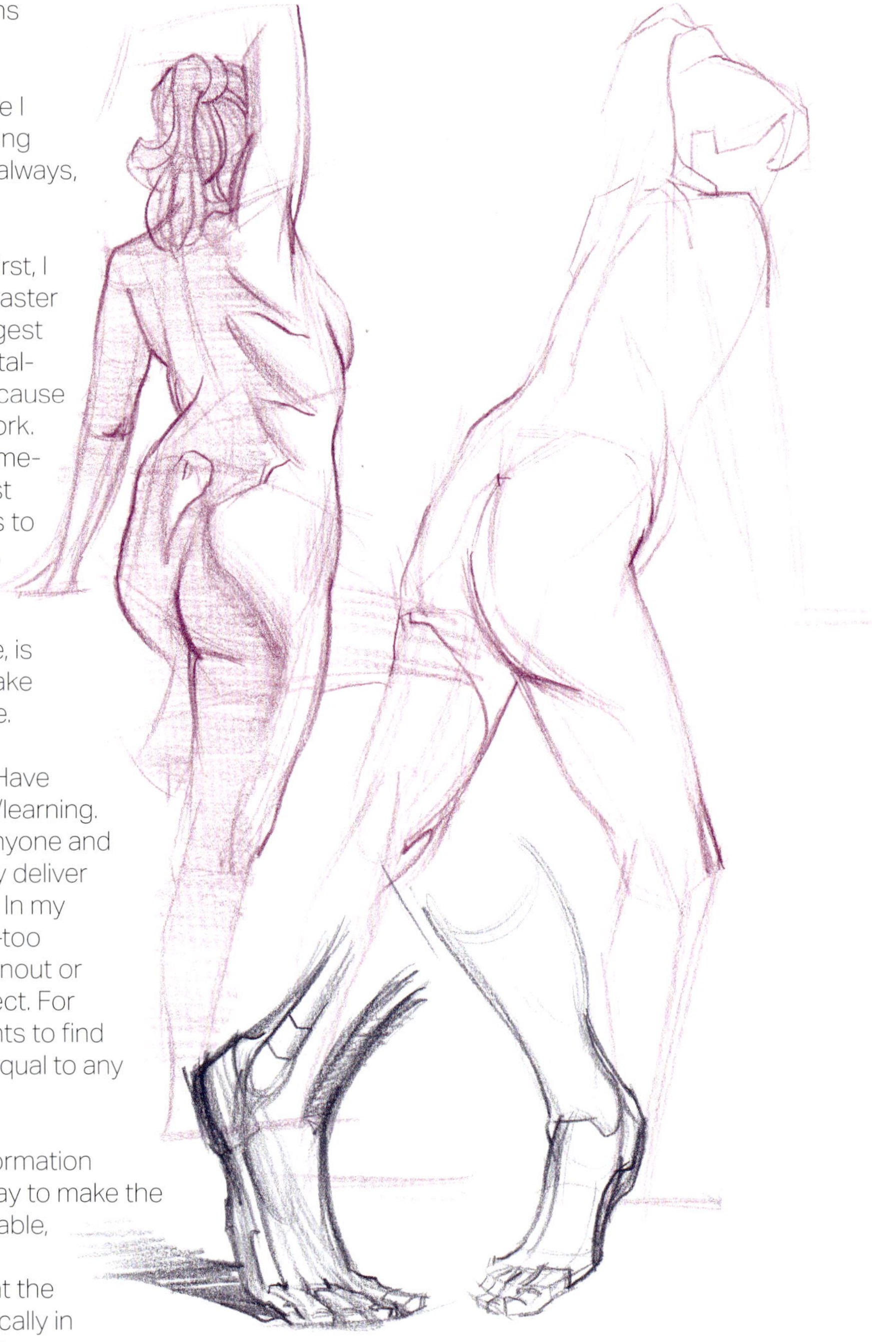

I say this for a couple of reasons. First, I think it unlikely any of us will ever master gesture drawing. That's not to suggest any one of us are incapable or not talented enough, but more simply because it's not intended to be a finished work. It's only the first step or draft to somewhere else. Second, one of the best ways to improve gesture drawing is to move on to the rest of the drawing. Having a better understanding of what you intend to develop, and the steps you take to get there, is often the best way to reflexively make improvements at the gesture stage.

Finally, a word of encouragement. Have grace for yourselves when making/learning. This is a challenging practice for anyone and if you're at all like me, you can easily deliver a heaping amount of self-criticism. In my own experience this isn't healthy—too much self-criticism can lead to burnout or a loss of enthusiasm for your subject. For this reason, I always ask my students to find balance by celebrating their wins equal to any indulgence in self-criticism.

I hope that the description and information covered throughout goes some way to make the subject of gesture more approachable, with definable aims and practical solutions. Though I understand that the two approaches here vary dramatically in look and execution, I believe they share a common root and represent two viable interpretations for how to practice gesture. I encourage you to play with both and combine elements from each into a more customized practice tailored to your specific interests and style.

Best of luck!

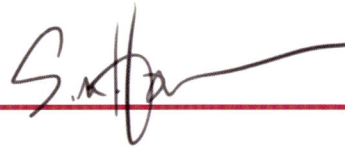

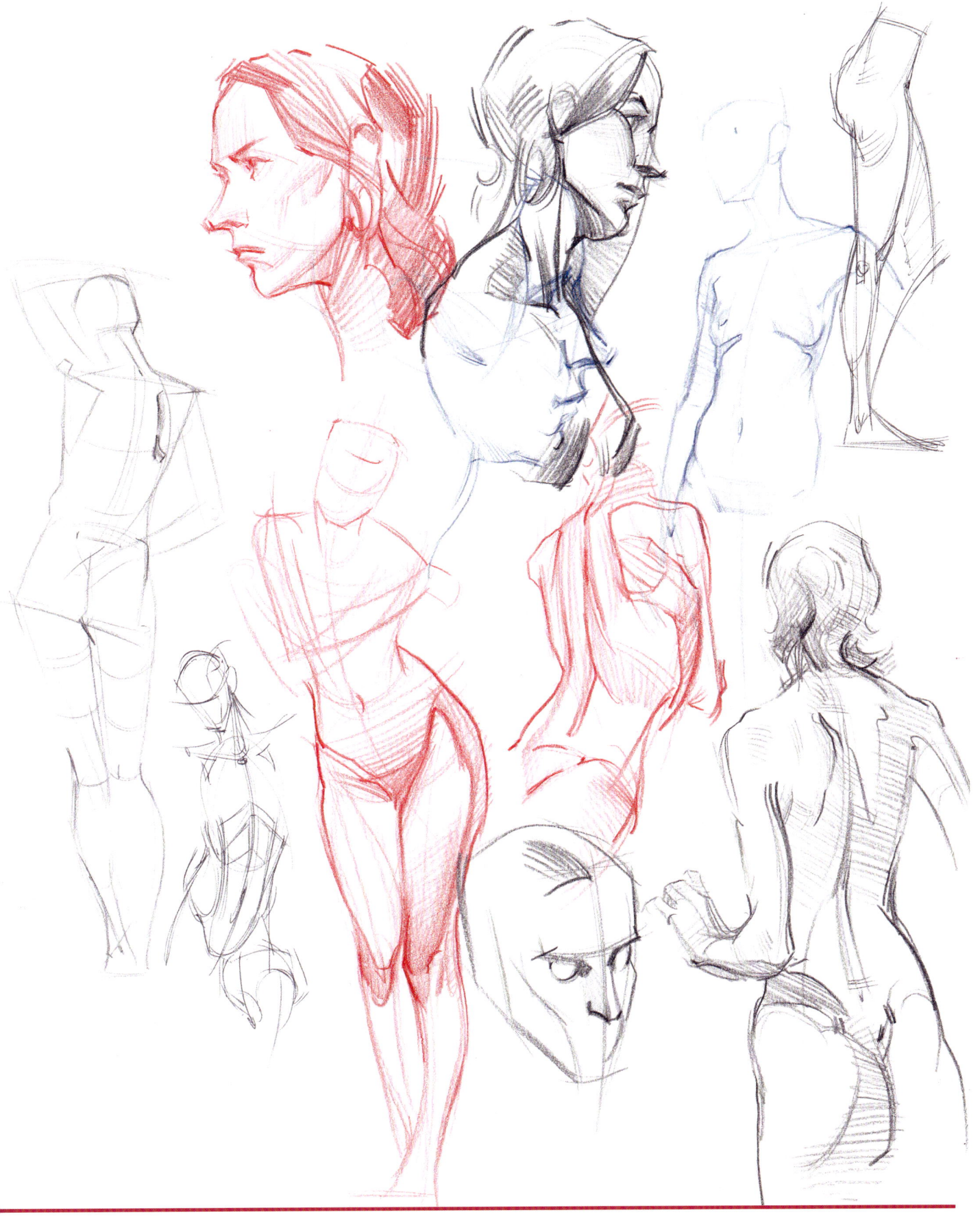

# BIBLIOGRAPHY

Da Vinci, Leonardo. *The Notebooks of Leonardo Davinci (Volume 1)*, edited by Jean Paul Richter. New York: Dover Publications, 1970.

Eisner, Will. *Comics and Sequential Art: Principles & Practice of the World's Most Popular Art Form.* Florida: Poorhouse Press, 1985.

Goman, Carol Kinsey. *The Nonverbal Advantage: Secrets and Science of Body Language atWork.* Berret-Koehler Publishers, Inc. San Francisco, 2008.

Hampton, S. Michael. *Figure Drawing: Design and Invention*. S. Michael Hampton, 2009.

Hendrix, John "The Neoplatonic Aesthetics of Leon Battista Alberti," in *Neo-PlatonicAesthetics: Music Literature, & the Visual Arts*, eds. Liana De Girolami Cheney and JohnHendrix. New York: Peter Lang Publishing, 2004.

Hogarth, Burne. *Dynamic Figure Drawing.* Watson-Guptill: New York, 1996.

Hogarth, William. *The Analysis of Beauty*. New York: Dover Publications, 2015.

Kemp, Martin. *Leonardo Da Vinci: Experience, Experiment and Design.* Princeton and Oxford: Princeton University Press, 2006.

Lee, Stan and John Buscema. *How to Draw Comics the Marvel Way.* Attria Books, 1984.

Loomis, Andrew. *Figure Drawing for All It's Worth.* New York: Viking Press, 1962.

Mattesi, Mike. *Force: Dynamic Life Drawing for Animators*. Focal Press: Massachusetts, 2006.

McMullan, James. *High Focus Drawing: A Revolutionary Approach to Drawing the Figure.* Echo Point Books: Vermont, 2018.

Navarro, Joe. *The Dictionary of Body Language: A Field Guide to Human Behavior.* New York: Harper Collins, 2018.

Navarro, Joe with Marvin Karlins, Ph.D., *What Every Body is Saying: An Ex-FBI Agent's Guide to Speed-Reading People.* New York: Harper Collins, 2008.

Pease, Alan and Barbara. *The Definitive Book of Body Language.* Bantam Dell: New York, 2004.

Prokopenko, Stan. Proko.  Fun and Informative Lessons, *www.proko.com/.* Accessed 27 July 2024.

Rose, Bernice. *Drawing Now.* New York: The Museum of Modern Art. 1976.

Vilppu, Glen. *Vilppu Drawing Manual: Gesture and Construction.* Vilppu Studio, 1997.

# QR LIBRARY

Handsome Squidward
Holds the Secret
https://scnv.io/EMWh

Life Drawing Session
https://scnv.io/xCYO

Gesture Drawing Lecture
https://scnv.io/8DQq

Basics of Gesture Drawing
https://scnv.io/yXNW

Gesture Student Feedback
https://scnv.io/Iebt

Common Questions
https://scnv.io/mQ9p

More Common Questions
https://scnv.io/NiPT

Capture the Energy of Any Pose
https://scnv.io/s6jC

Head Drawing
https://scnv.io/kxTQ

Anatomy and Structure
of the Hand
https://scnv.io/uSnv

How to Draw the Foot
https://scnv.io/TCz

Gesture and Process
https://scnv.io/oSmz

Gesture Drawing Demonstration
https://scnv.io/cnqe

A Shape-Based Approach
https://scnv.io/3xFd

Basics of Composition
https://scnv.io/VUe4

Composition Study
https://scnv.io/n21l

From Gesture to Lighting
https://scnv.io/rkHT

Shading Gesture Easy
https://scnv.io/Rdph

# ABOUT THE AUTHOR

Michael Hampton is an artist and long-time educator in the fields of figure drawing and anatomy. He has lectured and led workshops at school and companies such as Anatomy Tools, Laguna College of Art and Design, Proko.com, Blizzard Entertainment, IDEA Academy, and Lucas Film. In 2009, Michael self-published *Figure Drawing: Design and Invention*, a textbook used for analytical figure drawing classes at many schools worldwide, as well as a reference book at various game/animation companies. Michael received a BFA in Illustration from Art Center College of Design, an MFA in Fine Arts from Claremont Graduate University, and a PhD in Art History at University of California Riverside.

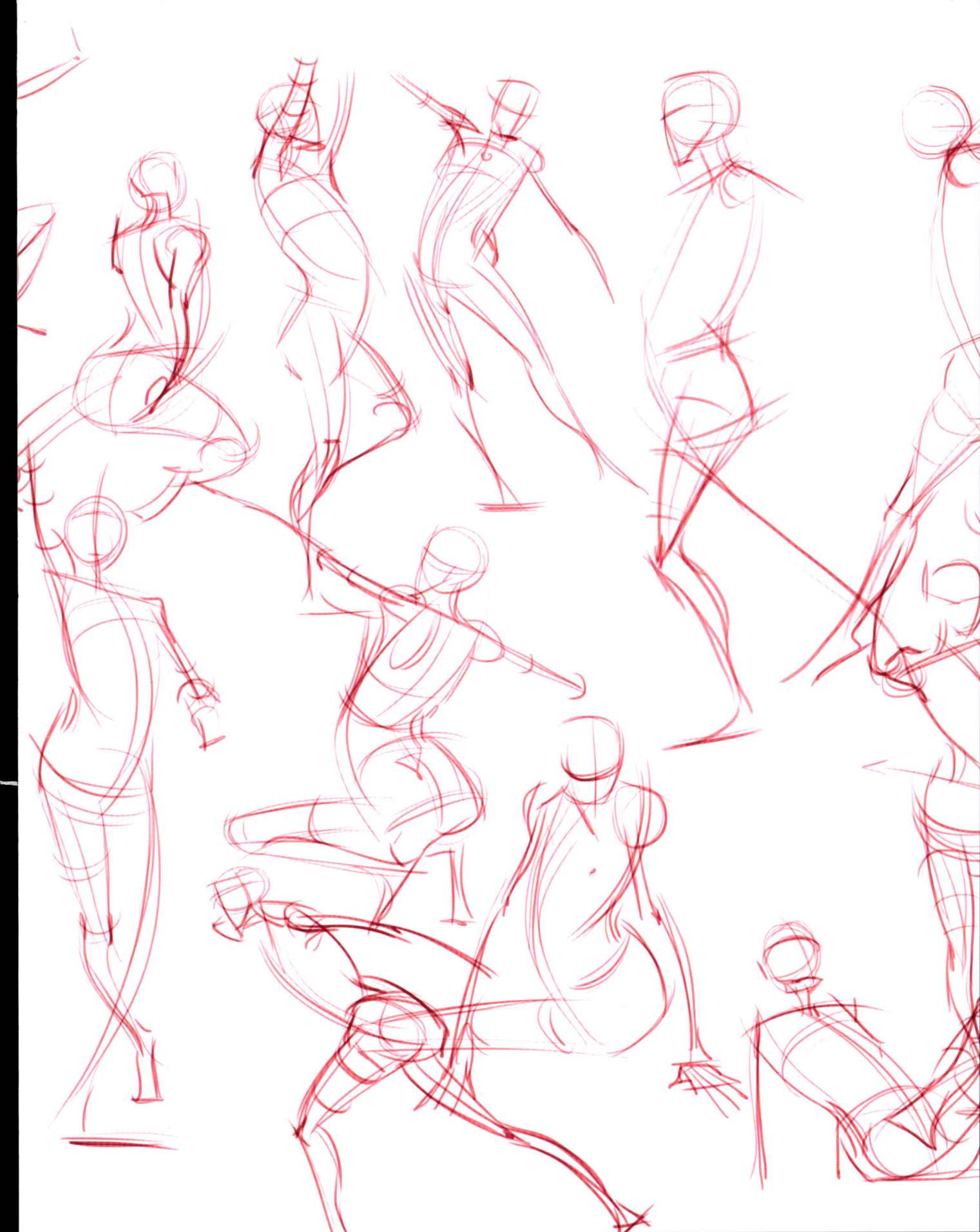

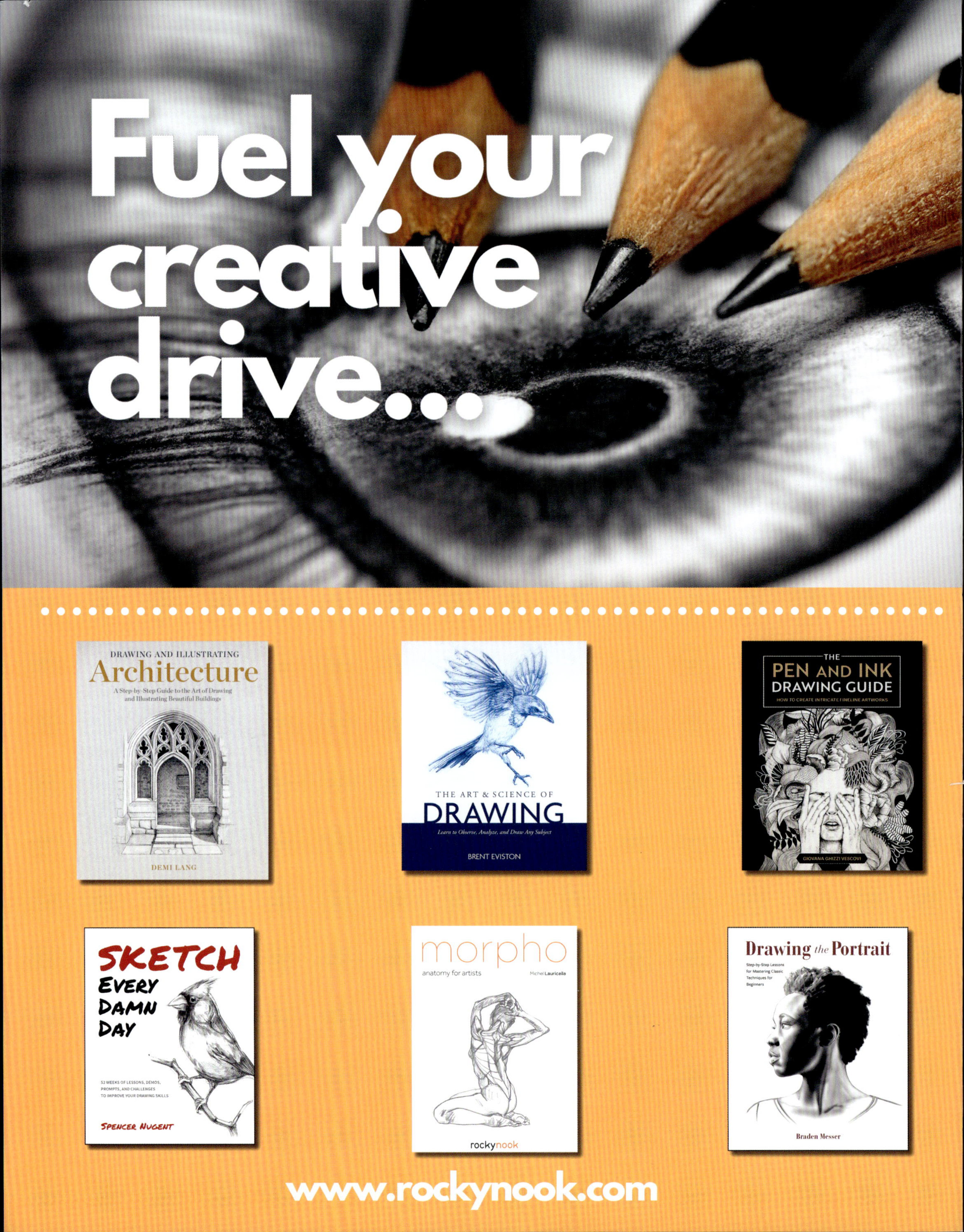

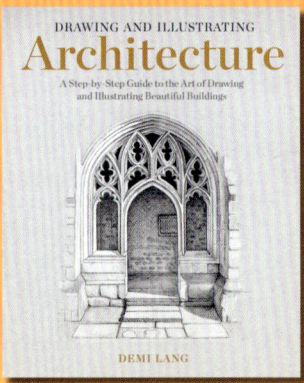
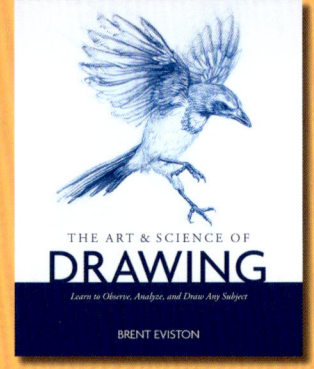
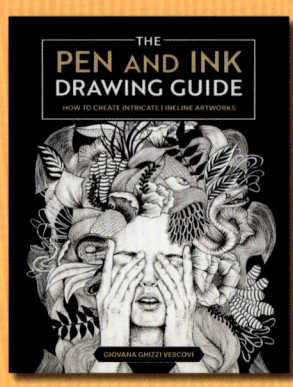
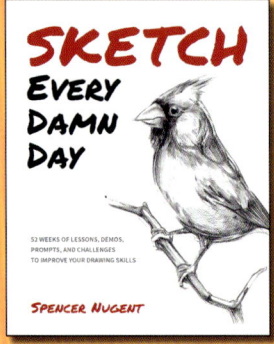
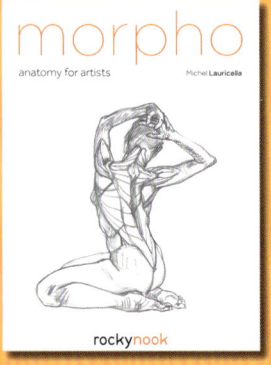
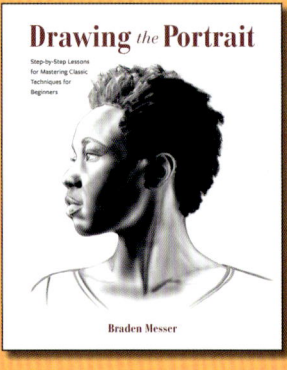